SAINT AUGUSTINE AND THE DONATIST CONTROVERSY

SAINT AUGUSTINE
AND THE
DONATIST CONTROVERSY

BY
GEOFFREY GRIMSHAW WILLIS

Eugene, Oregon

Wipf and Stock Publishers
199 W 8th Ave, Suite 3
Eugene, OR 97401

Saint Augustine and the Donatist Controversy
By Willis, Geoffrey G.
Copyright©1950 SPCK
ISBN: 1-59752-142-6
Publication date 4/11/2005
Previously published by SPCK, 1950

CONTENTS

Preface — page ix

Introduction — xi

CHAPTER I

THE HISTORY OF DONATISM BEFORE THE TIME OF SAINT AUGUSTINE

1. Introduction — 1

    The failure of the Church to realize perfect holiness on earth gave rise to the opposite attitudes of liberalism and rigorism in Church discipline.

2. The persecution of Diocletian and the schism at Carthage — 3

    The persecution of Diocletian endeavoured to destroy Christianity by the seizure of all sacred writings; and when peace returned the Church was faced with the disciplinary problem of how to deal with the *traditores* who had betrayed the faith by thus surrendering books. There were those in Carthage who favoured a liberal policy, and among them was the newly elected bishop, Caecilianus, who thereby attracted to himself the odium of the puritan party, who were opposed to any compromise. They proceeded to the election of a schismatic bishop, Maiorinus, and with his consecration a schism was inaugurated.

3. The appeal to the Emperor — 6

    After appeals to Constantine, who remitted the question to the Church for conciliar decision, the matter was decided in favour of Caecilianus.

4. The spread of Donatism in the fourth century — 8

    The schism, however, spread, gathering to itself those who were for social and political reasons opposed to the Roman government and hostile to those in Africa who supported it; and in the course of the fourth century achieved widespread power in Africa, not without the use of considerable violence.

5. Saint Optatus of Milevis — 23

    The only considerable surviving work against the Donatists in the fourth century is that of Saint Optatus, who wrote the history of the schism in a work revised towards 390, and which (with its appendix of ten documents concerning the schism) became the principal historical foundation for Saint Augustine's work.

CONTENTS

CHAPTER II

THE SITUATION AT THE TIME OF SAINT AUGUSTINE'S PRIESTHOOD

1. The power and influence of Donatism   *page* 26

   By the time that Saint Augustine was ordained priest, Donatism had acquired in some parts of Africa, and not least in the diocese of Hippo, a clear predominance; and from the beginning of Augustine's ministry, the division of the Church was an unceasing preoccupation to him.

2. Internal schisms of Donatism   31

   But about this time Donatism was beginning to show the fissiparous tendency which weakened it from inside while its Catholic enemies were opposing it from without.

CHAPTER III

SAINT AUGUSTINE'S STRUGGLE WITH THE DONATISTS

1. Priesthood, 391–395   36

   During his priesthood Saint Augustine initiated his anti-Donatist campaign, but confined it at this time to the diocese of Hippo.

2. The period 395–400   40

   After his consecration in 395 to the episcopate he extended his campaign to the whole African Church and at this time began for the first time to consider the advisability of an appeal to the civil power against the Donatists.

3. The period 400–405   49

   During these five years Augustine became convinced that it was necessary to appeal to the State; and the period concluded with the promulgation of the first Edict of Unity.

4. The period 405–411   60

   This policy continued during the next period and culminated in the summoning of a Conference at Carthage to discuss the matter under government auspices.

5. The Conference of Carthage, 411   70

   Marcellinus, the imperial commissioner, tried the case, and pronounced judgement in favour of the Catholic Church.

6. After the Conference   76

   The work of Saint Augustine after the Conference was designed to facilitate the return of the schismatics to the Church.

CONTENTS

CHAPTER IV

SAINT AUGUSTINE'S DOCTRINE OF THE CHURCH

1. The doctrine of the Church and Ministry before Saint Augustine   *page* 93

    In the course of this controversy, it fell to Saint Augustine to work out more fully than his predecessors the doctrine of the Church. Saint Cyprian, following Saint Irenaeus and others, had arrived at a rigid theory of a Visible Church, recognized by its catholicity and by its communion with Catholic bishops. This view, in its main essentials, had dominated since that time in the Western Church, and was held by Saint Optatus, the immediate predecessor of Saint Augustine in this controversy.

Excursus. Saint Cyprian and the Roman Primacy   110

2. Saint Augustine on the Church and Ministry   113

    Saint Augustine was compelled by the challenge of Donatism to consider afresh the four notes of the Church: (*a*) its unity, (*b*) holiness, (*c*) catholicity and (*d*) apostolicity; and to maintain that its bond of unity is charity, of which schism is the denial.

3. Saint Augustine's development of the doctrine of the Church   120

    His thought is governed partly by the particular form of the Donatist insistence upon empirical holiness, and by an ardent pastoral desire for the reunion of African Christianity. We find, therefore, in him a certain modification of the Cyprianic point of view, and the development of the doctrine of the Invisible Church, which eases his practical problem.

CHAPTER V

CHURCH AND STATE

1. The development of Saint Augustine's theory of coercion   127

    The political violence of Donatists also forced upon Augustine's consideration the grave question of how far it is permissible to use coercion for the establishment of Christian unity; and his thought shows a gradual and steady development towards approval of such coercion in certain circumstances.

2. The relations of Church and State   135

    The development of this argument about compulsion obviously involves some consideration of the whole attitude of Augustine towards the problems raised by the relations between Church and State, and between the *ciuitas superna* and the *ciuitas terrena*.

CONTENTS

CHAPTER VI

SAINT AUGUSTINE'S DOCTRINE OF THE MINISTRATION OF THE SACRAMENTS

1. Earlier views *page* 145

   On the administration of the sacraments the Donatists pleaded the view held by Saint Cyprian on the irregularity and invalidity of all sacraments conferred outside the fold of the Church; but transferred the emphasis from the necessity of union with the Church to the necessity of purity of life in the individual minister; thus destroying the true balance of Saint Cyprian's thought.

2. Saint Augustine's view 152

   Saint Augustine answered this problem by distinguishing between the validity and the regularity of sacraments, concentrating especially on the sacrament of baptism.
   (a) Distinction between validity and regularity of sacraments
   (b) The baptismal question
   (c) Other sacraments

CHAPTER VII

CONCLUSION

1. The controversy with the Donatists 169

   The intensely pastoral outlook of Saint Augustine influenced his whole approach to the long controversy; and all the action he took against the Donatists was co-ordinated with his literary campaign on the subject of the schism.

2. The doctrinal principles involved 172

   The controversy elicited from Saint Augustine great contributions to the doctrines of the nature of the Church, on the relations between Church and State, and of the principles governing the ministration of sacraments.

3. The importance of these principles for the future 177

   Saint Augustine's teaching on these matters rooted itself very firmly in subsequent theology; and can be illustrated in medieval theology, and in the formularies of the Church of England as well as in its great theologians of the sixteenth and seventeenth centuries.

4. Conclusion 187

Bibliography 188

Indices 193

PREFACE

The controversy with the Donatists was not the least important of the literary and theological struggles in which Saint Augustine found it his duty to engage during his episcopate. In any account of his life's work it must claim a vital place, for it occupied his attention constantly for over thirty years, and the unification of the Church of North Africa was one of the greatest achievements of a man who could lay claim to so many great achievements. Yet it has claimed surprisingly little attention from English writers. There is much about it in compendious foreign works, such as Dr Harnack's *Dogmengeschichte* and M. Monceaux's *Histoire littéraire de l'Afrique chrétienne*. Yet in this century it appears that the only English work devoted exclusively to it is Dr W. J. Sparrow Simpson's *Saint Augustine and African Church Divisions* (London, 1910). There seems room, therefore, for a somewhat fuller treatment of the subject in English. I have endeavoured to provide this in the present work, and to set forth the struggle between Catholicism and Donatism as seen from both the historical and the theological standpoints. A study of the theological issues will lead us to consider the nature of unity and of schism in the Church, the relations of Church and State, and the nature of the Church's authority in ministering the sacraments of Christ. As considered from the historical point of view, the Donatist controversy presents a most interesting picture of the life of Africa in the fourth and fifth centuries of our era, and of the struggle there waged between African nationalism and Roman imperialism, and between the nationalistic and catholic conceptions of the Church. Such a study would appear to have much to teach us in the present time, and is in any case worth pursuing for its intrinsic interest.

My grateful thanks are due in the first place to Dr E. F. Jacob, Sub-Warden of All Souls, without whose encouragement this study would never have been undertaken, and without whose generous interest and constant guidance and counsel it would never have been brought to completion; to Dr W. H. C. Frend, for invaluable suggestions concerning the material of the first chapter; to the Reverend R. J. H. Hill, who read the work in typescript and proffered most

PREFACE

useful criticisms; to the Reverend J. D. C. Fisher, who undertook the drudgery of proof-reading; to the Clarendon Press, Oxford, and to Messrs Macmillan, for permission to quote from F. Homes Dudden's *The Life and Times of Saint Ambrose* and from *Essays on the Early History of the Church and the Ministry* (ed. H. B. Swete) respectively; and to the S.P.C.K. and its Editorial Secretary, the Reverend F. N. Davey, for their help and care in publication.

G.G.W.

DERBY
May 1949

INTRODUCTION

'To the present writer it seems indisputable that, whether Augustine be the greatest Latin writer or not, he is the greatest man who ever wrote Latin.' Such is the glowing tribute of a contemporary scholar, Professor Alexander Souter, to the fascination of Saint Augustine's writings.[1] There is in the Saint's mind such vastness of scope and versatility of genius and penetration of thought, that the study of his life and works has ever since his day been a perennial fount of Christian wisdom. There are few matters of theology on which he has nothing to say, few controversies of historical theology in which there is no benefit to be sought in a reading of some part of his extensive work. But though prolific in his output, he is in no exact sense a writer of systematic theology. His approach is essentially casuistical: he writes not so much in the role of a theologian or a philosopher—though he is great in both fields—as in that of a pastor of souls. It was in this field that he desired above all to excel.[2] When he reviewed his life's literary work, in the *Retractations*, written after an episcopate of over thirty years, when he had passed his seventieth year, it was with reference to his responsibility for the flock and to the whole Church in which he was called to be a bishop, that he adjudicated and, if necessary, corrected his writings. Who can doubt that in the last three weeks of his life, when he had the seven penitential psalms inscribed in large letters on cards which were hung on his bedroom wall, that he might use them as the basis of his final self-examination, he judged his life by the criterion of a pastor's responsibility for the flock committed to his charge? To that responsibility all his writings after his ordination may be referred.

The subject of this inquiry is Augustine's dealing with one of the principal anxieties which beset the greater part of his episcopate, namely his struggle with the Donatist schism in Africa. In any account of his life it must claim a vital place, not only because of its intrinsic importance, but also because it occupied his attention for thirty years. The unification of the African Church, rent in two by this devastating schism, was in large part one of the greatest achievements of a man who could lay claim to so many great achievements. The essence of the problem which faced Saint Augustine was simple and by no means novel.

[1] A. Souter, in *J.T.S.*, vol. XI, p. 150.
[2] See H. I. Marrou, *Saint Augustin et la fin de la culture antique* (Paris, 1938), pp. 335–9.

INTRODUCTION

It was one which has recurred time and again in Christian history, and may not unfairly be described as an inevitable and fundamental problem of ecclesiastical discipline. That problem is how to reconcile the holiness of the Church as the Body of Christ with the actual sinfulness of its members here on earth. It is a problem which will remain ineluctable as long as the Church is *in uia*, and can only disappear when it is *in patria*. Professor Michael Ramsey suggests that three main solutions have been attempted in Christian history.[1] The first is that of the puritans, among whom the Donatists must be numbered. It is to regard the true Church as the society of those who are morally perfect. Professor Ramsey sums up the traditional objection to this solution in the following words:

> It does violence to the true meaning of the Church. For the holiness of the Church is the holiness of the Spirit whereby the members are made holy. To use visible standards of morality as a test of membership is to transfer the merit and glory from Christ to the members themselves, and to set forth the Church as a society of the moral rather than a family of the redeemed.[2]

The second solution is to identify the kingdom of God with the Church on earth; and this fails because the kingdom of God is greater than the visible society on earth. In reaction against this second view is the third solution, which is to identify the true Church with the Church Invisible, and this also fails in that it does not provide a place for the ministration of the word and sacraments within the Visible Church on earth. Saint Augustine's controversy with the Donatists is an attempt to effect a synthesis between the sanctity of the Church and the imperfection of its actual members on earth.

The Donatist controversy in its theological aspect leads us to consider the meaning of the unity and sanctity of the Church, and the evil of schism to which is opposed the good of charity, binding the members in one with each other and with Christ the head of the Body. It involves also the consideration of the source of grace in the sacraments, and poses the question whether anything depends upon the personal sanctity of the minister of a sacrament, or whether the whole virtue of the sacrament derives from God alone. What is the effect, if any, of the unworthiness of the minister of a sacrament? This problem Saint Augustine answered by distinguishing between the validity and the regularity of a sacrament. The argument is principally conducted in the sphere of holy baptism, which was in the forefront of the dispute

---

[1] A. M. Ramsey, *The Resurrection of Christ* (London, 1943), pp. 96–8.
[2] Ibid. p. 97.

INTRODUCTION

because of the Donatist insistence on rebaptizing all who came over to their fold. This fact is yet another illustration of the pastoral preoccupations of Augustine in respect of this controversy.

But side by side with these theological considerations there are the historical problems involved in the struggle. Donatism was a great social force in Africa by the end of the fourth century; and the sect was in some regions stronger and more numerous than the Catholic Church. The puritan outlook of the Donatists went to great excesses, and affected personal life and relationships in African society very deeply. It also provided an effective rallying-point for many who were not interested in the theological problems involved, but were disaffected for political and economic reasons against the Roman power. The Catholic Church was regarded by many Africans as the ally of the imperial power of Rome, and was included therefore in the hatred which they felt for that power on non-theological grounds. The rebellious machinations of Donatists, and the atrocious cruelty with which they were carried into effect, combined to force the Catholics, as it were, into the arms of the State, and to impel them for the protection of their persons and property to seek the recognition and support of the civil power. Measures for the suppression of Donatist depredations were only partly successful, and in the end the Church was compelled to petition for a Conference in which the whole matter might be examined and, if it were decided in favour of the Church, settled by the extirpation of the schismatics. This policy was eventually successful, but the pursuing of it compelled Augustine to an exposition of the whole question of the relations of Church and State. His teaching on this matter is not his least contribution to this wearisome dispute.

This domination of the pastoral outlook in Augustine's mind, coupled with his insistence as a rhetorician on answering in detail the points raised by his opponents, influenced the whole course of his approach to Donatism. He has not given us a closely argued work on the doctrine of Church and sacraments: he has argued the particular points that events have forced upon his attention. And yet his output on this question is so varied and so great in bulk that he has been able to cover most of the ground involved in a consideration of Church, Ministry and sacraments, and of the relations between Church and State. As his contemporary controversy with the Pelagians led him to expound the Christian doctrine of sin and grace, of predestination and election, of marriage and original sin, so his dispute with the Donatists elicited from him his vast contributions to ecclesiology and the doctrine of sacraments. He bequeathed to the Church after his time

INTRODUCTION

two profound and perennial problems, those of the ministration of sacraments, and of the relations of the Christian Church and the semi-Christian State. He partly solved these problems, and suggested the main lines of principle on which solutions might be sought; and in the changing circumstances of subsequent ages men have turned again and again to his work for inspiration in solving them. They are problems which in the modern world press no less for a solution than in the fifth century. The former is even more acute than in his day because of the divisions of Christendom; the latter is daily increasing in urgency as State and Church increasingly diverge. And it may not be unprofitable for us to study afresh what this great doctor, in the vast scope of his erudition, and the profound subtlety and penetration of his thought, has to say about them.

ABBREVIATIONS USED IN NOTES

C.C.E.A.   *Codex Canonum Ecclesiae Africanae.* Printed in C. J. Hefele, *History of the Christian Councils*, trans. W. R. Clark (Edinburgh, 1872), pp. 468 sqq.

C.I.L.   *Corpus Inscriptionum Latinarum* (Berlin, 1887-1931).

C.S.E.L.   *Corpus Scriptorum Ecclesiasticorum Latinorum* (Vienna, 1866), in progress.

C.Th.   *Codex Theodosianus*, ed. Th. Mommsen (Berlin, 1905). (*Theodosiani libri XVI, cum constitutionibus Sirmondianis.*)

J.T.S.   *Journal of Theological Studies* (Oxford).

P.G.   *Patrologiae cursus completus. Series graeca*, ed. J. P. Migne (Paris, 1857-66), 161 vols.

P.L.   *Patrologiae cursus completus. Series latina*, ed. J. P. Migne (Paris, 1844-55), 221 vols.

The Latin enumeration of the Psalter, according to the reckoning of the Vulgate, is used throughout this work in text and citations.

CHAPTER I

THE HISTORY OF DONATISM BEFORE THE TIME OF SAINT AUGUSTINE

1. *Introduction*

In the Apostles' and Nicene Creeds we express our belief in the Church as holy. It is so because it is the Body of Christ, and shares in the holiness of God, and also because in its ideal condition it will have complete empirical holiness as well. But since it dwells on earth, and is composed of men who are at varying stages along the road which leads ultimately to entire holiness, it is obfuscated in this present world by a certain proportion of evil within its own ranks. Therefore, from the earliest days, the Church has been faced with the problem of discipline among its members. The logical extremes of its condition would be complete actual holiness, so that nobody who had not attained such holiness would be numbered among its members; or else complete carelessness as to the quality of the lives of its members. Neither of these conditions would be satisfactory, and therefore the principal disciplinary problem of the Church in every age is to strike the balance between them. Where is the line to be drawn which separates those whom, in spite of imperfections, we may call true Christians, and those whom we consider to have fallen below the minimum standard of holiness which we think allowable in a Christian? The answer which men make to this question will depend upon their temperament and environment, and on the view which they take of the position of the Church in relation to the world.

Speaking generally, two main views have held the field throughout the Church's history. The first has been what is described by the moral theologian as the 'rigorist' view.[1] It tends to refuse absolution and restoration to all those who are guilty of grave sins; whereas the 'liberal' view, which ultimately and on the whole has prevailed, allows restoration even after grave sins when the sinner displays a proper

---

[1] On rigorism in the early Church, see O. D. Watkins, *History of Penance* (London, 1920); K. E. Kirk, *The Vision of God*, Bampton Lectures, 1928 (London, 1931), pp. 221–9, 506–7; T. G. Jalland, *The Church and the Papacy*, Bampton Lectures, 1942 (London, 1944), pp. 131, 132, 157, 158, 169, 209; H. B. Swete (ed.), *Essays in the Early History of the Church and the Ministry* (London, 1921), pp. 39, 149, 155 n., 156, 157, 163, 359–76.

penitence and desire for restoration. When under Constantine the Church became a *religio licita*, and freedom of worship was assured, the Church tended to develop from a society of elect, who were prepared, if need be, to face deprivation and death for their faith, to a society to which it involved little risk to belong; and it is not surprising that this toleration led to a general lowering of the moral standard of Christianity, and to its partial assimilation to a world with which it was now, as never before, on good terms. The two tendencies of rigorism and liberalism are illustrated in the New Testament by our Lord's command to Saint Peter to forgive his brother seventy times seven,[1] and by the declaration of the author to the Hebrews that it is impossible for those who by baptism have put on Christ and become partakers of the Holy Ghost to be reconciled after grave sin, 'seeing they crucify to themselves the Son of God afresh, and put him to an open shame'.[2] The history of the discipline of penance in the early centuries is set in the framework of a conflict between these two contrasted attitudes.

Those who laid considerable emphasis on the need of purity of life and belief among Christians were inclined to adopt the rigorous attitude towards those who were guilty of grave sins such as schism, heresy, apostasy, idolatry, homicide and unchastity. Some thought that no absolution should be given for such sins, and others were prepared to allow one reconciliation to the offenders. This question was being discussed as early as the middle of the second century, when it is mentioned in the *Shepherd* of Hermas. Hermas rather grudgingly allows one act of repentance for serious sins.[3] The tendency of the Church of Rome, which in dogmatic questions was comprehensive rather than exclusive, was similarly liberal in disciplinary matters. At the beginning of the third century the Roman Bishop Callistus (218–223) announced that it was his practice to absolve sins of the flesh after due penance.[4] For this he was violently assailed by the rigorist and puritan writers. Tertullian maintained that idolatry, homicide and unchastity, with certain other grave sins, are irremissible except by God.[5] This view was supported by a later anti-pope, Hippolytus, who, after the death of Callistus, attacked him for his liberalism.[6]

On the whole, rigorism in discipline appealed to the African mind, and we find it in Cyprian as well as in Tertullian, and later in the African Donatists; for the Africans, in moral as in dogmatic theology, liked that which was clear-cut. The Roman mind was more liberal;

[1] Matt. xviii. 21, 22. [2] Heb. vi. 4–6.
[3] Hermas, *Pastor*, mand. IV, 1, 3. [4] Tert. *De pudic.* 1.
[5] Ibid. 2 sq., 18 sq., 21. [6] Hippol. *in Prov.* XXIV, 50 sq.

but liberalism in discipline never went far in any part of the early Church, as it was destined to do after the fifth century. Until then the invariable rule of the Church was to allow one penance only to those guilty of capital sins; and that penance was so severe in character that it was customary to defer it until the approach of death.[1]

Persecution of the Church always brought to the fore the problem of disciplinary treatment of those who lapsed into idolatry and apostasy. During the Decian persecution in the middle of the third century Carthage and Rome agreed in allowing restoration after penance to the *libellatici*, who had obtained from the magistrate a certificate saying that they had offered sacrifice; but to *sacrificati*, those who had actually and publicly offered pagan sacrifices, only at the point of death.[2] This arrangement won general acceptance, and commended itself to the general Christian mind. Of course it was displeasing to the extreme rigorists, and many of these were attracted to the schismatic sect of Novatian, which eventually came to deny the right of the Church to absolve any mortal sin.

2. *The persecution of Diocletian and the schism at Carthage*

The long peace of the Church which followed the Decian persecution was shattered in 303 by Diocletian, and a fresh persecution was again the source of a dispute about discipline. The intervening period had been one of growth in the Church generally, and in Africa the number of bishoprics had increased by as many as one hundred.[3] Christianity was gaining ground: everywhere it began to affect the upper classes more profoundly. Diocletian's persecution aimed at suppressing Christianity not by the compulsory offering of sacrifice, as Decius had tried to do, but by the seizure of its sacred writings. Therefore those clergy and others who apostatized were not now *libellatici* or *sacrificati*, but *traditores*. We have seen in our own day that persecution is apt to lead to charges of treachery when at length deliverance comes. In the early centuries the acute disciplinary problem at the end of each persecution gave impetus to the rigorist cause. It was not otherwise in the fourth century, for it was out of such a situation that Donatism arose. Some of the apostates in the persecution, like the *libellatici* of the Decian persecution, resorted to subterfuges as a means of appearing to obey

---

[1] K. E. Kirk, *Vision of God*, pp. 227, 275.
[2] E. W. Benson, *Cyprian, his Life, his Times, his Work* (London, 1897), pp. 79–84.
[3] A. Audollent, art. 'Donatisme', in *Dictionnaire d'histoire et de géographie ecclésiastiques*, col. 754.

the imperial decree while at the same time saving their own consciences. Among them was Mensurius, then Bishop of Carthage. In a letter to Secundus, Bishop of Tigisis and Primate of Numidia, he related how he ordered to be deposited in the Basilica Nouorum at Carthage certain heretical works, which were surrendered to the representatives of the proconsul Anulinus under the guise of holy scripture.[1] Such an action was not unnaturally assailed by the rigorist party, and was the primary origin of the Donatist schism.

Two years later a small council of Numidian bishops, about twelve in number, met at Cirta on 5 March 305,[2] with a view to electing a successor to Bishop Paulus of Cirta, who had been a *traditor* at the beginning of the persecution and had since apparently died.[3] They assembled in the private house of Vrbanus,[4] under the presidency of Secundus, Bishop of Tigisis. The president began by inquiring into the fitness of the assembled bishops to act as consecrators; and immediately charges of *traditio* were made against Donatus of Mascula, Victor of Russicade, Marinus of Aquae Tibilitanae, Donatus of Calama, Purpurius of Limata, and Menalius.[5] Four of these admitted their guilt, and Purpurius also confessed to the murder at Milevis of his sister's children, and threatened to murder likewise anyone who might oppose him. At the same time he counter-charged the presiding bishop with the crime of *traditio*. The council then thought it prudent to abandon this line of inquiry and to proceed forthwith to the election. They elected as the new bishop of Cirta Siluanus, subdeacon to Paulus, who had been involved with him in the act of *traditio*; and, in spite of the protests of the church of Cirta, they consecrated him. The record of this council is authentic, although it was declared by the Donatists at

---

[1] Aug. *Breu. Coll.* III, xiii, 25.

[2] The record of this council was attacked as false by the Donatists at the Conference of Carthage in June 411, on the ground that the document bore a date. It was the practice of Montanists, Novatianists, and Donatists not to use consular dates, through their intense hostility to the employment of civil forms: another example of their excessive puritanism. See Benson, op. cit. p. 364, n. 1.

[3] C. J. Hefele, *History of the Christian Councils*, E. T. (W. R. Clark, Edinburgh, 1872), vol. I, ch. III, § 11, pp. 128 sq. See Optatus, I, 13, 14; Aug. *Breu. Coll.* III, xvii; *C. Cresc.* III, xxvii, 29, 30.

[4] Vrbanus Carisius (Opt. I, 13, 14), or Vrbanus Donatus (Aug. *C. Cresc.* III, xxvii, 30).

[5] Opt. I, 13, 14; Aug. *C. Cresc.* III, xxvi, 29, xxvii, 30; *C. Gaud.* I, xvi, 17, xxxvii, 47; *De unico bapt.* XVII, 31; *Ep.* XLIII, ii, 3; *C. Litt. Pet.* I, xxi, 23; *Ad Don. post coll.* XIV, 18. In *C. Cresc.* III, xxvii, 30, he gives a nearly complete text of the *acta* of this council.

the Conference of Carthage in 411 to be a forgery, on the grounds that, as we have seen, it bore a date, and also that no council could have assembled at a time of persecution.[1]

In 311 Mensurius had gone to Rome from Carthage to defend his deacon, Felix, on a charge of libel against the consul, Maxentius: he succeeded, but died on the return journey, leaving the see of Carthage vacant at a most critical time. When peace was restored in the next year, 312, the Archdeacon of Carthage, Caecilianus, was chosen by the unanimous vote of the people, and consecrated Bishop of Carthage by Felix, Bishop of Aptunga, and others.[2] But there was a considerable party in the Church of Carthage which disliked him because they were rigorists, and Caecilianus had agreed with his bishop, Mensurius, in adopting a lenient policy towards those who lapsed in the persecution. This party immediately raised opposition against him. Its ringleaders were the priests Botrus and Caelestius,[3] supported by the fanaticism of an opulent and factious woman named Lucilla, who had an old quarrel with Caecilianus because he had forbidden her favourite superstition of bringing to Mass the bone of a martyr, which she kissed before communicating.[4] Trouble also arose between the new bishop and those to whom Mensurius, on departing for Rome, had entrusted church treasures and sacred vessels. They gave them up reluctantly to Caecilianus, but joined the opposition against him. This party sought the help of certain Numidian bishops (since Numidia had a reputation for rigorism) and no fewer than seventy of them assembled in council, probably at Lucilla's house, under the chairmanship of Secundus of Tigisis. It is not known on what grounds they claimed to take part in the election and consecration of a bishop of Carthage. Their successors, Donatists, claimed at the Conference of Carthage that it was because a primate should be consecrated by a primate; but the Bishop of Carthage seems usually to have been consecrated by his comprovincial bishops, as the Bishop of Rome was traditionally consecrated by his neighbour the Bishop of Ostia.[5] Perhaps it was because Carthage ranked as a quasi-patriarchal see for the whole of Africa. This synod at Carthage, a somewhat rowdy one,[6] decided that the consecrator of

[1] See n. 2, p. 4, supra; and Aug. *Breu. Coll.* III, xvii, 31–3; *Gesta Coll. Carthag.* III, 351–5, 387–400, 408–32, 452–70 (in *P.L.* XI, 1223 sq.)

[2] Opt. I, 18.

[3] Opt. I, 18; Aug. *Ps. c. part. Donati*, vv. 42–51.

[4] Opt. I, 16, 18, 19: 'schisma igitur illo tempore confusae mulieris iracundia peperit, ambitus nutriuit, auaritia roborauit.' Aug. *C. Ep. Parm.* I, iii, 5.

[5] Aug. *Breu. Coll.* III, xvi, 29.

[6] Aug. *De unit. eccl.* xxv, 73: 'seditiosum turbulentumque concilium'.

Caecilianus, Felix of Aptunga, had been a *traditor* in the persecution,[1] and the notorious Purpurius of Limata advanced the suggestion that they should invite Caecilianus to the synod with a view to giving him confirmatory consecration, and then break his head by way of penance.[2] But the faithful at Carthage kept Caecilianus back from venturing himself into their company, though he himself said that if it was indeed true (as they alleged) that Felix was a *traditor*, they could themselves come and consecrate him as if he were still in deacon's orders.[3] In the end this gathering of *traditores* consecrated Maiorinus, a Carthaginian reader,[4] no doubt the candidate proposed by Lucilla (since Optatus describes him as *domesticus Lucillae*),[5] who had bribed the Numidian bishops at a cost of 400 pieces of gold each, a vast sum of money; and thus set up a schismatic church at Carthage, inaugurating the division of African Christianity which was only finally to be healed when at the beginning of the seventh century Christianity itself in Africa succumbed to the Arab invasion. The seventy bishops then sent a circular to all the African churches, asking them to break off communion with Caecilianus.[6]

3. *The appeal to the Emperor*

In the same year, 312, was published the Edict of Toleration, which concluded the Diocletian persecution. In Africa it was to apply to the Church which was in communion with Caecilianus, and in defence of their property the schismatics appealed to the Emperor for recognition. They lodged with Anulinus, the proconsul at Carthage, in 313, a document entitled *Libellus ecclesiae catholicae criminum Caeciliani, traditus a parte Maiorini*. This has not survived, but we have the text of the report forwarded to the Emperor by Anulinus, in which he says that a few days after he had sent on to Caecilianus a letter from the Emperor entitling him to claim from Vrsus, the *Rationalis*, or finance minister, of Africa, the sum of 3000 *folles* given by the Emperor for distribution to the Church,[7] he was approached by certain persons who gave him two memoranda, one open and one secret, to be sent to the Emperor. The secret one is lost; it was the *Libellus ecclesiae catholicae*. These were sent on 15 April 313; and the open one was produced at the Conference

[1] It was later shown that these charges were false. Aug. *Ep.* CXXIX, 4; CXLI, 8–10.
[2] Opt. I, 19.
[3] Opt. I, 19; Aug. *Breu. Coll.* III, xvi, 29.
[4] Opt. I, 15; Aug. *C. Ep. Parm.* I, iii, 5.   [5] Opt. I, 19.
[6] Opt. I, 19, 20; Aug. *De unit. eccl.* XXV, 73; *C. Cresc.* III, iii, 3; IV, vii, 9; *Ep.* XLIII, v, 14; pseudo-Aug. *C. Fulgentium*, XXVI.
[7] Eusebius, *Historia Ecclesiastica*, X, vi, 1.

of 411 by the Catholics, and in the Conference records a full text is given.[1]

The party of Maiorinus requested the Emperor to submit the dispute to the adjudication of the bishops of Gaul, chosen since they had largely escaped the furies of the recent persecution. The Emperor expressed his disapproval of such an appeal to the State in a letter to Miltiades, Bishop of Rome,[2] but appointed three Gallic bishops, Maternus of Cologne, Reticius of Autun, and Marinus of Arles, to judge the affair, under the presidency of the Bishop of Rome, Miltiades, and with fifteen Italian bishops as assessors. This synod sat at the Lateran, the residence of the Empress Fausta, for three days beginning on 2 October 313.[3] Caecilianus was invited to be present with ten bishops, and Donatus of Casae Nigrae with a like number, to represent the schismatics. The synod acquitted Caecilianus of *traditio*, and recognized him as lawful Bishop of Carthage.[4] On the other hand, it found that Donatus of Casae Nigrae in Numidia, the principal accuser of Caecilianus, had during the episcopate of Mensurius committed schism by rebaptizing Christians. Two bishops, Eunomius and Olympius, were sent to Carthage to announce the acquittal of Caecilianus, and they arrived in the next Lent. Caecilianus and Donatus were, however, detained for a time in Italy.

The proconsul, Anulinus, was then ordered to hold an inquiry in Africa concerning the conduct of Felix during the persecution; and at this inquiry, held on 15 February 314, Felix was found innocent of *traditio*, it being discovered that the charge against him rested on the false evidence of letters forged by a Roman official of state, who was summoned to Rome to answer for his misdemeanour.[5]

The Maiorinists then appealed to the Emperor against the decision of the synod of Rome, and he remitted the appeal in the same year to the Council of Arles,[6] which was a more or less general council of the Western Patriarchate, under the presidency of Marinus of Arles. It met on 1 August 314, and Caecilianus was again found innocent.[7] At the

---

[1] *Gesta Coll. Carthag.* III, 215–20; Aug. *Breu. Coll.* III, vii, 8, xii, 24; Opt. I, 22. It is quoted also in great part in Aug. *Ep.* LXXXVIII, 2; and mentioned in *C. Cresc.* III, lxi, 67; *De unico bapt.* XVI, 28; *Ep.* XLIII, v, 15; LXXXIX, 3; XCIII, iv, 13; CXXVIII, 2.

[2] Eusebius, *H.E.* X, v, 18–20.   [3] Opt. I, 22–4.

[4] Aug. *Breu. Coll.* III, xii, 24.   [5] Aug. *Ep.* LXXXVIII, 4.

[6] See the letter of Constantine to Aelafius, Vicar of Africa, in C. H. Turner, *Ecclesiae Occidentalis Monumenta Iuris Antiquissima* (Oxford, 1899–1939), vol. I, pp. 376 sq.

[7] C. J. Hefele, op. cit. vol. I, pp. 180 sq. Canons VIII, on rebaptism; XIII, on *traditio*; XIV, on false accusations; and XX, on the necessity of at least three bishops

same council Felix was also again pronounced innocent,[1] and his accusers were excommunicated till the day of their death. It was resolved also that bishops who could be proved by public records to have been *traditores* should be deposed, but that their ordinations should be recognized as valid.[2] The council reported its decision to the Bishop of Rome, Siluester,[3] and the Donatists now appealed to the Emperor to try the case in person.[4] It was an appeal from an ecclesiastical to a civil jurisdiction, which was to be so inconvenient to their successors in future polemics against Catholicism in Africa. The Emperor refused to hear the case; and ordered those who contumaciously refused to conform to the decision of the Council of Arles to be sent to court for punishment.[5] Some of the schismatics thereupon returned to the Church, but the majority remained obstinate. The Bishop of Carthage and his leading opponents were summoned to Rome, but for some unknown reason Caecilianus did not appear,[6] and the case was remitted to Milan, where it was tried in November 316, and Caecilianus finally acquitted. The churches of the Donatists were confiscated, but throughout the fourth century the party, nourished on religious faction and political hatred of the Roman domination, waxed stronger in Africa.

4. *The spread of Donatism in the fourth century*

The Donatists were led for many years by a powerful and unscrupulous bishop, Donatus, who is always mentioned as ruling the Donatist church at Carthage. It was for long usual to distinguish this Donatus from the Donatus of Casae Nigrae, whom we have met at the synod of the Lateran in 313, and to call him Donatus the Great. M. Monceaux has thrown doubt upon this.[7] And in fact we never hear of Donatus as residing at Casae Nigrae but at Carthage. The Donatus described as of Casae Nigrae (which may be his town of origin and not the seat of

---

at consecrations, are interesting in connexion with Donatism. There is some doubt about the number of bishops present at Arles; see C. H. Turner, op. cit. vol. I, pp. 397 sq. On the canons above mentioned, see ibid., pp. 373 sq.

[1] L. Duchesne, *Histoire ancienne de l'Église* (E.T.), *Early History of the Church* (London, 1922), vol. II, pp. 115-18.

[2] Canons XIII, XIV: Hefele, op. cit. vol. I, pp. 191, 192; Turner, op. cit. vol. I, pp. 390, 391.

[3] The text of the letter is given in Document IV of the Appendix to Optatus in *C.S.E.L.* vol. XXVI, pp. 206-8, and in C. H. Turner, op. cit. vol. I, p. 381.

[4] Aug. *Ep.* LXXXVIII; *C. Ep. Parm.* I, 6.

[5] Aug. *Ep.* LXXXVIII, 3.

[6] Ibid. XLIII, vii, 20.

[7] P. Monceaux, in *Revue de l'histoire des religions* (Paris, 1909).

his bishopric) disappears from history after the Lateran synod, and the party in Africa is thereafter led by Donatus the Great at Carthage. Saint Optatus identified the one with the other, and so did Saint Augustine; but at the Conference of Carthage the Donatists still maintained that the two persons were distinct. Donatus the Great held the Donatist see of Carthage for some forty years.

In 318 he gave the Donatist communion its first overseas bishop, establishing at Rome a bishop for the handful of Donatists there. He chose Victor of Garba. At Rome the Donatists were called *Montenses*, from the fact that to his flock of less than forty souls Victor ministered not in a church, for they had none, but in a cave outside the city.[1] Saint Optatus attacks this appointment as an act of schism, for Victor did not sit in the throne of Saint Peter, but in a *cathedra pestilentiae* of his own: 'erat ibi filius sine patre, tiro sine principe, discipulus sine magistro, sequens sine antecedente, inquilinus sine domo, hospes sine hospitio, pastor sine grege, episcopus sine populo.'[2] Down to the Conference of 411 the Donatists managed to maintain a bishop at Rome, though they established no see elsewhere outside Africa; and the succession at Rome was Victor, Boniface, Eucolpius, Macrobius (who was there when Optatus wrote in the middle of the century), Lucianus, and Claudianus.[3]

An inquiry was held by order of Constantine in 320 into the conduct of the Donatist leaders during the recent persecution, and the official record of this inquiry is partly preserved.[4] Secundus, who at the time of the persecution was a subdeacon of Cirta, was shown to be guilty of *traditio*, and a correspondence between him and various Donatist bishops came to light, in which Secundus was warned by them to be reconciled to his enemy the deacon Nundinarius, who knew too much about his past. In 320 Nundinarius produced this correspondence before Zenophilus, and the revelations discredited Secundus, thereby vitiating (on Donatist principles) the consecration of Maiorinus and undermining the whole theological foundation of Donatism.

But all this time, when by the various imperial inquiries the basis of the schism was being undermined, Donatism was a growing force, appealing to many Africans because of its successful opposition to the Roman power in Africa and to the Catholic Church, which strong African nationalists were inclined to look upon as an ally of the imperial power. An instance of this successful resistance, illustrating also the astonishing weakness of the Roman administration in Africa, is

---

[1] Opt. II, 4.   [2] Opt. II, 4.   [3] Opt. II, 4.
[4] *Gesta apud Zenophilum*, in Migne, P.L. XLIII, 793 sq.

provided in the next year (321) at Cirta, one of the most powerful centres of Donatist influence. The Emperor built there a basilica for the Catholics, and when it was finished the Donatists took possession of it. The protests of the local magistrates having been ineffective, complaint was made to Constantine. He sent a letter to Africa deploring schism, but was unable to enforce his decision, and instead promised to build another church for the Catholics to replace the one thus stolen. It is no wonder that the Donatists were encouraged in their opposition, or that they were able to gather to themselves the discontented elements of the African countryside.

Little is known of the Catholic bishops of Carthage during the century. By 347 Gratus had succeeded to Caecilianus, and by 356 Restitutus to Gratus. In 391 Genethlius, who had held the see for an unknown period, was succeeded by Aurelius, who was bishop at the time of Saint Augustine's consecration to Hippo.

In 347, when Gratus was Bishop of Carthage, the Emperor Constans made an effort to restore the shattered ecclesiastical unity of Africa by sending an imperial largess to the Christians there. This came by the hands of the imperial commissioners Paulus and Macarius,[1] who landed at Carthage, and were churlishly received by Donatus the Great, who inquired 'quid imperatori cum ecclesia?' and warned his people not to accept any alms offered. The commissioners travelled west into the country districts of central Numidia where Donatism was strongest,[2] and found increasing opposition to their mission. The Donatist bishops there organized a savage resistance, and they were led by Donatus, Donatist bishop of Bagai, a schismatic stronghold at the foot of the Aures mountains. He gathered his flock into a church, which he provisioned as for a siege, with a view to resisting what was described as a sacrilegious union of the Church. Ten bishops of the sect were sent to meet the two commissioners; and this meeting took place at Vegesela, where the bishops spoke in such an insolent manner that Paulus and Macarius had them immediately tied to pillars and flogged. At this they all moderated their tone, except Marculus, who was imprisoned, and was later to become one of the most famous of Donatist 'martyrs'. The commissioners now judged it imprudent to venture further into Numidia without military protection; and Siluester, Count of Africa, provided them with troops. With these they proceeded to Bagai, and

[1] Opt. III, 4. L. Duchesne, *Histoire ancienne de l'Église* (E.T.), *Early History of the Church* (London, 1922), pp. 191 sq.

[2] A. Berthier, *Les vestiges du christianisme antique dans la Numidie centrale* (Alger, 1943), describes excavations in this region.

Donatus led forth his troops of Circumcellions against them. A bloody battle ensued, in which the dissidents were overcome, and Donatus taken.[1] This encounter quietened the Donatist violence, and until the accession of the apostate Julian in 361 its excesses were restrained.

This is the first appearance in history of the marauding bands of Circumcellions.[2] They were lawless rebels who lived on their depredations in the country districts of Africa, wandering around the farmhouses (*circum cellas*), from which fact they derived their name *Circumcelliones*.[3] They are compared by M. Martroye[4] to the *Bagaudae* who created a peasant revolt in the time of Diocletian, and tyrannized Gaul.[5] The Circumcellions were mostly men of peasant origin, African in nationality, and usually speaking only Punic. They made profession of continence, and compared themselves to monks; but lived as brigands, armed at first with clubs, which they called *israeles*, since it was forbidden by the New Testament to take the sword.[6] But by Saint Augustine's time they had added slings, axes, stones, lances and swords.[7] They readily allied themselves to the Donatist cause, and claimed the title of 'saints', and were called by the Donatists *Agonistici*.[8] About 350 they were being led by Axido and Fasir, a couple of robbers who rejoiced in the title of 'captains of the saints',[9] but their leaders were frequently Donatist bishops, of whom the most notorious later on was the infamous Optatus of Thamugadi.[10] Any of their forces who fell in battle were adjudged to be martyrs, and the honours customary for martyrs in Africa were paid at their tombs.[11] Burial in churches was a common practice with the Donatists, and it is unusual to find

---

[1] Opt. III, 1.

[2] See F. Martroye, 'Une tentative de révolution sociale en Afrique: Donatistes et Circoncellions', in *Revue des questions historiques* (Paris, 1904, 1905), vols. 76, 77.

[3] *Philastri Brixensis Liber de haeresibus*, LXXXV, P.L. XII, 1197–8 (he calls them *circuitores*); Aug. *De haeres.* LXIX; *Ep.* CVIII, v, 14; *C. Gaud.* I, xxviii, 32.

[4] F. Martroye, op. cit.

[5] Le Nain de Tillemont, *Histoire des Empereurs* (Paris, 1700–38), vol. IV, p. 9.

[6] Aug. *Enarr. in Ps.* X, 5.

[7] Aug. *C. Ep. Parm.* I, xi, 17; II, lxxxviii, 195, xcvi, 222.

[8] Opt. III, 4; Aug. *Enarr. in Ps.* CXXII, 6. The fallen Circumcellions are often called *sancti* in their sepulchral inscriptions; see S. Gsell, in *Bulletin archéologique du Comité des travaux historiques* (1905), p. clxxxvi. Sometimes also they are similarly described as *iusti*, e.g. in *Corpus Inscriptionum Latinarum*, VIII, 7922, 10863, 18552. At Henchir-el-Guesseria was found over the church door an inscription, H(A)EC PORTA DOMI(N)I IUSTI INTRABUNT (Berthier, op. cit. pp. 103, 207).

[9] Opt. III, 4.   [10] Aug. *C. Litt. Pet.* II, ciii, 237.

[11] On the cult of martyrs in Africa, see Berthier, op. cit. pp. 191–205, 220–4.

a quire in any of their churches without traces of such burial. The remains are sometimes immured, and sometimes buried beneath the floor. In some cases remains of whole bodies have been discovered. Occasionally, however, in such reliquaries there are no traces of bones, but small collections of earth known to be brought from elsewhere (since it is different from the earth of the site). It may be the earth of the place where the martyr fell, or sometimes it is earth from the Holy Sepulchre, or from elsewhere in the Holy Land.[1] The very name *Circumcelliones* became a byword for terror and violence among all peaceable African citizens, and their cry of *Deo laudes* was more dreaded than the roar of a Numidian lion.[2] This war-cry has been found frequently in inscriptions.[3] M. Martroye holds that these Circumcellion outrages began when the Catholic clergy sought the support of the imperial authority, and were the natural outlet for a party which saw in Christianity the prospect of a new social order in Africa, free from Roman domination and taxation, and that the religious difference was used merely as a pretext for creating trouble.[4] There is considerable truth in the latter part of this statement; but it may be doubted whether the hatred of the orthodox clergy was due solely, or even primarily, to their appeal to the State. They would have been hated in any case as being Latin-speaking, and loyal citizens of the Empire; and, if not on this pretext, then on another, the chance would have been seized of relieving the inevitable tension between the native Punic outlook and the Catholic and Roman tendencies of the orthodox, who were strongest in the more highly civilized regions of the coast and in the towns.

[1] Cf. Aug. *De ciu. Dei*, XXII, viii, 6. See Berthier, op. cit. pp. 161, 191, 200 sq.
[2] Aug. *Enarr. in Ps.* CXXXII, 6.
[3] A. Audollent, 'Mission épigraphique en Algérie', in *Mélanges de l'École française de Rome* (1890), pp. 440 sq., especially Khenchela; Pierre Cayrel, 'Une basilique donatiste de Numidie' (Ksar-el-Kelb), ibid. (1934). *Deo laudes* is found in the following inscriptions: *C.I.L.* VIII, 2046, 2308, 10694, 10969, 17768, 18669, 22653. W. H. C. Frend, 'The Revival of Berber Art', in *Antiquity* (December, 1942), p. 351; 'Note on the Berber Background in the Life of Augustine', in *J.T.S.* (July–October 1942), vol. XLIII, nos. 171, 172, pp. 188–91: 'The Catholic Church in Africa could not survive the Roman cities, and the Roman villa-owning aristocracy. The strength of Christianity among the peasants lay in the Donatist church. Here they could at one and the same time vent their antipathy to their Latin-speaking masters, and express beliefs which had inspired their forefathers, beliefs which indeed form the basis of North African religion to-day' (e.g. the cult of martyrs). For other references to Donatist epigraphy, see Paul Monceaux, *Histoire littéraire de l'Afrique chrétienne*, vol. IV, ch. iv; and A. Berthier, op. cit. pp. 77, 206, 207, etc.
[4] F. Martroye, op. cit.

In any case the attacks of the Circumcellions were not directed solely against the Catholics. When the rebels felt strong enough, they assailed the pagans as well. Professor J. H. Baxter has shown in a most interesting article[1] that a letter of the pagan grammarian Maximus of Madaura to Saint Augustine is concerned with the Circumcellion outrages, and with the Donatist pseudo-martyrs who perished in the *tempora Macariana*.[2]

Professor Baxter gives some very significant comparisons between the phraseology of this letter and facts about the Circumcellions known to us from Saint Optatus as well as from Saint Augustine,[3] and uses them to illustrate the animosity of the Donatists, mainly drawn from the Punic population, against the State as well as against the State religion. Their ferocity may have been practised on Maximus himself, which would account for the bitterness of his references. The Circumcellions were, suggests Professor Baxter, 'diis hominibusque odiosa nomina', because they attacked pagan as well as Catholic property.

After the battle of Bagai in 347 the two rebel leaders, Donatus of

[1] J. H. Baxter, 'The Martyrs of Madaura', in *J.T.S.* (October 1924), pp. 21 sq.
[2] *Apud* Aug. *Ep.* XVI, 2. See also A. Audollent, 'Mission épigraphique en Algérie', in *Mélanges de l'École française de Rome* (1890), on Tixter and on Tebessa.
[3] Professor Baxter makes the following comparisons:

cunctis...diis immortalibus. It was not usual to exalt martyrs to be the rivals of the gods, but the Donatists did this. Opt. II, 21: 'personas nostras iam pro Deo habere noscuntur.' Cf. Opt. II, 16, 22, 23.

alio interminato numero. This suits the Circumcellion bands. Cf. Opt. III, 4; Aug. *C. Gaud.* I, xxix, 33.

conscientia nefandorum facinorum. Cf. Opt. II, 19 on Felix: 'inter crimina sua et facinora nefanda'; Aug. *Ep.* CXXIV, 2: 'horrenda facinora' (cf. *C. Cresc.* I, 28); *Ad Don. post coll.* XVII, 22: 'apertissima facinora et scelera'; *C. Cresc.* III, xliii, 47: 'tam magna scelera'; *C. Gaud.* I, xxxvi, 46: 'nefanda scelera'; *De unico bapt.* VIII, 14: 'manifesta flagitia et facinora'; *De unit. eccl.* LIV: 'sceleratissima latrocinia'; *Breu. Coll.* III, viii, 13: 'scelera quibus uiolenter saeuiunt nefarieque uiuunt', etc.

specie gloriosae martyris. The collocation of this with the last is found over and over again in the charges levelled against the Donatists, e.g. Aug. *Ep.* LXXXVIII, 8; CV, 5; *C. Litt. Pet.* II, 184; *C. Gaud.* I, xxvi, 29; xxvii, 31; *C. Cresc.* III, xlii, 46.

dignum moribus factisque suis exitum...reppererunt. He refers to either death or suicide. Cf. Aug. *Breu. Coll.* III, viii, 13; *Ep.* LXXXIX, 2.

maculati. Cf. Aug. *Ep.* LII, 3; CLXXXV, 15; *C. Cresc.* III, xlviii, 52; *De unico bapt.* VIII, 14.

busta. The funeral orgies are often mentioned, e.g. Aug. *De unit. eccl.* L.

stulti. S. Augustine calls them *imperiti*: the ignorant rank and file (*Ep.* XCVII, 2; CXVIII, 32; CXXXIV, 4; CLXXXV, ii, 6; *In Ioan. Evang. tract.* IV, 16; *C. Cresc.* III, lxviii, 78, etc.

So, concludes Professor Baxter, it is almost certain that Miggin, Saname, Namphamo, Lucitas, were Circumcellions who perished during the *tempora Macariana*.

Bagai and Marculus, who had both been arrested, died. According to the Donatist account of this, they were executed, Donatus being thrown down a well and Marculus from a rock.[1] This account is contained in the extant *Passio Marculi*.[2] It says that Marculus, one of the ten Donatist bishops, had been beaten, and then taken round Numidia for four days before being imprisoned at Noua Petra; and that later, on a Sunday at dawn, 29 November 347, he was thrown from a rock. Saint Optatus contents himself with saying that the deaths of Donatus and Marculus were claimed by the Donatists as martyrdoms, but that the opponents of unity cause their own downfall:[3] Saint Augustine says that it is uncertain whether they threw themselves down or were thrown down, but that in any case self-precipitation of this kind was a common practice with the Donatists,[4] which they attempted to justify by the example of Razias, narrated in II Maccabees xiv.[5] M. Paul Monceaux has suggested that they were judicially executed with the sword, precipitation not being an usual method of Roman execution, and that their bodies were then thrown down to prevent their being salved for relics.[6] If this was the object, it was not attained, for in 411 Datiuus, the then Donatist bishop of Noua Petra, claimed at the Conference of Carthage that he had no Catholic bishop in his town because they had there the relics of this same Marculus, whom God would avenge, he said, in the day of Judgement.[7]

Severe repression of Donatists ensued, and Saint Optatus says that their remaining bishops fled, and, if not, were exiled; and their churches seized.[8] Among these bishops was Donatus the Great, who was exiled from Carthage, and died in exile between 350 and 355.[9] Peace being thus established, Paulus and Macarius on their return to Carthage attended a public thanksgiving in the principal basilica.[10] Shortly afterwards, apparently in 348, a council met at Carthage under the Bishop, Gratus, to deal with matters of ecclesiastical discipline resulting from this unification.[11] Some Donatist bishops conformed at this time, among them Optantius, Donatist bishop of Madaura in Numidia, who was allowed to divide that diocese with its Catholic bishop, Antigonus.

[1] Opt. III, 6; Aug. *In Ioan. Evang. tract.* XI, 15.
[2] Printed in Ellies Dupin, *Optatus* (Paris, 1845), pp. 302 sq.
[3] Opt. III, 6.
[4] Aug. *C. Litt. Pet.* II, xx, 46; *C. Cresc.* III, xlix, 54. See infra, p. 15.
[5] Aug. *C. Gaud.* I, xxxi, 36–9.
[6] P. Monceaux, *Histoire littéraire de l'Afrique chrétienne*, vol. v, ch. ii.
[7] *Gesta Coll. Carthag.* I, 187.   [8] Opt. III, 4.
[9] Opt. III, 3.   [10] Opt. III, 12.
[11] Hefele, op. cit. vol. II, pp. 184–6.

Later on he contrived to usurp some of the jurisdiction of Antigonus.¹ But not many of the Donatists thus submitted, and those who did not were more and more embittered. They would not correspond with Catholic clergy, or salute them.² If they were strong enough to take over any Catholic churches, they evicted the Catholics, and washed with salt and water the pavements on which they had walked, and even the walls.³ They constantly attacked the Catholics in their sermons,⁴ and spied on their clergy, with a view to exposing the smallest fault.⁵ There was at this time an outburst of the dominating Donatist passion for pseudo-martyrdom by suicide, if it was impossible to seek death by legal process. Whole companies threw themselves from rocks, for they despised hanging, since Judas the traitor had thus died.⁶ Even women practised this folly, and the anniversaries of such 'martyrs' were observed with riots of drunkenness and immorality at their tombs.⁷ Those who thus intended to die gave invitations to their friends, who assembled and brought supplies of food to fatten the victims for their impending sacrifice.⁸ This practice is evidenced archaeologically by the discovery in recent investigations of at least three collections of inscribed memorial stones at the foot of precipices in central Numidia, which was always a great Donatist stronghold. M. Berthier suggests with much probability that these cemeteries below precipices are the resting-places of such Donatist suicides.⁹ But they did not kill themselves if they could persuade the authorities to do it. One device was to attack magistrates on the road.¹⁰ Saint Augustine tells us that one magistrate thus attacked had the hands of the Circumcellions tied with a view to arresting them. They willingly submitted, and he then went

---

¹ *Gesta Coll. Carthag.* I, 126.   ² Opt. I, 4; IV, 5.   ³ Opt. VI, 6.
⁴ Opt. IV, 5.   ⁵ Aug. *Ep.* LXXVIII, 5.
⁶ Opt. III, 4: 'inde etiam illi qui ex altorum montium cacuminibus uiles animas proiicientes se praecipites dabant.' Aug. *C. Litt. Pet.* I, xxiv, 26; *De haeres.* LXIX: 'ad hanc haeresim in Africa et illi pertinent, qui appellantur Circumcelliones, genus hominum agreste et famosissimae audaciae, non solum in alios immania facinora perpetrando, sed nec sibi eadem insana feritate parcendo. nam per mortes uarias maximeque praecipitiorum et aquarum et ignium se ipsos necare consuerunt; et in istum furorem alios quos potuerint sexus utriusque seducere, aliquando ut occidantur ab aliis, mortem, nisi fecerint, comminantes.' *Philastri Brixensis Liber de haeresibus,* LXXXV (*P.L.* XII, 1197-8); Le Nain de Tillemont, *Mémoires pour servir à l'histoire ecclésiastique des six premiers siècles* (Paris, 1701-12), art. xxxvii.
⁷ Aug. *C. Ep. Parm.* III, iii, 18.
⁸ Theodoretus, Episcopus Cyrensis, *Haereticarum fabularum compendium,* IV, 6 (*P.G.* LXXXIII, 423).
⁹ A. Berthier, op. cit. pp. 215-18.   ¹⁰ Aug. *Ep.* CLXXXV, iv, 15.

away and left them.¹ Sometimes ordinary travellers were stopped, and invited to kill them.² If they were unwilling, they were threatened with murder themselves; but one young man, thus accosted, tied up the Circumcellions, and, having flogged them, went his way.³ Saint Optatus tells us that they sometimes paid men to kill them.⁴

As bandits they were extraordinarily cruel. They attacked and robbed by night the houses of priests: they stabbed people, or blinded them with vinegar. When they found that people recovered from this, they took to adding quicklime to the vinegar.⁵ In robbing a house they poured out on to the floor any wine that they could not take away. The rebaptism of Catholics was sometimes enforced by such violent means.

From 347 until the accession of Julian in 361 Donatism was proscribed in Africa, but thus continued its violent course. Under the Apostate, however, the law changed. Donatism was now tolerated, and those who had been banished by Constantius were recalled.⁶ This did not include the Donatists banished by Constans, and they petitioned Julian in 362 for an amnesty.⁷ The signatories of this petition included Rogatianus, Pontius, and Cassianus.⁸ The reason for this toleration is not clear: most of the ancient historians think that Julian did it in the hope that it would weaken Christianity in Africa by encouraging internal dissensions;⁹ but M. Martroye makes the interesting suggestion that he tolerated them to rob them of any good pretext for hostility to his government, and to make them interested in the maintenance of the existing order without incurring much danger of strengthening Christianity.¹⁰ The text of his rescript¹¹ says nothing about church buildings, but they seem to have been restored to the Donatists, for we hear of their washing them with salt water, giving the altar wine to their workmen, and committing other sacrileges, which included throwing the chrism out of the window, and the Host to the dogs,

---

¹ Aug. *Ep.* CLXXXV, iv, 15.
² Aug. *De haeres.* LXIX.   ³ Theodoretus, loc. cit.
⁴ Opt. III, 4.   ⁵ Aug. *C. Cresc.* III, xlii, 46.
⁶ Socrates, *Historia Ecclesiastica*, II, xxxviii (*P.G.* LXVII, 328); Rufinus, *Historia Ecclesiastica*, I, xxvi (*P.L.* XXI, 498).
⁷ Opt. II, 16; Aug. *C. Litt. Pet.* II, xcvii, 224.
⁸ Ibid. II, xcvii, 224.
⁹ E.g. Socrates, *H.E.* III, 1 (*P.G.* LXVII, 367 sq.); Rufinus, *H.E.* I, xxvii (*P.L.* XXI, 498); Sozomen, *H.E.* V, 5 (*P.G.* LXVII, 1225 sq.); Ammianus Marcellinus, XXII, 5.
¹⁰ F. Martroye, op. cit.
¹¹ Quoted in Aug. *C. Litt. Pet.* II, xcvii, 224.

which thereupon most fittingly went mad, and bit their masters.[1] A renewed outburst of hatred against the Catholics was to be expected, and Optatus describes it.[2] At Tipasa, in Caesarean Mauretania, men were torn in pieces, women ill-treated, children murdered, and abortions performed in the interests of Donatism by two Donatist bishops, Vrbanus of Formae and Felix of Idicra. At Castellum Lemellense, in Mauretania Sitifensis, the Catholics endeavoured to retain their basilica, and took refuge in it; but the Donatists went on to the roof, stripped off the tiles, and threw them down on the occupants, two of whom, Primus and Donatus, were killed, and are mentioned in the Roman martyrology under 9 February.[3] No answer was given to the protest made with regard to this incident by Primosus, the Catholic bishop there. Saint Optatus was a contemporary witness of many of these acts of violence.

This was a short-lived triumph for Donatism, for in 363 Valentinian I succeeded; and in the next year, when Catholicism was again a tolerated religion, the Donatists, along with the Manichaeans, were exempted from the act of toleration;[4] and, by a law of 20 February 373, addressed to Iulianus, proconsul of Africa, Valentinian deposed bishops who had been guilty of rebaptizing.[5] This legislation was evidently not carried into effect in Africa, for Donatism continued to increase by leaps and bounds.

This expansion of Donatism was in no small measure due to the leadership it found in its new bishop of Carthage, who succeeded to the chair of Donatus the Great in 361. This was Parmenianus, a foreigner, probably from Gaul or Spain, who may well have met the great Donatus when he was exiled there.[6] He was almost the only recruit whom the Donatist sect had from overseas.[7] But he achieved such fame that the Donatists were sometimes known as Parmenianists.[8] During his episcopate, which lasted till about 390, Donatism grew to be about as strong as the Church in Africa, and in Numidia was definitely stronger.[9] He inaugurated his episcopate by writing a long work in five books against the Catholic position;[10] and it was this work that Optatus refuted in his six books on the history of Donatism. The work of Saint Optatus was published about 366 or 367, and was revised many

---

[1] Opt. II, 17–19; VI, 1–7.   [2] Opt. II, 17–19.   [3] Opt. II, 18.
[4] C.Th. XVI, v, 1, v, 3.   [5] Ibid. XVI, vi, 1.
[6] P. Monceaux, op. cit. vol. v, ch. v.
[7] Opt. I, 5, 10; II, 7; III, 3; Aug. C. Ep. Parm. I, ii, 2; Serm. XLVI, viii, 17.
[8] Aug. De haeres. XLI; C. Ep. Parm. I, iv, 9.
[9] Gesta Coll. Carthag. I, 165; Aug. Ep. CXXIX, 2, 6; Enarr. in Ps. XXI, 26; Serm. II. in Ps. XXXVI, 19.
[10] Opt. I, 5, 6.

years later. Both Catholics and Donatists speak of Parmenianus as a straightforward man, much respected and of great ability, who did not stoop to deceit or violence, as did so many Donatist prelates.[1] He was considered a good orator[2] and was also the author of a collection of psalms for the instruction of his people, which have been lost, but are said to have been very popular and to have been sung lustily in the Donatist churches.[3] The only two works of his about which we know anything were the great treatise against the Catholics, published in the time of Julian, and the letter to Tyconius, which was written about 378.[4]

The former was one of the most important of all Donatist polemical works; and Saint Optatus thought it worth while to answer it in detail.[5] It is from his quotations that we are in part able to reconstruct the book. It may have been called *Aduersus Ecclesiam Traditorum*; and in five books it dealt with the questions at issue. But Optatus complains that it had no logical order.[6] In the first book Parmenianus seems to have dealt with baptism,[7] before proceeding to the Donatist thesis concerning the unworthiness of ministers.[8] The second book, on the unity of the Church,[9] brought him to the core of the subject, and he tried to show that the Donatist was the only true Church.[10] The third book attacked the *traditores*,[11] and the fourth complained of the iniquity of the imperial attempt to establish unity,[12] and of the improbity of the Catholics in appealing to the State on a purely religious matter.[13] This led Parmenianus on to elaborate the persecutions alleged to have been suffered by the schismatics;[14] and his fifth book expounded some texts of Scripture alleged to bear on the subject.[15]

The letter to Tyconius answered from the rigid Donatist standpoint the work of Tyconius the Donatist exegete. Saint Augustine was asked about 400 to compose a refutation of this *Epistula ad Tyconium*, and his *Contra Epistulam Parmeniani* is the response to this request.[16] What we know of the letter of Parmenianus is derived from this treatise. The letter was concerned first of all with the statement of Tyconius that the

[1] Opt. I, 4, 5, 9; IV, 9; Aug. C. Ep. Parm. II, vii, 13.
[2] Aug. C. Cresc. I, ii, 3. [3] Aug. Ep. LV, xviii, 34.
[4] Monceaux, op. cit. V, vi, 2, 3. On Tyconius, see infra, pp. 19 sq.
[5] Opt. I, 4–6. [6] Opt. I, 6, 7. [7] Opt. I, 5, 6; V, 1.
[8] Opt. V, 4, 6, 7. [9] Opt. I, 6. [10] Opt. II, 1, 2, 8, 10–13.
[11] Opt. I, 5, 6. [12] Opt. I, 6; III, 4; IV, 1. [13] Opt. I, 22.
[14] Opt. I, 5, 6; II, 14, 15, 18, 19; III, 1, 4, 6, 8, 11, 12; VI, 3, 4; VII, 6.
[15] Opt. I, 5, 6; IV, 1.
[16] Aug. Retract. II, xvii; Ep. XCIII, x, 43; C. Ep. Parm. I, i, 1, ii, 2; II, xiii, 31, xxii, 42; III, iii, 17, etc.

Church is always universal in its extension. Parmenianus denies that this is always so, since the oversea churches had during the fourth century forfeited their claim to catholicity by remaining in communion with an African church which on the puritan theory of the Donatists was purely a congregation of *traditores*, and therefore lacking in the holiness which must characterize a truly Catholic Church.[1] He admits that during the persecution there had been *traditores* in every country, but adds that only in Africa had the 'Catholic' Church broken off relations with them, as it should have done all over the world.[2] On this theory the holy Church throughout all the world is now reduced to the pure Church in Africa of the Donatists.[3] If this is admitted, it follows that the imperial condemnation of Donatism was erroneous. Constantine, misled by the Catholics, and particularly by the venerable Hosius, Bishop of Cordova, was unjustified in condemning the Donatists.[4] And to this error he added the crime of using force to repress the Church.[5] Parmenianus, having disposed of his enemies on historical grounds, proceeded to expound his doctrine of the sacrament of baptism, which is the ancient African theory of Agrippinus and Saint Cyprian, that baptism can only be administered even within the true Church by men whose hearts are pure.[6] These dogmatic and historical considerations led Parmenianus to the conclusion of his epistle, which was that the two churches were irreconcilable.[7]

In Tyconius, the other great Donatist writer of the latter half of the fourth century, we have the unusual spectacle of a balanced writer who, though always remaining a Donatist, could see what was to be said on the other side of the question. He was a layman whose special interest was Scriptural exegesis. Gennadius says that he was 'Afer', that is, a native of Proconsular Africa, and that he was brought up a Donatist, and was learned in sacred and in secular studies.[8] Saint Augustine describes him as 'hominem et acri ingenio praeditum et uberi eloquio':[9] he was intelligent enough to know the weak points in Donatism, and honest enough to admit them,[10] thereby rendering

---

[1] Aug. *C. Ep. Parm.* I, ii, 2.   [2] Ibid. I, iii, 4, 5.
[3] Ibid. II, i, 1–3, ii, 4, iii, 6, 7, iv, 8, v, 10, vii, 13, viii. 15, ix, 18.
[4] Ibid. I, iv, 7, v, 10, vi, 11.   [5] Ibid. I, viii, 13, ix, 15, x, 16.
[6] Ibid. II, x, 20, 21, xi, 23, 24, xii, 26, xiii, 27–30, xiv, 32, xv, 33, xvi, 35, xvii, 36.
[7] Ibid. II, xviii, 37, xx, 39, xxi, 40, 41, xxii, 42, xxiii, 43; III, i, 1, ii, 4, 7, 9, 11, iii, 17, 18, iv, 20, v, 26; *C. Cresc.* III, lxxxi, 93; IV, lix, 71.
[8] Gennadius, *De uiris illustribus*, 18.   [9] Aug. *C. Ep. Parm.* I, i, 1.
[10] Gennadius, loc. cit.; Aug. *C. Ep. Parm.* I, i, 1; II, xxii, 42; III, iii, 17; *Ep.* XCIII, *⁌*, 43, 44; CCXLIX.

himself liable to attacks by Donatus[1] and to expulsion from the Donatist party.[2] He seems to have died about 390.

His two principal works of a polemical nature were entitled *De bello intestino*, published about 370, and the *Expositiones diuersarum causarum*, about 375. Fragments of these have been preserved by Saint Augustine, and show that they were both concerned with the catholicity of the Church.[3] Against the Donatists he objected the arrogance of their claim 'quod uolumus sanctum est',[4] and went so far as to maintain the Catholic opinion that the promises of God were made to an universal and not to a merely African Church[5] and that African crimes could not defile the Church overseas.[6] Like the Catholics, he taught that evil must be tolerated in the Church until it is finally severed in the Last Judgement.[7] He pointed to the Rogatist schism to show that, whatever their theory, the Donatists had themselves practised this toleration.[8] He also contested the practice of rebaptism, and showed that, as in the case of Deuterius, some Donatists had refused to practise it, but had not therefore been excommunicated by the Donatist sect.[9] He still thought, however, that Donatism was the true faith, but would have been prepared to unite the shattered Church of Africa by meeting the Catholics half-way; and for this reason Saint Augustine suggested that his logical course would have been to come over to the Church.[10]

The greatest work of Tyconius, on which his fame principally rests, is his work on Biblical exegesis, the *Liber Regularum*, published about 382, which we have almost intact.[11] This work expounds seven *regulae* for the understanding of Scripture, and gives special attention to the Old Testament. These *regulae* are as follows:

I. De Domino et corpore eius.   V. De temporibus.
II. De Domini corpore bipertito.   VI. De recapitulatione.
III. De promissis et lege.   VII. De diabolo et eius corpore.[12]
IV. De specie et genere.

---

[1] Aug. *Ep.* XCIII, x, 43–5; C. *Ep. Parm.* I, i, 1.
[2] Ibid. I, i, 1.   [3] Ibid. I, i, 1.
[4] Aug. *Ep.* XCIII, iv, 14, x, 43; C. *Ep. Parm.* II, xiii, 31.
[5] Aug. C. *Ep. Parm.* I, i, 1; *Ep.* XCIII, x, 44.
[6] Ibid. XCIII, x, 44.   [7] Aug. C. *Ep. Parm.* III, iii, 17.
[8] Ibid. II, xxii, 42.   [9] Aug. *Ep.* XCIII, x, 43.
[10] Aug. C. *Ep. Parm.* I, i, 1; *Ep.* XCIII, x, 44; *De doctrina christiana*, III, xxx, 42: 'contra Donatistas inuictissime scripsit, cum fuerit Donatista: et illic inuenitur absurdissimi cordis, ubi eos non omni ex parte relinquere uoluit.'
[11] F. C. Burkitt, 'The Book of the Rules of Tyconius', in vol. III, § 1 of J. A. Robinson, *Texts and Studies* (Cambridge, 1894).
[12] F. C. Burkitt, op. cit.; Aug. *De doctr. christ.* III, xxx, 42.

The work became a classic in Carthage and in Numidia, and in 396 Saint Augustine sent a copy of it to Aurelius, Bishop of Carthage, for him to study,[1] and he himself quotes it in several places.[2] In 385 Tyconius published the last work of his which is known to us, a mystical commentary on the Apocalypse, based on the Old Latin text, which he revised by referring to the Greek original.[3] Primasius appropriated this work, and published it as his own.[4] These works of Tyconius are interesting because of the use which Saint Augustine made of them both for exegetical rules and for a foundation of his doctrine of grace,[5] and of his doctrine of the two cities, of God and of the Devil, which he elaborated in the *De ciuitate Dei*.[6]

We must leave these literary controversies to trace the course of the struggle in the political and religious fields from the accession of Valentinian. It was shortly after this time that Donatism began to manifest the fissiparous tendencies which were afterwards to characterize it. We read of various sects within Donatism: there were Claudianists in Proconsular Africa, Urbanists in Numidia, and Rogatists in Mauretania Caesariensis. The Rogatists existed only at Cartenna, and were less fierce than the rest, having nothing to do with the Circumcellions.[7] Their leader, Rogatus, Donatist bishop of Cartenna, remained faithful to the Emperor in the revolts of Firmus and Gildo. Persecution by these rebels weakened the Rogatists, and in Saint Augustine's day, by 408, they had only ten or eleven bishops left.[8] This revolt of Firmus in Mauretania was due, according to Ammianus Marcellinus, to the incapacity of the Count of Africa, Romanus, whom nobody liked.[9] Firmus, a Moor, quarrelled with him, and instigated a successful revolt against Rome, showing once more the social and political animosity always ready to flare up in Africa.[10] The revolt lasted from 371 to 374,

[1] Aug. *Ep.* XLI, ii.

[2] E.g. Aug. *Quaest. in Heptateuch.* II, xlvii; *Ep.* CCXLIX; *De doctr. christ.* III, xxx, 42–xxxvii, 56.

[3] Aug. ibid. III, xxx, 42; Gennadius, *De uir. illustr.* 18.

[4] Primasius, *Commentarium super Apocalypsim Beati Ioannis*, *Prologus* (P.L. LXVIII, 793 sq.). A. Souter, 'Tyconius' Text of the Apocalypse: a partial restoration', in *J.T.S.* (1913), vol. XIV, pp. 338 sq.

[5] Tyconius, *Regula* III, in Burkitt, op. cit. pp. 17–19.

[6] Tyconius, *Comment. in Apoc.* passim; see N. H. Baynes, *The Political Ideas of S. Augustine's 'De ciuitate Dei'* (London, 1936), p. 5; J. N. Figgis, *Political Aspects of S. Augustine's 'City of God'* (London, 1921), pp. 46, 47. See infra, pp. 139 sq.

[7] Aug. *Ep.* XCIII; *C. Ep. Parm.* I, xi, 17; *C. Litt. Pet.* II, lxxxiii, 184.

[8] Aug. *Ep.* XCIII.   [9] Ammianus Marcellinus, XXVII, v, 2 sq.

[10] W. H. C. Frend, 'The Revival of Berber Art', in *Antiquity* (December, 1942), pp. 342, 343.

and began with the taking and firing of Caesarea, the pillage of Icosium, and the siege of Tipasa. Valentinian sent his best general, Theodosius, the father of the future Emperor, with troops from Pannonia and Moesia, to restore order. One of the allies of Firmus, Igmazen, chief of the tribe of the Isaflenses, seceded to Theodosius; Mascezel, the brother of Firmus, was overcome; and when Firmus hanged himself the revolt collapsed, and peace was restored to Mauretania, though the Circumcellion outrages continued.[1] At this time a series of edicts was promulgated against Donatism. Valentinian[2] and Gratian[3] prohibited rebaptism. The discontent in the country districts smouldered, to burst out afresh under the brigand bishop, the infamous Optatus of Thamugadi in Numidia, who is often called *Gildonianus* because of his alliance with the Count Gildo.[4] Gildo was a brother of Firmus, who had been appointed by Maximus, the usurper of the Western Empire, as Count of Africa, with the exceptional title of Master of Soldiers. He had been loyal to the Empire, and had fought in the Roman forces against his brother Firmus. Now for ten years he tyrannized Africa in conjunction with Optatus, and protected the Donatists.[5] At the end of this time he revolted against the young Emperor Honorius, then twelve years old, and against his regent Stilicho, with a view to transferring the province of Africa from the Western to the Eastern Empire. His first act was to prevent the sailing to Italy of the corn-ships from Africa, which was an act of war, since Italy drew most of its supply from that source; and therefore the Senate immediately declared Gildo a public enemy. Corn was obtained from Gaul and Spain; but Claudian speaks bitterly of the action of Gildo.[6] Stilicho immediately found an African chief to fight against Gildo: this was Mascezel,[7] who went from Italy to Africa with 10,000 men.[8] This force, such as it was, overcame Gildo's 70,000,[9] and Gildo hanged himself after a vain attempt to escape.[10]

[1] Aug. *Ep.* LXXXVIII; *C. Ep. Parm.* I, x, 16.
[2] *C.Th.* XVI, vi, 1 (20 February 373).
[3] Ibid. XVI, vi, 2 (17 October 377).
[4] Aug. *C. Ep. Parm.* II, xv, 34; *C. Litt. Pet.* II, ci, 232, ciii, 237; *C. Cresc.* III. xiii, 16. J. B. Bury, *History of the Later Roman Empire* (London, 1923), pp. 121 sq.
[5] Aug. *C. Ep. Parm.* II, ii, 4: 'Optatum Gildonianum, decennalem totius Africae gemitum'; *C. Litt. Pet.* II, lii, 120: 'sub cuius iniquitatibus Africa tota lugebat'.
[6] Claudianus, *Bellum Gildonianum*, vv. 58 sq.; e.g. v. 70: 'pascimur arbitrio Mauri.'
[7] Ibid. vv. 389 sq.
[8] Ibid. vv. 410 sq.; Orosius, *Historiarum libri*, VII, 36 (P.L. XXXI, 1156).
[9] Zosimus, v, ii.
[10] Orosius, ibid.; Zosimus, ibid.

Mascezel was then summoned to Milan, and received by Stilicho, who, however, had him thrown over a bridge and drowned as they crossed together.[1] Optatus of Thamugadi died in prison,[2] and was consequently acclaimed as a Donatist martyr,[3] and at the same time much Donatist property was confiscated.[4]

5. Saint Optatus of Milevis

The only considerable surviving anti-Donatist work before the time of Saint Augustine is the book of Saint Optatus, Bishop of Milevis, an old Numidian city on the borders of Mauretania, about twenty miles north-west of Constantina.[5] In his youth he had been a pagan, and had been well educated, especially in rhetoric and philosophy.[6] That is all we know of his life. Of his work on the history and theology of Donatism, it may be said that its date is fixed from internal evidence between October 366 and August 367.[7] For he says that he wrote sixty years after the persecution of Diocletian, that is, between 363 and 372; but Saint Jerome narrows this down to 364–367;[8] and, as we see from Optatus, II, 3, his book was written while Damasus was Bishop of Rome, which again narrows the field to the end of 366 or the first half of 367. The second edition was issued some twenty years later,[9] when Book VII was added, and it appears from some repetitions and other indications that Saint Optatus did not himself give the final touches to his work, but that it was patched up by a not very skilful disciple. The object of this seventh book was to answer the objections raised by the Donatists to the first six books.[10] It is noteworthy that this seventh book is not addressed to Parmenianus himself, but to the Donatists in general, with a view to seeking peace and unity.[11] The work of Saint Optatus was so important as an historical work of reference for the controversy that even the Donatists at the Conference did not disdain to appeal to it on questions of fact.[12]

---

[1] Zosimus, VIII.   [2] Aug. C. Litt. Pet. II, xcii, 209.
[3] Aug. Ep. LXXVI, 3; CVIII, ii, 5. On Optatus of Thamugadi, see also Aug. Ep. XLIII, viii, 24; LIII, iii, 6; C. Ep. Parm. II, iv, 8, vii, 13. A mosaic which lined the font in Optatus's cathedral church at Thamugadi is described by W. H. C. Frend, 'The Revival of Berber Art', loc. cit. p. 346.
[4] C.Th. IX, xxxiv, 3; IX, xl, 19.
[5] Eusebius Hieronymus, De uiris illustribus, CX; Aug. De unit. eccl. XIX, 50; C. Ep. Parm. I, iii, 5.   [6] Aug. De doctr. christ. II, xl, 61.
[7] P. Monceaux, op. cit. vol. V, pp. 248, 249.
[8] Opt. I, 15; Eusebius Hieronymus, De uir. illustr. CX.
[9] P. Monceaux, op. cit. vol. V, p. 250.   [10] Opt. VII, 1.   [11] Opt. VII, 1–3.
[12] E.g. Aug. Breu. Coll. III, xx, 38; Ad Don. post coll. XXXI, 54; Ep. CXLI, 9.

The first six books were the reply of Saint Optatus to the work of Parmenianus, which may have been entitled *Aduersus Ecclesiam Traditorum*.[1] They aimed at refuting the Donatist allegations levelled against the Church,[2] and also at exposing the weakness of the whole Donatist case.[3] By this means reconciliation might be sought.[4] The plan of the work is set out in Book I, ch. 7.

The first book opens with a long preface[5] setting out the plan and objects of the work. Then comes the subject proper to Book I, which is the origins of Donatism, and its condemnation by conciliar and imperial judgements.[6]

Book II invites the reader to consider which is the true Church in Africa. The tests applied are the catholicity of the African Church, and the holiness of its sacraments, its unity with the churches overseas, and with the see of Saint Peter in particular: its possession of the distinguishing marks of the Catholic Church, which are lacking in Donatism;[7] then the history of persecution through the century is adduced to show which Church possesses the true Christian charity.[8]

In the third book the question of appeal to the State is discussed, and it is shown that the Catholics have never asked for compulsory unity, but for defence against the unjust attacks of the Donatists.[9] The fourth book turns to the question of the Church's holiness, and the Donatists' claim that they alone possessed this qualification.[10] Book V deals with the administration of baptism, and the possibility of a sinner conferring the grace of God. Saint Optatus answers the Donatist case along the lines which Saint Augustine later followed, saying that the sacraments are the gift of God, and man is only the minister and not the giver of grace through them.[11] In the sixth book, the last of the original work, Saint Optatus gives an account of the sacrilegious violence of the Donatists.[12]

The appendix, Book VII, replies to criticisms made against the original work,[13] and then concludes with two discussions on texts,[14] and with an apology for Macarius, whom the Donatists alleged to have been received into Catholic communion.[15]

These books are of paramount importance as being the principal historical foundation for the writings of Saint Augustine against

[1] Opt. I, 5, 6.   [2] Opt. I, 7.   [3] Opt. I, 4.
[4] Opt. I, 1–3; II, 5; III, 9; IV, 1, 2.   [5] Opt. I, 1–12.
[6] Opt. I, 13–28.   [7] Opt. II, 1–13.
[8] Opt. II, 14–26.   [9] Opt. III, 1–12.
[10] Opt. IV, 1–9.   [11] Opt. V, 1–11.
[12] Opt. VI, 1–8.   [13] Opt. VII, 1–3.
[14] Opt. VII, 4, 5.   [15] Opt. VII, 6, 7.

Donatism. Saint Optatus quotes with accuracy from imperial and other documents, such as the *Gesta Purgationis Caeciliani et Felicis*,[1] the Edict of Union promulgated by Constans in 347,[2] the rescript of Julian in 362,[3] the letter of the *praefectus praetorio* Gregorius,[4] the speeches of Macarius,[5] the reports of various governors concerning the Donatists,[6] and the canons of certain African councils.[7] He gives us accounts of atrocities of which he was an eye-witness, or of which he had learned from credible witnesses.[8] He seems to have annexed to his work a corpus of ten documents relevant to the controversy,[9] and these, along with the history, are used by Saint Augustine in his writings.

It is therefore apparent how important the work of Saint Optatus is as preparing the ground for Saint Augustine. To some degree this is true theologically, especially in respect of the appeal to the State, the origin of the sanctity of sacraments, the evil of schism and the unity of the Church. These matters may well be examined at a later stage when we come to trace the development of Catholic teaching on them prior to the work of Saint Augustine.[10] But the dependence of Saint Augustine on the work of Optatus is even more obvious in matters of historical fact. Optatus co-ordinated for Augustine the documents relevant to the history of the schism, and provided a first-hand and trustworthy picture of Church conditions in Africa in the middle of the fourth century. Frequently Saint Augustine praises him,[11] and in one passage goes so far as to rank him with his beloved Saint Cyprian.[12] The work of Optatus may be summarized in the words of M. Monceaux:[13]

> Bref, l'évêque d'Hippone a perfectionné la machine de guerre; mais cette machine avait été conçue, exécutée, mise en mouvement par Optat de Milev, qui dans ce domaine a été le précurseur et le maître d'Augustin.

[1] Opt. I, 13, 14, 19, 20, 22–4, 26, 27.
[2] Opt. III, 1–3.   [3] Opt. II, 16.   [4] Opt. III, 3.
[5] Opt. VII, 6.   [6] Opt. II, 17.   [7] Opt. III, 4; II, 18, etc.
[8] E.g. Opt. III, 3–6; II, 16–19; VI, 1 sq.
[9] They are printed in Optatus, *C.S.E.L.* XXVI, 185 sqq. On their authenticity, see Carolus Ziwsa, 'Praefatio in Optatum', ibid. pp. xiii, xiv; and L. Duchesne, 'Le dossier du Donatisme', in *Mélanges de l'École française de Rome* (1890).
[10] See infra, pp. 106 sq.
[11] E.g. Aug. *C. Ep. Parm.* I, iii, 5; *De unit. eccl.* XIX, 50; *De doctr. christ.* II, xl, 61.
[12] Aug. *De unit. eccl.* XIX, 50.   [13] P. Monceaux, op. cit. vol. V.

CHAPTER II

THE SITUATION AT THE TIME OF SAINT AUGUSTINE'S PRIESTHOOD

After his stay of five years in Italy, Saint Augustine returned to Carthage at the end of 388, and was entertained there for a time by Innocentius, a former agent of the praetor of Africa. He then returned to Tagaste, his native town, where he sold the estate which his father Patricius had left him, and gave the proceeds to the poor.[1] He settled down for a period of study and meditation in an house on the outskirts of the town, in the company of a small religious community consisting of his son Adeodatus and his friends Alypius, Romanianus, Euodius and Seuerus, with others.[2] It was during this time that he received from Maximus of Madaura the letter which we have considered, mentioning the Donatist martyrs of the *tempora Macariana*, and sent an answer to it.[3] At this time also Adeodatus died. After three years of this life Augustine was invited in 391 to Hippo Regius by a friend who wished to talk to him about adopting the coenobitic life; and while he was staying there Valerius, the Bishop of Hippo, suggested in an address in church that as he was a Greek, and unable to preach fluently in Latin, he needed a learned presbyter who might assist him in that office. The people immediately clamoured for Augustine, and he reluctantly submitted to ordination to the priesthood, asking the Bishop, Valerius, for an interval for study until the ensuing Easter, that he might be better fitted for his ministry.[4] He took it up at Easter 391, and held it until in 395 he was consecrated Bishop-coadjutor of Hippo.

1. *The power and influence of Donatism*

From the beginning of his presbyterate he was faced with the menace of Donatism, which was at its strongest in his own province of Numidia. The efforts of the imperial power to restrain its violence, and forbid its augmentation by rebaptism, had failed, and Donatism was stronger now than ever before. It was not particularly strong in the towns, which were for the most part loyal to the Empire, but in the country districts, and some of the smaller towns, its successful propaganda had commended it to the Punic-speaking population, as an outlet for anti-

[1] Aug. *Ep.* CXXVI, 7. [2] Possidius, *Vita Augustini*, v.
[3] Aug. *Ep.* XVI, XVII. See supra, p. 13. [4] Aug. *Ep.* XXI.

Roman sentiment, and established it as a national African sect. People followed it for this reason when they were entirely ignorant of its theological basis. Its cult of the martyrs gave them what they had always loved from pre-Christian days, the rowdy feasts and celebrations held in their basilicas; and its anarchist tendencies provided an excuse for pillaging the property of the rich. The Donatists grew into the habit of investing their sufferings for unrighteousness and disorder with the glory of martyrdom. They were able to use marriage to accomplish conversions to their sect.[1] Landowners compelled their slaves to come with them into the Donatist communion, and anyone who left the sect was the object of special persecution and violence.[2] Lapsed clerics were sometimes induced to go over to them from the Church, and in some cases were raised to the episcopate.[3] Another reason for their popularity with the peasants was their use of Punic for preaching,[4] which, owing to the general ignorance of Latin, was a great attraction in the country districts. We find that in the appointment of a bishop for Fussala, on the division of the diocese of Hippo in 419, Saint Augustine had to find a Punic-speaking bishop for that town.[5]

The whole of the African provinces was organized into Donatist dioceses, often with their cathedral churches in the same towns as those of the Catholics, and in many other cases with their sees conterminous with the Catholic sees.[6] Most of their parishes had the sanctuaries of martyrs.[7] Sometimes they were able to steal churches from the Catholics;[8] but when they had to build new ones they built lavishly.[9] The epigraphical references to Donatist churches are always strikingly grandiloquent. Stones have been found in many places inscribed with the Donatist catchword, *Deo laudes*; and references to the righteous

---

[1] Aug. *Serm.* XLVI, vii, 15.
[2] Aug. *Ep.* LXXXVIII, 6–8; XCVII, 4; CV, ii, 3; CVIII, v, 6, xiv, 18; CXI, 1; CXXXIII, 1; CXXXIV, 2; CXXXIX, 1, 2; CLXXXV, vii, 30; Possidius, *Vita Aug.* xv.
[3] *Gesta Coll. Carthag.* I, 201.   [4] Aug. *In Ioan. Evang. tract.* II, 3.
[5] Aug. *Ep.* CCIX, 3.
[6] *Gesta Coll. Carthag.* I, 64, 65, 99–143, 149–210.
[7] *Conc. Carthag. anno* 348, Canon 2 (Hefele, op. cit. vol. II, p. 185); A. Berthier, op. cit. pp. 191–219.
[8] Aug. *C. Ep. Parm.* I, xiii, 20; *C. Litt. Pet.* II, xliii, 102, lviii, 132, xcii, 205, xcvii, 224.
[9] Opt. III, 1: 'basilicas fecerunt non necessarias'; Aug. *C. Ep. Parm.* I, xi, 18, xiii, 20; *Ep.* CXXXIX, 2. Berthier (op. cit. pp. 220 sq.) says that there were very numerous churches found in Numidia, but they may only be a sign of the ancient populousness of the Aures region. This is probably only part of the truth. See also F. Cabrol, *Dictionnaire d'archéologie chrétienne et de liturgie*, art. 'Afrique', § IV; and Aug. *Ep.* LXXVII, 3: 'numquid non et Africa martyrum corporibus plena est?'

are common. At Henchir-el-Guesseria, for example, is a stone inscribed 'H(A)EC PORTA DOMI(N)I IUSTI INTRABUNT'. One small chapel is described in an inscription as *praeclara et decora domus Dei*: another *domus Dei perfecta*. They are all examples of the gross arrogance which characterized the Donatist outlook, and arose no doubt from their exclusive claim to holiness.[1]

Their holy orders, both major and minor, were the same as those of the Church: their nuns, however, lived freely in the world, and not in communities.[2] They met in council like the Catholics. In worship they were for the most part like the Catholics: they had the same Mass,[3] celebrated daily.[4] But they were conservative, and ignored feasts of recent institution, for example the Epiphany, which had been generally adopted after the Diocletian persecution.[5] On the other hand they had numerous feasts of their own introduction, in commemoration of the martyrs of their sect. They did not adopt Saint Jerome's revision of the Latin Scriptures, preferring to continue using the Old Latin version which had hitherto been employed in Africa.

They laid stress on the necessity of holiness in Christians, to which they thought themselves to have the sole claim.[6] To the Catholic objection that the Church must be universal as well as holy they were content to reply with the text of the Song of Songs, 'ubi cubas in meridie', that is, in Africa, as they interpreted it.[7] To their belief in the possession of this exclusive holiness may be traced the strictness of their separation, in personal as well as in ecclesiastical matters, from the members of the true Church. They would not bury Catholics in their cemeteries;[8] Faustinus, a Donatist bishop of Hippo thirty years before Saint Augustine's time, had succeeded in preventing the bakers from baking bread for Catholics.[9] No Donatist must greet a Catholic,[10] or sit in the same room with one,[11] much less give his daughter in marriage to one.[12] Most of their bishops would not answer letters from

---

[1] A. Berthier, op. cit. pp. 206, 207.
[2] Aug. *Ep.* LXI, 2; C. *Ep. Parm.* II, ix, 19; C. *Litt. Pet.* III, xl, 48; C. *Gaud.* I, xxxi, 37, xxxvi, 46.
[3] Aug. C. *Litt. Pet.* II, xxxii, 72, xxxiii, 77; l, 115–liv, 123; *De unico bapt.* XI, 19; *Enarr. in Ps.* LIV, 16.
[4] Opt. II, 12. [5] Aug. *Serm.* CCII, 2.
[6] *Gesta Coll. Carthag.* III, 258; Opt. II, 1, 14; Aug. C. *Litt. Pet.* II, i, 2; *Serm.* II *in Ps.* XXXVI, 20.
[7] Cant. i. 6; Aug. *Ep.* XCIII, viii, 24, 25. [8] Opt. VI, 7.
[9] Aug. C. *Litt. Pet.* II, lxxxiii, 184. [10] Opt. IV, 5.
[11] *Gesta Coll. Carthag.* I, 144, 145; II, 3–6.
[12] Aug. *Serm.* XLVI, vii, 15.

Catholics,[1] and they would not admit Catholics to their churches.[2] The natural Catholic answer to this claim to holiness was to contrast it with the violent behaviour of the Circumcellions; and this they refused to answer, disclaiming responsibility for such outrages, although it was known that they encouraged and financed them,[3] and that the armed bands were not infrequently led by the Donatist clergy[4] and even in some cases by their bishops.[5]

The diocese of Hippo was especially infested with Donatism. Their church at Hippo was very rich, since its adherents had given lavishly to it;[6] and its rural parishes extended over the diocese. At Fussala, for instance, at this time, there was not a single Catholic;[7] Sinitum had a Donatist bishop[8] and some large estates with their tenants had submitted to the sect, for example those of Celer, on which the Donatists had chapels.[9] The district around Hippo itself was infested with Circumcellions, who even penetrated into the town.[10] Their basilicas were the scenes of dancing, drunkenness and other orgies.[11] At Hippo their principal martyr was Leontius, a bishop who had been martyred under Diocletian, and in whose honour they held uproarious feasts, which could be heard across the street in the Catholic Basilica Leontiana.[12] Some of the Donatist laity, in defiance of the strict rules of the sect, were not unfriendly towards Saint Augustine. Donatists as well as Catholics requested him to debate with Fortunatus the Manichee,[13] and during his priesthood Donatists attended his sermons.[14] The Donatist bishops endeavoured to restrain such friendliness.[15]

At this time the State was trying to stem the advance of Donatism. A constitution of Theodosius imposed a fine of ten pounds of gold

---

[1] Aug. *C. Litt. Pet.* I, i, 1,; *Ep.* XXXV, 1; XLIII, 1; LXXXVII, vi, 10; CVII, 1.
[2] Aug. *Serm.* XLVI, xiii, 31.
[3] Aug. *Ep.* CVIII, vi, 18; CLXXXV, iv, 16; *C. Ep. Parm.* I, xi, 17; *C. Litt. Pet.* I, xxiv, 26.
[4] Aug. *Ep.* CV, ii, 3; CVIII, v, 14; CXXXIII, 1; CXXXIV, 2; *C. Cresc.* III, xliii, 47; IV, li, 61; *Breu. Coll.* III, 11, 21, 22; *Ad Don. post coll.* XVII, 22.
[5] Aug. *Ep.* XLIV, iv, 9; *Enarr. in Ps.* x, 5; Opt. II, 18, 19.
[6] Aug. *In Ioan. Evang. tract.* VI, 25.
[7] Aug. *Ep.* CCIX, 2.   [8] Ibid. XXIII.
[9] Ibid. CXXXIX, 2.   [10] Possidius, *Vita Aug.* X.
[11] Aug. *Ps. c. part. Donati*, vv. 84, 137-55; *C. Ep. Parm.* I, xi, 17, 18; *C. Litt. Pet.* I, xxiv, 26; II, lxv, 146, lxxiv, 186, lxxxviii, 195, xcvi, 222; *Enarr. in Ps.* CXXXII, 3, 6; *Ep.* XXIII, 6, 7; XXIX, 1; XXXV, 2; XLIII, viii, 24; LXXXVIII, 1; CVIII, v, 14; CXXXIII, 1; CXXXIV, 2; CLXXXV, iv, 15.
[12] Aug. *Ep.* XXIX, 11.
[13] Possidius, *Vita Aug.* VI, VII.   [14] Ibid. VII.
[15] Ibid. IX, x sq.; Aug. *Ep.* XXIII, XXXIII-XXXV; *Serm.* XLVI, vii, 15.

upon any heretic who secured ordination.[1] This law was used by Saint Augustine about 400 against Crispinus of Calama, to restrain him from rebaptizing people by force.[2] In 403 Crispinus was fined ten pounds of gold under this law, but the Catholics intervened, and had the fine remitted.[3] On 18 July 392, a law had been promulgated threatening deportation to those who troubled the Catholic Church,[4] and on 15 April 394 there comes another constitution to restrain heretics (including Donatists) from consecrating bishops;[5] and by a law of 9 July 394 heretics are forbidden to meet, ordain, or conduct propaganda.[6] All these laws of Theodosius against meeting, worship and ordinations among heretics were confirmed by his sons on 13 March 395;[7] and on 30 March of the same year, they reiterated these provisions.[8] By a law of 3 September 395 all who did not hold the Catholic faith in every detail were classed as heretics, and became liable to all the penalties imposed upon heretics.[9] In the spring of the same year (23 March 395) a rescript addressed to Hierius, the Vicar of Africa, by Honorius had confirmed the rights and privileges of the Catholic Church.[10] The frequent reiteration of laws, so commonly noticed throughout the Codex, seems to indicate that they were laxly enforced, and that the imperial government was powerless to impose its will. All this time in Africa, Donatism was flourishing and tyrannizing the province.[11] For instance, the basilica of Hasna was sacked by the Circumcellions in 395.[12]

During Saint Augustine's priesthood there was held at Hippo in 393 the first of the many synods presided over by Aurelius, Bishop of Carthage. It is noteworthy because Saint Augustine, though still a priest, was invited to address the assembled bishops, which he did in the words of his still extant work *De fide et symbolo*.[13] Some of the abridged canons of this council, contained in the *Codex Canonum Ecclesiae Africanae*,[14] appear to have reference to Donatism. Thus Canon 12 of these prohibits the marriage of sons of bishops and clergy with

[1] *C.Th.* XVI, v, 21 (15 June 392). [2] Aug. *Ep.* LXVI, 1.
[3] Possidius, *Vita Aug.* XIV; Aug. *Ep.* LXXXVIII, 7; CV, ii, 4; *C. Cresc.* III, xlvii, 51.
[4] *C.Th.* XVI, iv, 3. [5] Ibid. XVI, v, 22.
[6] Ibid. XVI, v, 24. [7] Ibid. XVI, v, 25.
[8] Ibid. XVI, v, 26. [9] Ibid. XVI, v, 28.
[10] Ibid. XVI, ii, 29.
[11] Aug. *Ep.* XXXIV; XXXV; LXXXVII, 8; XLIV, v, 12.
[12] Ibid. XXIX, 12.
[13] Possidius, *Vita Aug.* VII. For the records of this council, see Hefele, op. cit. vol. II, pp. 394 sq.
[14] Hefele, op. cit. vol. II, pp. 467, 468.

heathens, heretics and schismatics;[1] Canon 14 says that bishops and clergy shall not choose for their heirs those who are not Catholic Christians, even though they may be relatives; Canon 17 that no man may be ordained bishop, priest or deacon who has not first made all his household Catholic Christians; and by Canon 29 bishops and clergy are forbidden to have meals in church, except when necessary for the refreshment of guests, and then none of the laity shall be admitted. The last canon seems to have in mind the possible imitation of the riotous feasts of the Donatists, held in churches, which were dear to all the common people of Africa. Canon 37 reaffirms the old rule of the Councils, that no Donatist clerics shall be received into the Church except into lay communion, unless they can show that they have never practised rebaptism, or that they wish to come over with their whole congregation. Men baptized in infancy by the Donatists are not thereby to be deprived of the privilege of Catholic ordination.

2. *Internal schisms of Donatism*

It was probably only the violence of the Circumcellions and the political and social animosity which inspired all Donatists that enabled them thus to flourish in the face of the schismatic tendencies within their own ranks, which were specially manifest at this time. The Rogatists, as we have seen,[2] were separated as long ago as 370, and were the mildest of the Donatist sects; they came to an end in 420, when their chief bishop, Vincentius Victor, joined the Catholic Church.

In the year 391 the Catholic and the Donatist bishops of Carthage both died. Genethlius, the Catholic, was succeeded by Aurelius; and the Donatist, Parmenianus, by Primianus.[3] Primianus soon antagonized some of his own party, especially by tolerating the schismatic Claudianists, who were followers of Claudianus, one of the Donatist bishops of Rome, who had been turned out by Pope Damasus, and had come to Carthage, where he quarrelled with his fellow-Donatists, and went out of communion with Parmenianus.[4] On his succession to the see, Primianus received Claudianus into his communion without enforcing any penance. One day the faithful Donatists made a disturbance in the basilica because the Claudianists came to communion, and they were violently expelled by Primianus. This was the principal cause of

[1] Ibid. vol. II, p. 398; J. P. Migne, *Dictionnaire des Conciles* (Paris, 1847), vol. I, p. 474.
[2] P. 21 supra.
[3] Aug. *Ep.* XLIII, ix, 26; *C. Cresc.* IV, iv, 7; *Serm.* II *in Ps.* XXXVI, 19, 20.
[4] Opt. II, 4.

antagonism to Primianus within his own sect; but other causes were alleged by his enemies. It was said that he had refused communion to the priest Demetrius, unless he disinherited and disowned his son; and that he had shut up the priest Fortunatus in a sewer on the ground that he had administered clinical baptism without episcopal permission.[1] These dissidents found a leader in the person of Maximianus, a relative of Donatus the Great, and one of the deacons of Primianus, a man of much better education than his bishop, who saw in him a possible rival. Primianus immediately excommunicated Maximianus, along with three other deacons.[2] Maximianus was never summoned to appear before his bishop, and was in fact sick at the time. The council of elders in Primianus' church thereupon protested to him concerning his treatment of the Claudianists and Maximianists, but they received no satisfaction from him. The events of 312 were re-enacted: Maximianus, supported by some wealthy lady, attracted to himself a party of dissidents, which held a council at Carthage in 392, composed of forty-three Donatist bishops, who cited Primianus to appear before them. He refused to come, and when they attempted to meet in a basilica he sent a gang of his followers, who evicted and stoned them.[3] Primianus then secured the support of the civil power in restraining them from the use of any Donatist property for their meeting, and they therefore met in a private house, belonging to the disaffected Demetrius, on the outskirts of the town. They condemned Primianus, but did not order his deposition: they gave him an opportunity for recantation, and then notified the decision to all the Donatists.[4] Primianus retaliated by an attack on Demetrius for having received the forty-three bishops into his house, and at the same time contrived to have the houses of a number of his opponents sacked. He also filled with his own followers the sees of the forty-three bishops.[5] Against Maximianus he instituted legal proceedings for the recovery of an house then occupied by him, and was successful after an action tried before the legate of the proconsul.[6] On 24 June 393, the dissident bishops met in augmented numbers in the Council of Cabarsussa in Byzacium, under the chairmanship of Victorinus of Munaciana.[7] Saint Augustine says that there were one

[1] Aug. *Serm.* II *in Ps.* XXXVI, 20.
[2] Aug. *Ep.* XLIII, ix, 20; *Serm.* II *in Ps.* XXXVI, 19, 20.
[3] Ibid. XXXVI, 20.
[4] Aug. *Ep.* XLIII, ix, 26; *Serm.* II *in Ps.* XXXVI, 19, 20; *C. Cresc.* IV, iv, 7; *Gesta cum Emer.* IX. [5] Aug. *Serm.* II *in Ps.* XXVI, 20.
[6] Aug. *C. Cresc.* IV, xlvii, 57; *Serm.* II *in Ps.* XXXVI, 18, 19.
[7] Migne, *Dictionnaire des Conciles*, vol. I, p. 393; Aug. *Ep.* CXLI, 6; CLXXXV, iv, 17; *Serm.* II *in Ps.* XXXVI, 20; *C. Cresc.* IV, vi, 8; *De haeres.* LXIX.

hundred bishops present, but the synodal letter is subscribed by only fifty-five men. The charges preferred at this council against Primianus were as follows: that he had illegally appointed bishops in the room of bishops still alive; that he had admitted the sacrilegious to the communion of the saints; that he had instigated the priests to make a plot; that he had had the priest Fortunatus thrown into a sewer; that he had excommunicated Demetrius, and persecuted him for having received the bishops into his house in 392; that he had sent a gang of ruffians to ravage the houses of the faithful; that he had stoned bishops and clergy; that the elders had been attacked in the basilica; and that he had misappropriated property. They found these charges proved, and therefore deposed and excommunicated him: 'decreuimus omnes sacerdotes Dei, praesente Spiritu sancto, hunc eundem Primianum...a sacerdotali choro perpetuo esse damnatum, nec, eo palpato, Dei ecclesia aut contagione aut aliquo crimine maculetur.'[1] They also threatened with excommunication all his friends who did not submit before a date appointed. When they had communicated this decision to all the Donatist churches, they returned to Carthage, and there elected Maximianus bishop of Carthage; and twelve of them consecrated him,[2] making three rival bishops of Carthage, and dividing the Donatist flock, much to the delight of the Catholics.[3] Save in Byzacium, which was Maximianist, most Donatists remained faithful to Primianus: all Numidia did so. On 24 April 394 he called a Donatist council to meet at their great Numidian stronghold, Bagai. It was the greatest schismatic council yet held, and numbered 310 bishops; they recognized Primianus as lawful bishop of Carthage, and condemned the twelve consecrators of Maximianus, giving them till the following Christmas to submit.[4] Inconsistently with their often reiterated principles they promised to recognize the sacraments of the Maximianists who returned to their fold.

There followed a great campaign to obtain possession of Maximianist basilicas and other property.[5] Primianus himself instituted

[1] Aug. *Serm.* II in *Ps.* XXXVI, 20.
[2] Ibid. XXXVI, 20; *C. Cresc.* III, lii, 58 sq.; IV, vi, 7, xxxi, 38 sq.; *Gesta cum Emer.* IX; *Ep.* CVIII, ii, 5; CLXXXV, iv, 17.
[3] Aug. *C. Cresc.* IV, i, 1, xlvii, 57; *Ep.* CXLI, 6; *De haeres.* LXIX; *Ep.* XLIII, ix, 26; LIII, iii, 6; CVIII, iv, 13.
[4] Migne, *Dictionnaire des Conciles*, vol. I, p. 254; Aug. *C. Cresc.* III, liii, 59; IV, xxxi, 38 sq., xxxvii, 44 sq.; *C. Ep. Parm.* II, iii, 7; *Gesta cum Emer.* IX–XI; *Ep.* LI, 2; LIII, iii, 6; CVIII, ii, 4 sq.; CXLI, 6. The text of their decision is collated by M. Petschenig in *C.S.E.L.* vol. LIII, pt. iii, pp. 276–7.
[5] Aug. *C. Cresc.* III, lii, 58, lvi, 62; IV, iii sq.; *Breu. Coll.* III, xi, 22; *Ep.* CVIII, ii, 5.

proceedings for the recovery of the basilica of Maximianus at Carthage, and obtained it in 394; but it was, by whom we do not know, burned down and utterly destroyed.[1] Primianus, claiming to be the only orthodox bishop of Carthage, tried to proceed against the Maximianists under the laws against heretics; but the proconsul said that he knew no Catholic Bishop of Carthage save Aurelius.[2] Primianus was able, however, to enlist the help of Optatus of Thamugadi, who with Gildo ravaged Numidia for him, and even penetrated into Proconsular Africa to attack Maximianist strongholds. Under his threats two Maximianist bishops, Felicianus of Musti and Praetextatus of Assuras, returned to the Primianist fold. They were confirmed in their sees, and their sacraments recognized.[3] But others did not submit, and they had to bear severe Primianist persecution. Saluius, the Maximianist bishop of Membressa, in 397 refused to give up his basilica, and was attacked by the Primianists of Abitina, who suspended dead dogs round his neck, and paraded him through the streets of their city.[4] Rogatus, who succeeded Praetextatus at Assuras, became Catholic, and the Circumcellions arrested him, and cut out his tongue and amputated one hand.[5]

Between 394 and 397 many actions of the Primianists against the Maximianists succeeded in the courts.[6] Owing to this pressure Maximianism never penetrated beyond the borders of Byzacium and Proconsular Africa; in Numidia the only schismatics were the Primianists, who held councils at Constantine and at Milevis.[7]

The Maximianists thus formed a considerable schism; in 411 they unsuccessfully claimed the right to send representatives to the great Conference at Carthage, but they disappeared later in the general overthrow of schismatics in Africa. Primianus, however, remained the principal Donatist leader, and his communion the principal Donatist communion until in turn it was outlawed, and it had as

[1] Aug. *Ep.* XLIV, iv, 7; *C. Cresc.* III, lix, 65; IV, i, 1, iii, 3, xlvi, 55; *Enarr. in Ps.* XXI, 31.
[2] Aug. *Enarr. in Ps.* XXI, 31.
[3] Aug. *Ep.* LI, 4; LIII, 36; CVIII, ii, 5; CLXXXV, iv, 17; *C. Cresc.* III, xv, 18, lx, 66; IV, i, 1; *Gesta cum Emer.* IX; *De haeres.* LXIX.
[4] Aug. *C. Ep. Parm.* III, vi, 29; *C. Cresc.* IV, xlix, 59.
[5] Aug. *Gesta cum Emer.* IX.
[6] Aug. *C. Ep. Parm.* I, x, 16, xi, 17, 18, xiii, 20; II, iii, 7; *C. Litt. Pet.* II, lviii, 132; *C. Cresc.* III, lvi, 62, lix, 65; IV, iii, 3, iv, 5, xlviii, 58, lxvi, 82; *Gesta cum Emer.* IX; *Ep.* LI, 2–5; LXX, 2; LXXVI, 3, 4; CVIII, ii, 5, iv, 13, v, 14.
[7] Aug. *Ep.* XXXIV, 5.

many bishops as the Catholics.[1] For the purpose of Catholic propaganda the Maximianist schism was a most fortunate occurrence. It gave the Catholic apologists a conclusive answer to the Donatist contention that schism and other sins invalidate the sacraments conferred by a minister guilty of them, for the Donatists had received back into communion the schismatics from their own sect; and it provided one more example of a Donatist appeal to the State for the compulsory suppression of their opponents, an appeal which they were never tired of accusing the Catholics of employing against themselves.

[1] Aug. *C. Cresc.* IV, lviii, 69, 70; *Ep.* cxxix, 6; *Breu. Coll.* I, xiv; *Gesta Coll. Carthag.* I, 165, 213–17.

CHAPTER III

SAINT AUGUSTINE'S STRUGGLE WITH THE DONATISTS

1. *Priesthood, 391–395*

It was during this period of his priesthood at Hippo that Saint Augustine began his prolonged campaign against Donatism. At first he confined his action to the diocese of Hippo, and approached the question from the pastoral point of view: the flock committed to his bishop's care must be defended from the contamination of schism. So it is fitting that his first work concerning Donatism should be the *Psalmus contra partem Donati*, published at the end of 393, after the Council of Hippo of 8 October 393, which, as we have seen,[1] enacted several canons concerned with the menace of Donatism. Of the *Psalmus* he says:

> Wishing even the lowliest and most ignorant people to know about the case of the Donatists, and to fix it in their memory, I wrote an alphabetical psalm to be sung to them, and took it down to the letter V, omitting the last three letters, and adding in their place a sort of epilogue, as though their mother the Church were addressing them.

The *hypopsalma* or refrain ('omnes qui gaudetis de pace, modo uerum iudicate') is not included in the alphabetical order, which begins after the preface.[2] Such psalms had proved very popular among the Donatists, and been an useful method of instructing the unlearned. Parmenianus, as we have seen, had composed some, which the Donatists bawled in their churches.[3] The alphabetical scheme may have been borrowed from the Old Testament, where it occurs in Psalm cxix. Saint Augustine's *Psalmus* was not written in metre, lest the exigencies of prosody should compel the writer to use words not in colloquial use among the members of his congregation.[4]

---

[1] Supra, pp. 30, 31.   [2] Aug. *Retract.* I, 20.
[3] Supra, p. 18; Aug. *Ep.* LV, xviii, 34.
[4] Aug. *Retract.* I, 20: 'ideo autem non aliquo carminis genere id fieri uolui, ne me necessitas metrica ad aliqua uerba quae uulgo minus sunt usitata compelleret.' On the *Psalmus* see also H. J. Rose, 'Saint Augustine as a forerunner of mediaeval hymnology', in *J.T.S.* (July 1927), vol. XXVIII, pp. 383 sq.; P. Monceaux, op. cit. vol. VII, ch. iii; F. J. E. Raby, *A History of Christian Latin Poetry* (Oxford, 1927), pp. 20 sq.

The metre is accentual, and not quantitative, and, though it makes frequent departures from its scheme, it is on the whole to be described as accentual trochaic tetrameters, similar, as Professor Rose points out, to the *Stabat mater dolorosa* ascribed to Jacoponi da Todi. And its lines rime throughout on the syllable *-e* or the diphthong *-ae*. It is of twenty alphabetical strophes of twelve verses each, with assonance in all the verses. Each verse is divided by a caesura into two equal hemistiches of eight syllables, in each of which the penultimate syllable is stressed. In view of this regularity of construction it may be asked why Augustine says that it is not a *carmen* at all. He seems to confine that term to the strictly classical verse based on quantitative prosody, and such it is not. In his sermons he is very fond of rime at all periods; and no doubt thought that in compositions intended to be heard and not read it had the advantage of marking clearly to the hearer's ear the close of a period or verse. Accentual verse had been known in Latin before: the Saturnian verse was accentual, and there were traces of this left in the earlier comic poets. And so in the *Psalmus contra partem Donati*, to quote the words of Professor Rose:

> ...no fewer than three great streams meet. There is first the popular tradition, native to Latin, so far as we can see, that the proper cadence to sing was an accentual rhythm of some sort; secondly the ecclesiastical tradition...that the Psalms were the proper model, which meant that the rhythm should be a parallelism of sense rather than of sound...thirdly the tradition of rhetorical prose, which for centuries had taught balance and antithesis, in sense and sound alike, as essentials of a literary style, and which made a contribution of its own in the shape of rime.[1]

So much for the form and purpose of this *Psalmus*. What of its content? Its refrain is an appeal to those who love peace, the watchword of the Catholic Church in Africa during the Donatist upheaval, to attain it by pursuing truth:

> omnes qui gaudetis de pace, modo uerum iudicate.[2]

The preamble attacks the basic theory of Donatism, its insistence on the actual empirical holiness of the Church Militant, and with Scriptural references maintains that judgement must await the great day of the Lord.[3] Then the origins of the schism are discussed, and an appeal is

---

[1] H. J. Rose, op. cit.
[2] The word *pax* and texts containing it are extremely common in the epigraphy of North Africa at this period. E.g. *C.I.L.* VIII, 1214, 9708, 9710, 9712, 10946, 10947, 21497, 21498.
[3] Aug. *Ps. c. part. Donati*, vv. 1–13.

made for unity.¹ This exhortation to concord begins the next section, which then goes on to attack the shameless ferocity of the Circumcellions, and reminds the flock that sinners must be tolerated until the Last Judgement. It concludes with a reminder of the folly of thinking that baptism is man's gift rather than God's.² This brings us to the end of letter V; and the conclusion³ represents the Church calling all her children to herself:

> My children, what complaint have you against your mother? Why have you left me? You accuse your brethren, and I am rent in twain. When the nations oppressed me, I bore much with grief. Many deserted me, but they did it in fear; but no one compelled you to rebel against me. You say that you are still with me, but this is patently false. I am called Catholic; you are described as being of the party of Donatus. The Apostle commanded me to pray for the kings of the earth: you are envious that there are still kings in the Christian religion. If you are my children, why are you envious that my prayers are heard? You have forgotten the prophets, who foretold that great kings of the earth should send gifts to the Church. What have I, your mother, done to you? I expel the evil ones when I am able; those whom I cannot expel I am compelled to tolerate. I tolerate them either until they are healed, or until they are separated at the last. If you tolerate the evil, why do you not do so in my unity, where no man rebaptizes, or raises altar against altar? You tolerate so many evil ones, but for no good reward, because you prefer to suffer for Donatus what you ought to be suffering for Christ.
>
> > cantamus uobis, fratres, pacem si uultis audire.
> > uenturus est iudex noster: nos damus, exigit ille.⁴

About the same time, at the end of 393 or in early 394, came the first controversial treatise on Donatism, entitled *Contra Epistulam Donati haeretici, liber unus*.⁵ This is lost, but Saint Augustine tells us in the *Retractations* that it was written about the same time as the *Psalmus* in answer to a letter of Donatus the Great, successor of Maiorinus in the Donatist chair at Carthage, to prove the falsity of the contention of Donatus that true baptism was found only in his own communion. Augustine confesses that in this treatise he wrongly attributed to Donatus the Great, whom he here distinguishes carefully from Donatus of Casae Nigrae, the introduction of the practice of rebaptizing Christians.

Two letters of Saint Augustine referring to Donatism belong also to this period of his priesthood. About 392 he writes in a very conciliatory tone to Maximinus, Donatist bishop of Sinitum in the diocese of Hippo,

---

¹ Ibid. *vv.* 15–129. ² Ibid. *vv.* 131–257.
³ Ibid. *vv.* 259–89. ⁴ Ibid. ad fin.
⁵ Aug. *Retract.* I, 21.

to tell him that he hears that Maximinus has been rebaptizing Christians: and to invite him to discuss the question.[1] It is sinful, he adds, to rebaptize an heretic who has received Christian baptism, but to rebaptize a Catholic is a criminal enormity.[2] There is one baptism in the Church, which cannot be repeated; and it is impossible, as well as unnecessary, to separate the wheat from the chaff in the Church here on earth: that must await the final Judgement. Three years later he writes to his old friend Alypius, now Bishop of their native Tagaste, to tell him how he has at length succeeded in persuading the Hipponensian Catholics to abandon their indulgence in the riotous feasts with which in Africa it was usual, for Catholics as well as for Donatists, to celebrate the feasts of martyrs, and which were called *Laetitiae*.[3] The favourite feast at Hippo was that of Leontius, a former bishop there, who fell in the last persecution, and in whose honour one of the basilicas of the town was consecrated.[4]

Saint Augustine recurs to this subject in a sermon expounding Psalm xxxv, and delivered at this time,[5] and in another exposition on a psalm[6] he dwells at length on the earthly condition of strife and suffering which afflicts the Church, and contrasts it with the peace of her eternal abode, which in all his writings, and especially later on in the *De ciuitate Dei*, is never far from his thoughts.[7] At the end of his discourse, commenting on the *uiri sanguinum et dolositatis* of the psalm, he leads his congregation to think of the violence of the Circumcellions, and then to reflect how much worse is the spiritual murder of a soul committed by those who rebaptize.[8] Those who commit this crime did not hesitate, however, to say that the feet of their Maximianist enemies

---

[1] Aug. *Ep.* XXIII. Maximinus later embraced the Catholic faith (Aug. *Ep.* CV), and was confirmed in the tenure of his see. (See also Aug. *De ciu. Dei*, XXII, viii.)

[2] Aug. *Ep.* XXIII, 2: 'rebaptizare igitur haereticum hominem, qui haec sanctitatis signa perceperit quae christiana tradidit disciplina, omnino peccatum est; rebaptizare autem catholicum, immanissimum scelus est.'

[3] Ibid. XXIX. On the feasts of martyrs, see also Aug. *Serm.* CCCLV, 4; *Ep.* XVI, 2; *C. Faustum* XX, xxi; *Serm.* CCLII, 44; CCLXXIII, viii; Cypr. *Ep.* XXXIV, 3; *C.I.L.* VIII, 8641; A. Audollent, 'Mission épigraphique en Algérie', in *Mélanges de l'École française de Rome* (1890), pp. 440 sq., 468 sq.

[4] Aug. *Serm.* XIII, 2.   [5] Aug. *Enarr. in Ps.* XXXV, 14.

[6] Ibid. LIV, 26.

[7] John Burnaby, *Amor Dei: A Study in the Religion of S. Augustine* (London, 1938), p. 55.

[8] Aug. *Enarr. in Ps.* LIV, 26: 'uiros sanguinum propter interfectiones dicit: atque utinam corporales et non spirituales! sanguis enim de carne exiens, uidetur et horretur; quis uidet sanguinem cordis in rebaptizato? illae mortes alios oculos quaerunt.'

were swift to shed blood;[1] and yet the Maximianists do not make use of Circumcellions. Nevertheless these violent schismatics shall not live out half their days, and the flock is urged in the words of the psalm to put its trust in God.

'Of Saint Augustine's priesthood also is an Easter sermon in which a discussion of the net cast into the sea and filled with good and bad fish, not separated until the net is drawn to land, leads him to mention the necessity of tolerating heretics and schismatics in the Church until the final Judgement separates them from the righteous.[2]

During the four years of his priesthood, Saint Augustine has thus laid, with special reference to the diocese of Hippo, the foundations of his long campaign against Donatism, now, on his consecration, to be carried beyond the borders of the diocese into the province of Numidia, and indeed the whole Church of North Africa; and which was eventually to result in the overthrow of the schismatics. He has traced, in the *Psalmus*, the history of the schism; he has begun his polemical work with the answer to the letter of Donatus; he has exhorted the flock to unity; he has cautioned them against hastiness of judgement and premature separation of good men from evil; he has broached the controversy as it concerns the ministration of sacraments; he has condemned the outrageous violence of the Circumcellions; he has finally set before his hearers the peace of the City of God to which all true Christians must aspire 'among the sundry and manifold changes of the world'. Almost his whole case against Donatism (the important exception being the question of appeal to the State) is here in germ: it will remain for him as Bishop of Hippo to amplify and extend what is in essence already in his mind. At the end of 395 he was consecrated Bishop-coadjutor of Hippo, with right of succession to Valerius on his death, by Megalius, the Primate of Numidia; and at once took up this extended campaign against the African schism, which must now occupy our attention.

EPISCOPATE

2. *The period 395–400*

Saint Augustine's accession to the episcopate brought upon him the increased violence of the schismatics, who recognized in him a formidable enemy, and several attempts were made on his life.[3] In 397 and

---

[1] *Sentent. Conc. Bagaien.*: C.S.E.L. vol. LIII, pt. iii, pp. 276, 277.
[2] Aug. *Serm.* CCLII, iii, 3, iv, 4.
[3] Possid. *Vita Aug.* X, XIII; Aug. *Ep.* XXXV, 4; *Enchir.* V, 17.

398 he went to Thubursicum Numidarum to hold conferences with the Donatists and their bishop Fortunius.[1] The fury of the Circumcellions increased, and numerous assaults were made on the Catholic clergy.[2] Among the victims was the deacon Nabor, on whom Saint Augustine wrote an acrostic epitaph in hexameters.[3] On one occasion, as Saint Augustine was returning from a pastoral visit in his diocese, his men took him along the wrong road by accident, and thereby avoided an ambush of the Donatists placed on the usual route.[4]

At this time the Donatist bishop of Carthage, Primianus, attended festivities in Numidia at Thamugadi, on the anniversary of the consecration of the infamous Optatus to that see.[5] While there, he was present at a council, which reversed much of what had been enacted at Bagai a few years before. It looked as if the Primianists were victorious at last, but the only winner was Optatus, who had dragged the Primianists into an alliance with his friend the rebel Gildo; and thereby involved them in the penalties of the imperial constitutions enacted after Gildo's defeat against the partisans.[6] For such a benefit the Primianists had bartered their theological principles, and given the Catholics a complete answer to the Donatist argument concerning the purity of ministers. During the rest of his episcopate, as we shall see, Augustine was not slow to press home this advantage.[7]

The third Council of Carthage assembled on 28 August 397 in the *secretarium* or sacristy of the Basilica Restituta at Carthage, under the presidency of the Bishop, Aurelius.[8] Canon 12 forbade the marriage

[1] Possid. *Vita Aug.* x; Aug. *Ep.* XXXIII, XXXIV, LI.
[2] Aug. *Ep.* XXXV, 2, 4; XLIII, viii, 24; *Enarr. in Ps.* LIV, 26; *in Ps.* CXXXII, 6; *C. Ep. Parm.* I, xi, 17 sq.; II, iii, 6, 7; III, iii, 18; *C. Litt. Pet.* I, xxiv, 26; II, xiv, 33, lxv, 146, lxxiv, 186, lxxviii, 195, xcvi, 222; Possid. *Vita Aug.* x, xi.
[3] De Rossi, *Inscriptiones christianae*, II, 461:
> Donatistarum crudeli caede peremptum
> Infossum hic corpus pia est cum laude Nabori(s).
> Ante aliquot tempus cum Donatista fuisset,
> Conuersus pacem pro q(ua) moreretur amauit.
> Optima purpureo uestitus sanguine causa,
> Non errore perit, non se ipse furore peremit:
> Verum martyrium uera est pietate probat(um).
> Suscipe litterulas primas, ibi nomen honoris.

[4] Aug. *Enchir.* v, 17; Possid. *Vita Aug.* XII, XIII.
[5] Aug. *Ep.* CVIII, ii, 5; *C. Litt. Pet.* II, xxiii, 53.
[6] *C. Th.* VII, viii, 7, 9; IX, xxxix, 3, xl, 19, xlii, 16, 19.
[7] See, for example, Aug. *Ep.* LI, iv; LIII, iii, 6; CVIII, ii, 6; CLXXXV, iv, 17; *C. Cresc.* III, xvi, 19 sq.; IV, i sq.
[8] J. P. Migne, op. cit. vol. I, pp. 474 sq.

of Catholics with heretics and schismatics, and Canon 48 allowed converted Donatists who had been baptized by schismatics in infancy to be admitted to holy orders.

The third work of his episcopate which Saint Augustine notices in the *Retractations* is the book *De agone christiano*, which appears to have been written in 396, and purports to give a simple explanation of the rule of faith and of the Christian life.[1] In it he warns his readers against listening to the blandishments of certain types of heretics, and includes among these the Donatists, who claim that the true Church is confined to their own supporters. This arrogant and wicked presumption is patently falsified by the notorious divisions within their own Donatist ranks.[2]

In 397 there followed the two books *Contra partem Donati*, which are not extant. In his notice of them in the *Retractations*[3] the Bishop tells us that in them he mentioned, apparently for the first time in his works, the possibility of an appeal to the State for the reunion of the African Church. At the time of writing the *Contra partem Donati* he repudiated any such appeal, and at the end of his life, in writing the *Retractations*, he says that he has now changed his mind, because he has now realized, as he had not in 397, the extent to which the unrestrained violence of the Donatists would be prepared to venture, or what improvement might be wrought in them by a rightful discipline.[4]

Probably in the next year, 398, comes his first considerable work on the schism, *Contra Epistulam Parmeniani*, in three books. In the preface to this work he tells us that there has come to his notice a letter of the late Donatist bishop of Carthage, Parmenianus, written against the Donatist exegete Tyconius; and it is this letter which he proposes to answer in these three books. He hopes to show how Parmenianus in his answer to Tyconius had misused Scriptural texts to refute the position which that exegete had taken up, namely that the Church, as we see from Scripture, must be catholic and world-wide, and cannot be confined to one corner of the earth.[5] This led Tyconius to contradict the Donatist thesis that the evil in the Church contaminates it; and this is the important question specially taken up by Saint Augustine in his

[1] Aug. *Retract.* II, iii.   [2] Aug. *De agone christ.* XXIX, 31.
[3] Aug. *Retract.* II, v.
[4] Ibid. II, v: 'in quorum primo libro dixi, non mihi placere ullius saecularis potestatis impetu schismaticos ad communionem uiolenter arctari. et uere tunc mihi non placebat, quoniam nondum expertus eram, uel quantum mali eorum auderet impunitas, uel quantum eis in melius mutandis conferre posset diligentia disciplinae.'
[5] Aug. *C. Ep. Parm.* I, i, 1.

work.¹ Tyconius came to the conclusion that since the Church is seen in Scripture to be truly universal, it follows that it must contain a mixture of good and evil, not to be finally separated until the Last Judgement. Saint Augustine commends this view, and, after considering and elucidating the texts quoted by Tyconius in support of it, he passes to the history of the schism, and, relying on the material collected by Saint Optatus, shows how Caecilianus was proved innocent.² From this there follows logically a discussion of the intervention of the secular power in ecclesiastical affairs,³ and we notice an inclination of Saint Augustine's opinion towards approval of such intervention which (to judge from the meagre notice in the *Retractations*) had been absent from the *Contra partem Donati* of the previous year. It is the first stage in the development of Saint Augustine's view on this vital and difficult question, a development which it will be our duty to trace at a later point in this study.⁴ In the second book against the letter of Parmenianus, he proceeds to consider the texts relied on by Tyconius and disputed by Parmenianus, and this occupies him to the end of the work.

In this second book Augustine promises to devote a later work to the elucidation of the controversy on baptism.⁵ This promise was fulfilled two years later, in 400 or thereabouts, with the seven books *De baptismo contra Donatistas*,⁶ one of the longest of all his works on the controversy, and one of the most significant. He is concerned in it not merely with expanding his teaching on baptism with special reference to the Donatist theory, but also with discussing the authority of Saint Cyprian in the matter, to which the Donatists were fond of appealing, and with showing that it not only provides no true foundation for the Donatist case, but actually furnishes the principal refutation of it.⁷ Book I attempts to show that baptism can be given outside the Church by the hands of heretics and schismatics, and this since it is not their gift, but the gift of Christ; but that if so received it is of no spiritual profit to the recipient until on his return to the true fold the sacrament revives and for the first time becomes profitable to salvation. In Book II Augustine comes to the argument derived from Saint Cyprian, and discusses at length the authority of the great African Father in the baptismal controversy. This is contained in Book III, with a special discussion of Saint Cyprian's Epistle to Iubaianus,⁸ which extends through

¹ Aug. *Retract.* II, xvii.
² Aug. *C. Ep. Parm.* I, iv, 6–9, v, 10, vi, 11.
³ Ibid. I, viii–xiii.   ⁴ Infra, pp. 127 sq.
⁵ Aug. *C. Ep. Parm.* II, xiv, 32.   ⁶ Aug. *De bapt.* I, i, 1.
⁷ Ibid. and *Retract.* II, xviii.   ⁸ Cypr. *Ep.* LXXIII.

Book IV, and into the first part of Book V, which is completed with a discussion of other epistles of Saint Cyprian bearing on the question. The last two books (VI and VII) contain a detailed examination of the judgements of the eighty-seven bishops of the Council of Carthage of 1 September 256, which, under the chairmanship of Saint Cyprian, determined the baptismal question.

The next anti-Donatist work, mentioned in the *Retractations* immediately after the *De baptismo*, is the *Contra quod attulit Centurius a Donatistis*, which has not survived. It was Saint Augustine's very brief answer to some work of Donatist polemics handed to him by a layman Centurius, and of which the subject is not indicated.[1]

The first book of the *Contra Litteras Petiliani* falls just within the period 395–400. Petilianus was the son of Catholic parents, born about 365, and bred at Cirta in Numidia,[2] and trained for the bar.[3] While he was a catechumen, he was seized by the Donatists, and forcibly rebaptized and ordained.[4] He remained, however, in the Donatist fold, and at about the age of 30, in 395, became their bishop of Cirta, his native town. He was one of the most able supporters of their sect, and at the Conference of Carthage was one of their seven chosen representatives.[5] About 400 he wrote to the Donatist priests and deacons a letter against the Catholics, and these three books of Augustine are the answer to it.[6] The first of them was written, Saint Augustine informs us, as an answer to the first part of the work of Petilianus, which was all that at that time had come into his hands, and which he thought to require an immediate answer. Unlike the second and third books, which are addressed to Petilianus personally, and answer him point by point, the first book is a pastoral to Augustine's own flock.[7]

Twelve epistles of Saint Augustine concerned with Donatism are to be assigned to this period, and show the expansion of his campaign against the schism which characterizes these first years of his episcopate. They are all marked by the persuasiveness of argument and friendliness of approach with which the Bishop's campaign commenced. At the start of his episcopate at Hippo, Saint Augustine invited Proculeianus, the Donatist bishop in the town, to an amicable discussion of the whole matter. He said that his diocesan, Valerius, was away, but that he would

---

[1] Aug. *Retract.* II, xix.
[2] Aug. *C. Litt. Pet.* II, civ, 239; *Serm. ad Caes. eccl. pleb.* 8.
[3] Aug. *C. Litt. Pet.* III, xvi, 19.
[4] Ibid. II, 104; *Serm. ad Caes. eccl. pleb.* 8.
[5] Aug. *C. Litt. Pet.* I, i, 1; III, i, 1; *De unit. eccl.* 1; *C. Cresc.* I, i, 1.
[6] Aug. *C. Litt. Pet.* I, i, 1.   [7] Aug. *Retract.* II, xxv.

certainly approve of such a discussion, which was necessary by reason of the grievous domestic disturbances which the schism was causing.[1]

Shortly after, he wrote to one Eusebius about the case of a violent young man in the town who was accustomed to beat his mother, and had even threatened to murder her. The Donatists had received this doubtful character into their communion without even imposing any penance. In the course of his letter, Saint Augustine again offered to discuss the schism with accredited Donatist representatives; and hoped that all men might come to the knowledge of the truth, and embrace the Catholic faith of their own accord.[2]

In a further letter[3] to Eusebius, Saint Augustine asked him to urge his bishop, Proculeianus, to take action against the man who beat his mother. The Donatist had answered that Proculeianus knew nothing about the matter. Saint Augustine mentions here also the case of a sub-deacon, called Primus, who was removed from his order for disobeying rules about access to nuns. He went over to the Donatists, and was rebaptized. Two nuns went over with him, and now Primus enjoyed rioting in the drunken bands of the Circumcellions. Perhaps, suggests the Bishop, Proculeianus knows nothing of this either. In any case, it is time for him to restrain the violence of his clergy against the Catholics.

At the end of 397 or the beginning of 398 an epistle to a certain Glorius, and others, discusses at length the conversion and reception of heretics, the origins of the schism, and the imperial judgements against the early Donatists, the violence of the modern Circumcellions, and the iniquity of schism.[4]

It is written (Saint Augustine concludes), 'The Lord said unto my lord, Thou art my Son; this day have I begotten thee. Ask of me and I will give thee the heathen for thine inheritance, and the utmost parts of the earth for thy possession.' Whosoever does not communicate with this inheritance disinherits himself; whoso fights against this inheritance acknowledges himself a stranger to the household of God.[5]

A little later Saint Augustine wrote again to the same men.[6] He described his meeting with Fortunius, Donatist bishop of Thubursicum Numidarum. Augustine had gone to see Fortunius, on account of the latter's great age, but the conference was conducted with difficulty because the crowd who came to see the spectacle would not preserve silence. After some hours Augustine tried to get the reporters to take

[1] Aug. *Ep.* XXXIII.
[2] Ibid. XXXIV.
[3] Ibid. XXXV.
[4] Ibid. XLIII.
[6] Ibid. XLIV.
[5] Ibid. XLIII, ix, 25.

some minutes, but they were unwilling, and some of his own friends did this for him. Fortunius maintained that the schismatics were shown to be in the right by the fact that they had suffered persecution, and Augustine answered that, if they had suffered, they had suffered for their wrongdoing, and not for righteousness' sake.[1] Before Fortunius and Augustine parted, another conference was arranged. We do not know whether it was held.

About 398 Saint Augustine wrote to another Donatist bishop, Honoratus, accepting gladly his suggestion that they should discuss the schism by letter, and thus avoid the turbulence of a public conference.[2] This letter is concerned with the Donatist contention that the Holy Catholic Church is now confined to Africa. Epistle LI is part of a similar discussion by letter: it is written to Crispinus, the Donatist bishop of Calama, and is to be dated 399 or 400. Saint Augustine expresses his willingness to meet Crispinus now that they are both in Numidia, and says that he had determined to discuss nothing except in writing, to avoid any possibility of mistake or misinterpretation. The matters discussed in his letter to Crispinus include the readmission of the Maximianists Felicianus and Praetextatus to the Donatist communion, and the use of compulsion against the schismatics. Augustine illustrates from the Donatist treatment of these two schismatics of their own the inconsistency with which the Donatists apply their professed principles to schisms within their own body.

At the same time Saint Augustine wrote to his Donatist kinsman Seuerinus, urging him to return to Catholic unity.[3] In 400 Fortunatus, Alypius and Augustine wrote to the Catholic Bishop of Constantina, Generosus, replying to a letter sent to Generosus by a Donatist priest to say that an angel had appeared to him from heaven to assure him that the schismatics were in the right. The argument of their letter is that the Donatists are not catholic, because they are not in communion with the whole world, and with Saint Peter's successors in the see of Rome; and they also contrast with the audacious claims of the Donatists their treatment of their own Maximianist schismatics.[4]

In 400 also Saint Augustine sent two letters to Celer, the great Numidian landowner, urging him to avoid the errors of the Donatists,[5] and, now that he has studied the origins of the schism with the help of a pamphlet lent to him by Augustine,[6] to commend Catholic unity in the district of Hippo, and in particular among his own friends.[7]

---

[1] Ibid. XLIV, ii, 3, 4, iv, 7.   [2] Ibid. XLIX.
[3] Ibid. LII.   [4] Ibid. LIII.   [5] Ibid. LVI, 2.
[6] Ibid. LVII, 1.   [7] Ibid. LVII, 2.

During the first five years of his episcopate, Saint Augustine was assiduous in warning his own congregation by sermons against the Donatists, and in pleading for church unity. In an exposition of Psalm x, he uttered a general warning against the dangers of heresy and schism;[1] and a particular caution against the Donatist error in admitting only those sacraments which are conferred by holy men,[2] quoting against them the malediction of Jeremiah[3] pronounced against those who put their trust in men. How can men from Mesopotamia, who have never heard the names of Caecilianus and Donatus, be considered polluted by the Donatists, and rebaptized if ever they come to Africa?[4] Men's righteousness is to be recognized by their works, and if this test be applied to the Circumcellions, their violence will show whether they can reasonably claim to be holy. From such persecution the Church must take her refuge under the shadow of God's wing.[5] Saint Augustine returns in a sermon on Psalm lvii to the inconsistency of the Donatists in accusing Catholics of persecuting them,[6] when they themselves violently expelled the Maximianist schismatics from their basilicas; and verse 7, 'the Lord hath smitten the jaw-bones of the lions in pieces', brings once more to the preacher's mind the thought of the war-cry of the Circumcellions, *Deo laudes*, more dreaded than the roaring of Numidian lions.[7]

In Psalm cxxiv, 'the hills that stand around Jerusalem' are interpreted mystically as the great leaders in the Church; some are good, and some, like Donatus, Maximianus, Photinus and Arius, are evil, but are mentioned among the 'hills' since they are eminent. But upon such hills men come to shipwreck.[8] And at the end the exposition returns, in commenting on the words 'but peace shall be upon Israel', to the recurrent refrain of all Saint Augustine's work at this time of upheaval, the contemplation of the vision of the heavenly Jerusalem, which is the vision of peace.[9] In a sermon delivered one Good Friday during this period, Augustine pictures the Son, now enthroned at the Father's right hand, being offered as his inheritance, not all the nations which the Psalmist assigned to him, but Africa only.[10] The Bishop then calls upon his flock to think of the greatness of the sacrifice commemorated that

---

[1] Aug. *Enarr. in Ps.* x, 1, 4. [2] Ibid. x, 5.
[3] Jer. xvii. 5. [4] Aug. *Enarr. in Ps.* x, 5.
[5] Ibid. x, 6. [6] Ibid. LVII, 15.
[7] Ibid. (cf. CXXXII, 6).
[8] Ibid. CXXIV, 5. [9] Ibid. CXXIV, 10.
[10] Aug. *Enarr.* II *in Ps.* XXI, 1: 'possidenti enim uniuersum orbem terrarum pars offertur; et dicitur sedenti ad dexteram Patris, Ecce quid hic habes: et pro tota terra ostenditur illi sola Africa.' See also ibid. XXI, 24, 26.

day, to remember that the Donatists in their church are saying the same psalm, and to consider whether it is only Africa which has been redeemed by the offering on Calvary.[1] He concludes a sermon which he acknowledges to have been long[2] with an appeal to the flock to remain under the banner of Christ who has redeemed it.[3]

In a sermon against the idolatry prevalent at Carthage, Augustine urges his people to abstain from its contamination, but not to take the law into their own hands, and indulge in idol-breaking. Violence of that type is more proper to the Circumcellions, who must have some kind of violent activity, and who, if they are unable to persecute other people, are content to lay violent hands upon themselves.[4]

At this period also Augustine again urges the necessity of tolerating evil in the Church until the Last Judgement, of correcting the wicked without falling into the snare of pride, and of preserving unity at all costs.[5] Christians should endeavour to keep the unity of the spirit in the bond of peace; and the Donatists are to be condemned for trying to anticipate Christ's judgement, and separate wheat from tares here and now.[6] If it is true, as they say, that the love of many has waxed cold, and that there are now more tares than wheat on the Master's threshing floor, it is still necessary to wait until he himself separates them.[7] But in the meantime the faithful Christian, though necessarily mingled in the Church with the unfaithful, must strive to keep himself pure in heart, for it is a greater evil to split the unity of the Church and separate from good men in our attempts to eradicate the wicked in this world than it is to tolerate them until the ultimate and final separation.[8]

This period, 395–400, covering the first five years of Saint Augustine's episcopate at Hippo, shows the beginning on a large scale of his anti-Donatist campaign. During this time he was principally, but not entirely, concerned with Donatism in his own diocese. The campaign was launched there on the lines which it was to follow until it eventuated in the final overthrow of Donatism. The period witnesses the first

---

[1] Ibid. XXI, 28: 'quid mihi dicis, o haeretice? non est pretium orbis terrarum? Africa sola redempta est?'

[2] Ibid. XXI, 32: 'multa diximus, fratres.'

[3] Ibid. XXI, 31: 'sic et qui baptismum habent Christi, si ueniunt ad unitatem, non mutamus titulos, aut delemus titulos; sed agnoscimus titulos regis nostri, titulos imperatoris nostri. sed quid dicimus? o domus misera, ille te possideat cuius titulos habes: Christi titulos habes, noli esse Donati possessio.'

[4] Aug. *Serm.* LXII, xi, 17.   [5] Ibid. LXXXVIII, xviii, 19–21.

[6] Ibid. LXXXVIII, xix, 21.   [7] Ibid. LXXXVIII, xix, 22.

[8] Ibid. LXXXVIII, xxii, 25.

two considerable polemical works on the subject, the *Contra Epistulam Parmeniani* and the *De baptismo contra Donatistas*, which is a full exposition of the controversy in its relation to the sacrament of baptism. The epistles of the period show Saint Augustine endeavouring to heal the schism by discussion with representatives of the schismatics of the theological problems involved; the sermons contain warnings to his flock of the dangers of schism, and of the uncharitable feelings which engender it. At the same time we see the beginnings of approval of appeal to the State, which in earlier works Saint Augustine had expressly repudiated, but which was to be developed between 400 and 405, and still more after 405, and was destined to be the means by which the unification of the African Church was eventually accomplished.

3. *The period 400–405*

Two councils assembled under Aurelius at Carthage in 401, again in the *secretarium* of the Basilica Restituta.[1] At the first, on 16 June, the President, in his opening speech, lamented the dearth of Catholic clergy in Africa, both in major and minor orders, which was occasioned by the schism, and possibly also by the lack of Punic-speaking clergy, necessary to the country districts where Latin was comparatively little spoken by the ordinary people. The remedy suggested by Aurelius was the ordination of converted Donatists, but as such ordinations were forbidden in various places abroad, it was decided to ask the Bishops of Rome and of Milan, Anastasius and Venerius, for their opinion. The Council concurred, and it was also proposed to approach the Emperor to urge him to exterminate paganism in Africa.

When the second council met in the same place on 13 September, the reply of the Bishop of Rome was read, in which he exhorted the African Christians to remain steadfast in the face of the Donatist menace, but apparently made no practical suggestions. The Council proceeded to enact certain canons on the question of the schism. Canon 1 ordered that the Donatists should be dealt with gently, but that at the same time the secular magistrates should be requested to take action against the violence of the Maximianists. In spite of the decision abroad against the ordination of converted schismatics, Canon 2 allowed Donatist clergy to retain their orders in the interests of ecclesiastical peace; and Canon 3 ordered discussions to be held with the Donatists to this end. An exception was made by Canon 12 in the case of those who had been rebaptized by the Donatists: in no case were they to receive Catholic orders. In accordance with these recommendations Saint Augustine

[1] Hefele, op. cit. vol. II, pp. 421 sq.; Migne, op. cit. vol. I, p. 494.

received into the Catholic ministry a number of Donatist clergy in his diocese.¹

But the obstinacy of the Donatists, who did not in the least desire reunion, frustrated these irenic measures. The seventh African council met under Aurelius on 27 August 402, in the *secretarium* of the basilica at Milevis.² Like the Councils of Carthage which we have considered, it was a general council of the African provinces. Canon 2³ concerned Maximianus, Bishop of Vaga. He was a converted Donatist, who had been elected bishop of the see. When divisions arose at Vaga on this account, he offered in a letter to the Council to resign. Their second canon accepted this resignation, and ordered the Church of Vaga to proceed to another election. The choice again fell on a converted Donatist, a brother of Maximianus, Castorius, to whom Alypius and Augustine wrote, as we shall see, to urge him to accept the see.⁴

A further step towards reunion was taken by the eighth synod of Carthage, assembled under Aurelius in the Basilica of the Regio Secunda on 25 August 403.⁵ Saint Augustine was present, as he had been at all the synods of Carthage since his consecration. Two canons enacted by this synod bear on Donatism.⁶ The first enjoins that every Catholic bishop in his own city, either alone, or in conjunction with his colleague of a neighbouring diocese, shall enter into communication with the Donatist leaders and, with the assistance of the imperial magistrates, choose representatives and hold a discussion. At the same time, by the second of these canons, Aurelius submitted for acceptance by the synod a letter summoning the Donatists to take part in such discussions through the African provinces, with a view to coming to a brotherly agreement on the points at issue.

In the next year, when the obstinacy of the Donatists had stultified these advances, the ninth Council of Carthage (June 404) took the first official step towards a formal appeal to the State for the protection of the Catholic Church in Africa, and thereby initiated a course of action which in 411 was to secure the official condemnation of Donatism in the Conference of Carthage.⁷ The bishops Thasius and Euodius were sent to the Emperors Arcadius and Honorius for this purpose, and in Canon 93 of the African Codex we have the instructions that were

¹ Aug. *Ep.* LXI, 1, 2; CCXLV, 2.
² Hefele, op. cit. vol. II, p. 427; Migne, op. cit. vol. I, p. 1316.
³ No. 88, of the *Codex Canonum Ecclesiae Africanae*.
⁴ Aug. *Ep.* LXIX.
⁵ Hefele, op. cit. vol. II, p. 439; Migne, op. cit. vol. I, p. 495.
⁶ C.C.E.A. 91 and 92.
⁷ Hefele, op. cit. vol. II, p. 440; Migne, op. cit. vol. I, p. 496.

given to these delegates. They were to inform Honorius that the Donatists had rejected the offer of the previous year, and, instead of sending representatives to a discussion, had proceeded to all kinds of violence. They therefore petitioned for imperial protection for the Church and its ministers, and for the enforcement of the imperial laws against heretics enacted by Theodosius. The delegates also took a letter to the Emperor, signed by Aurelius on behalf of the Council, in which the secular magistrates are requested to protect the Catholics until further order is taken by the Emperors. Before the emissaries arrived Honorius had published a severe edict against the schismatics, threatening their laity with fines and their clergy with exile. Afterwards, in February 405, he issued further edicts against the Donatists, and in support of Church unity.[1] The second of these, that of 12 February 405, is called the first Edict of Unity. It forbade rebaptism, under penalty of arrest and confiscation of goods; prohibited dissidents from receiving or making donations or legacies; decreed for the first time the assimilation of schismatics to heretics for legal purposes; and ordered all churches to be handed over to the Catholics.[2] In some towns, among them Carthage, the Donatists were almost entirely suppressed, but they continued to survive in others. On 5 March 405 the Emperor ordered the edict of unity to be publicly exhibited everywhere.[3]

The appeal of the Catholic bishops against Donatist persecution had thus won an imperial response, and by the acts of the tenth synod of Carthage in the same year (23 August) we learn that there had been numerous conversions at Carthage as a result of the edict. The synod ordered all the ecclesiastical provinces of Africa to send plenipotentiary delegates to the proposed Council of Union. It was also resolved to ask the civil magistrates to apply the edict in places other than Carthage; and letters of thanks were sent to the Emperor for his intervention.[4]

This period of Saint Augustine's struggle against Donatism, which saw the first-fruits of the policy of coercion adumbrated in the *Contra Epistulam Parmeniani* in 398, concludes in the last month of 405 with a rescript from the Emperors to Diotimus instructing him to prosecute Donatists everywhere with the utmost rigour.[5] Outward unity was established for a time even in the diocese of Hippo, and when the

[1] *C.Th.* XVI, v, 37, 38.
[2] Ibid. XVI, ii, 2, v, 38, vi, 3–5; cf. *C.C.E.A.* 94, 99, 117, 119; Aug. *Ep.* LXXXVIII, 5–10; CLXXXV, vii, 26.
[3] *C.Th.* XVI, v, 39.
[4] Hefele, op. cit. vol. II, p. 441; *C.C.E.A.* 94.
[5] *C.Th.* XVI, v, 39 (8 December 405).

Donatist basilica there was confiscated, Saint Augustine pasted up on its walls one of his latest polemical works, the *Probationum et testimoniorum contra Donatistas liber*.[1]

The first work of the third period is the second book *Contra Litteras Petiliani*. The first book, written about 400, had been addressed in general to the Catholics of the diocese of Hippo; but, as we have seen,[2] the remaining two books answered the letter of Petilianus point by point, and it is from the quotations of Petilianus which Augustine answers in turn that we are in part able to reconstruct the letter of Petilianus.[3] In the interval between Books I and II of this work, Saint Augustine had read the second part of Petilianus' *Epistula ad presbyteros et diaconos*, and Book II answers this work in detail. It will be seen from the title of Petilianus' work that it was in form a pastoral letter to the clergy of the diocese of Constantina.[4] Its three principal subjects were baptism, schism, and persecution. Petilianus plunged straight into his subject by saying that he would discuss baptism, and by laying down the Donatist thesis that its validity depends upon the worthiness of the minister: 'conscientia namque sancte dantis attenditur, quae abluat accipientis.'[5] This theory would stigmatize as void not merely baptism, but all Catholic sacraments; and Petilianus in fact states that the Catholics can confer no Christian sacraments since they are the successors of *traditores*;[6] and moreover since they continue to prove themselves impure by persecuting the Donatists.[7] It is because Catholic sacraments are thus held to be impure that men coming from the Church to Donatism are baptized, as being still heathens.[8]

The teaching of Petilianus with respect to schism follows the conventional Donatist lines. He argues that the Catholics in Africa have put themselves outside the true Church by their laxity under the persecution of Diocletian[9] and thereby voided all their sacraments.[10] The

[1] Aug. *Retract*. II, xxvii.   [2] Supra, p. 44.
[3] This reconstruction is printed in Monceaux, op. cit. vol. VI, pp. 311-28.
[4] Aug. *C. Litt. Pet.* II, i, 2.
[5] Ibid. II, ii, 4, iii, 6, iv, 8, v, 10: (Petilianus dixit) 'bis baptisma nobis obiiciunt ii qui sub nomine baptismi animas suas reo lauacro polluerunt, quibus equidem obscenis sordes cunctae mundiores sunt, quod peruersa munditia aqua sua contigit inquinari. conscientia namque sancte dantis attenditur, quae abluat accipientis. nam qui fidem sciens a perfido sumpserit, non fidem percipit sed reatum. omnis enim res origine et radice consistit, et, si caput non habet aliquid, nihil est; nec quidquam bene regenerat, nisi bono semine regeneretur.'
[6] Petil. II–XII (according to the numbering of the reconstruction by Monceaux, op. cit. vol. VI, pp. 311-28).
[7] Petil. VIII–X, XIII–XV.   [8] Petil. XVI–XXVII.
[9] Petil. XXVIII–XXXII.   [10] Petil. XXXIII–XXXVI.

violence of which he accuses contemporary Catholics (while ignoring the atrocities of the Donatist bands, and even praising the patience of their sect under persecution from the Catholics) proves that the Catholics are the true heirs of the original *traditores* and persecutors.[1]

This leads Petilianus to the third argument of his pastoral, that the Catholics are the only persecutors of their opponents: he multiplies Biblical quotations against persecutors,[2] and denounces the appeal to the secular power.[3]

This work, in spite of its violence, is free from personal attacks on Catholics, and acquired considerable prestige among the Donatists.[4] It is answered in detail by Saint Augustine in *Contra Litteras Petiliani* II.

As soon as this work was published, Saint Augustine wrote, in 401 or 402, a pastoral letter against the Donatists, entitled officially *Ad Catholicos epistula contra Donatistas*, and commonly known, from its subject, as the *De unitate ecclesiae*. It is not mentioned in the *Retractationes*, possibly because it is an epistle rather than a formal treatise, but is included in the Index of Augustine's works compiled by his friend and biographer, Possidius.[5] That it was addressed to the faithful of the diocese of Hippo appears from the greeting:

> Augustinus episcopus dilectissimis fratribus ad nostrae dispensationis curam pertinentibus, Salus quae in Christo est, et pax unitatis et caritatis eius sit uobiscum, et integer spiritus uester et anima et corpus in diem Domini nostri Iesu Christi seruetur.

He begins by reminding them how in a former pastoral letter[6] he answered the small portion of the letter of Petilianus which had reached him at that time; and how since then[7] he has sent Petilianus a detailed answer to his letter.[8] In the present work he desires to discuss where the true Church is to be found.[9] For this purpose he begins with some words about the unity of Christ and the Church,[10] supporting his teaching by citations from the Old and New Testaments.[11] At the end of this section he admits the imperfection of the Church's holiness in this world, and teaches that it cannot be perfected until the Last Judgement shall have weeded out all impurities.[12] But in the meantime it would be futile to let the Church's work of salvation come to a standstill; and

---

[1] Petil. XXXVII–XLIII.
[2] Petil. XLIV–L, LV, LVI.
[3] Petil. LI–LIV, LVII, LVIII.
[4] Aug. *De unit. eccl.* I, I.
[5] Possid. *Index op. Aug.* III.
[6] Aug. *C. Litt. Pet.* I.
[7] In *C. Litt. Pet.* II.
[8] Aug. *De unit. eccl.* I, I.
[9] Ibid. II, 2.
[10] Ibid. IV.
[11] Ibid. IV–XIV.
[12] Ibid. XV–XX.

God carries out this work through the sacraments conferred in his Church, by himself, and not by his ministers, although through their administration.[1]

In chapter 1 of the *De unitate ecclesiae* Saint Augustine says he has dispatched his answer to the letter of Petilianus, but has had no further reply from him. Such a reply, however, was already prepared, though it had not yet been sent; and it was in the form of a personal letter to Saint Augustine.[2] It drew from the Bishop his third and last book against Petilianus, which quotes the latter's epistle, though not so fully as his pastoral 'ad presbyteros et diaconos' is quoted in Book II. Enough, however, is quoted for us to know that the latest work of Petilianus consisted of criticism of Augustine's first book against him, a discussion of the Catholic objections to the Donatist conception of baptism, considerable personal abuse of Augustine, and a final exhortation to the Donatist flock. In attacking Augustine, Petilianus made a wide and unscrupulous use of the *Confessions*, published some five years before, and charged him with sacrilege, with introducing into Africa the coenobitic life, and with being a Manichaean and a sophistical, dishonest controversialist. Petilianus had exhausted his anti-Catholic arguments, and was compelled to fall back upon personal abuse of his opponent, after the manner of those who have little to offer by way of relevant argument.

The third book of Saint Augustine against Petilianus brought into the controversy the Donatist layman Cresconius,[3] who took up the cudgels on behalf of Petilianus, in a letter addressed to Saint Augustine personally.[4] Cresconius had only seen *Contra Petilianum* I, and so must have written at the end of 401 or in early 402. For some unknown reason, it was over three years before Saint Augustine received this letter, and he did not answer it till 405, since he mentions the imperial edict of unity of 12 February 405.[5] His answer was in the form of a letter to Cresconius in four books, entitled *Contra Cresconium*.[6] In the first three books all the matters raised by Cresconius are answered, but before they were published the author realized that the whole case of Cresconius in the matter of schism was undermined by the Donatist reception of their own schismatics, the Maximianists; and the fourth book was added to point this out.[7] Cresconius was a contemporary of

[1] Ibid. XXI-XXIII.
[2] Aug. *C. Litt. Pet.* III, 1, 61.
[3] Aug. *C. Cresc.* II, iv, 7; IV, xxxiv, 41.
[4] Aug. *Retract.* II, lii.
[5] Ibid.; *C. Cresc.* III, xliii, 47, xliv, 48, xlvii, 51.
[6] Aug. *Retract.* II, lii.
[7] Ibid. II, lii; *C. Cresc.* IV, 1.

Saint Augustine, born about 350 in 'Africa proconsularis', and proud therefore to call himself 'Afer in Africa'.[1] As a grammarian, he paid much attention in his work to small details of expression and style.[2] Saint Augustine tells us that he answered the letter of Cresconius in order in his first three books, and again, from the standpoint of the Maximianist schism, in his fourth book; and so, as the order of the original and the second letter agrees, we are sure that we know the order of the letter sent by Cresconius.[3] It appears from this that Cresconius opened with a bitter criticism of the attitude adopted by Augustine against Petilianus.[4] Then came the three great questions under discussion, first that of baptism,[5] secondly the legitimacy of schism,[6] thirdly the iniquity of persecuting the Donatist church.[7] Cresconius then imitated Petilianus by concluding with a violent personal attack on Augustine,[8] in the course of which he alleged that he was still a Manichee.[9] Saint Augustine's reply was constructed on the same lines. Book I is on the use of dialectic in religious controversy, Book II on rebaptism, and on the authority of Saint Cyprian in the matter, Book III on State repression, the crime of *traditio*, and the holiness of the Church. The *Contra Litteras Petiliani* and the *Contra Cresconium* are among the best examples we have of the thoroughness of Saint Augustine's literary method in combating the schismatics.

A large number of the epistles and sermons of this period is also concerned with Donatism. One letter, written about the end of 401, congratulates the senator Pammachius, the husband of Paulina, and friend of Saint Jerome, on the success with which he has extirpated Donatism on his African estates, and induced his tenants, especially in consular Numidia, to return to the Church.[10] Would that such action were more widespread! An epistle of about the same date advises a fellow-bishop, Theodore, on the reception of Donatist converts to the Church.[11] It is important, says Saint Augustine, to distinguish between heresy and schism. The Donatists are schismatics, and are not at peace with the people of God, because they do not possess the unity and truth of the Catholic Church. But they are to be brought by persuasion into

---

[1] Aug. *C. Cresc.* IV, lxxi, 83; cf. ibid. III, xxv, 28; IV, xliii, 51.
[2] Ibid. III, lv, 61, lxxi, 83, lxxiii, 85; IV, xi, 13.
[3] Aug. *Retract.* II, lii; *C. Cresc.* IV, i, 2.
[4] Aug. *C. Cresc.* II, ii, 3 sq.; IV, ii sq.   [5] Ibid. I, xxi, 26 sq.
[6] Ibid. III, xii, 15 sq.; IV, xxiv, 31 sq.
[7] Ibid. III, xli, 45 sq.; IV, xlvi, 55 sq.
[8] Ibid. III, lxxviii, 90 sq.; IV, lxiv, 78 sq.
[9] Ibid. III, lxxx, 92.   [10] Aug. *Ep.* LVIII.
[11] Ibid. LXI.

that unity, in order that they may begin to profit by the sacraments which they now possess to no purpose. God will graft them in again, and, possessing Christian unity, they will enjoy the blessings of Christian charity.

At the beginning of 402 Saint Augustine had further correspondence with the Donatist bishop of Calama, Crispinus, with whom, two or three years previously, he had offered to discuss the schism personally or by letter.[1] He now expostulates with him for rebaptizing by force eighty tenants on an estate he had recently bought in the Mappalia at Carthage.[2] Crispinus is warned that the legal penalty for this action is a fine of ten pounds of gold, and exhorted to remember also the moral claims of Christian unity. Crispinus did not reply to this letter; but Augustine took no legal action against him. However, his friend Possidius, who was Catholic Bishop of Calama, attacked Crispinus.[3] In 403 Possidius held a public debate with Crispinus before the municipal authorities, according to the resolution of the Council of Carthage of 25 August of that year.[4] Crispinus appeared, but refused to join in any discussion.[5] On one of his episcopal journeys Possidius was attacked by a band of Donatists led by the priest Crispinus, who may well have been a relative of the schismatic bishop of Calama. He took refuge in an house, and was besieged there, and wounded in the struggle when the schismatics tried to set the house on fire.[6] When he returned to his see he brought the matter before the city magistrates, but could secure no redress from bishop Crispinus. Nevertheless, he succeeded in having the bishop summoned before the court of the proconsul, under the law of Theodosius against the heretical clergy. The proceedings were defended, but Crispinus was found guilty, and fined ten pounds of gold. On appeal to the Emperor the findings were upheld, but the penalty was remitted at the desire of Possidius.[7]

At the end of 402 Augustine joined with his friend the Bishop of Tagaste, Alypius, in writing to Castorius, a lawyer converted from Donatism. They praised the devotion of the Catholic Bishop of Vaga, Maximianus, in resigning his see in the interests of Christian peace, and asked Castorius to undertake the responsibilities of the bishopric in his

---

[1] Ibid. LI; supra, p. 46.
[2] Ibid. LXVI; cf. *C. Litt. Pet.* II, lxxxiii, 184.
[3] Possid. *Vita Aug.* XII; Aug. *Ep.* LXXXVIII, 7; CV, ii, 4; *C. Cresc.* III, xlvi, 50 sq.
[4] *C.C.E.A.* 91; cf. p. 50 supra.
[5] Aug. *C. Cresc.* III, xlvi, 50.
[6] Ibid. III, xlvi, 50; *Ep.* CV, ii, 4; Possid. *Vita Aug.* XII.
[7] Aug. *Ep.* LXXXVIII, 7; CV, ii, 4; *C. Cresc.* III, xlvii, 51; Possid. *Vita Aug.* XII.

brother's room.[1] Alypius and Augustine joined also in writing at the same time to the Donatist Naucclio, to urge the inconsistency of the reception into communion by the schismatics of the penitent Maximianist bishop, Felicianus of Musti.[2] At this time the inconsistency of the treatment of the Maximianists had become a cardinal argument against Donatism in Saint Augustine's writings, and we have met it in the works against Petilianus and Cresconius.

At the end of 403 Saint Augustine wrote a pastoral to all the Donatists.[3] In it he pictured the Catholic Church calling the erring schismatics back to her communion, and to peace and unity. The main points of the Catholic case are all here exhibited: the schismatics are asked to consider the impossibility of pronouncing final judgement in this world; they are reminded of the origins of their schism, and of its condemnation by imperial and ecclesiastical judgements; their inconsistent reception of the Maximianists is alleged against them; and they are urged to embrace truth and unity: 'euigilate ad salutem: amate pacem: redite ad unitatem.'[4]

About 405 Saint Augustine wrote to the provincial governor, Caecilianus, to congratulate him on the support he had given to the cause of Christian unity in Africa generally, while at the same time expressing regret that Numidia, and particularly the region of Hippo Regius, had not yet profited by his good offices. Caecilianus would be able to learn, either from the Numidian bishops, or from the priest who was the bearer of this letter, how necessary it was that the Donatists in those areas should be subjugated.[5]

A letter to Possidius, Bishop of Calama, probably to be dated about 401, and concerned chiefly with the propriety of feminine adornment and cosmetics, concludes with a refusal to give definite authority to ordain men baptized by the Donatists, while not blaming Possidius for anything done under the pressure of emergency.[6]

A commentary of this period on Psalm xxxii,[7] delivered in September 403, shortly after Saint Cyprian's Day, concludes with an appeal to the Donatists to recognize that they are brethren of the Catholics, possessing the same faith and sacraments, and therefore bound to avoid rebaptism as sinful. Commenting likewise on Psalm xcv about the

---

[1] Aug. *Ep.* LXIX. [2] Ibid. LXX. [3] Ibid. LXXVI.
[4] Ibid. LXXVI, 2. [5] Ibid. LXXXVI.
[6] Ibid. CCXLV, 2: 'de ordinando autem qui in parte Donati baptizatus est, auctor tibi esse non possum: aliud est enim facere si cogaris, aliud consulere ut facias.'
[7] Aug. *Enarr.* II *in Ps.* XXXII, 29.

year 405, Saint Augustine speaks of the universal extent of the Christian salvation, wrought for all the nations, and not for select minorities;[1] and when he comes to verse 10, 'commoueatur a facie eius uniüersa terra: dicite in nationibus, Dominus regnauit a ligno', he asks whether it is a part of Africa, and not the whole earth, which is moved at God's presence, and whether it is not God who reigns from the Tree by his Passion, rather than the Donatists, who reign with the clubs, or *israeles*, of the Circumcellions.[2] Psalm cxxxii, 'Behold, how good and joyful a thing it is, brethren, to dwell together in unity', could only lead the preacher to apply the Psalmist's exhortation to the condition of the distracted African Church of his day. He contrasts the Catholic monks, with their cry *Deo gratias*, and the Donatist Circumcellions, with their war-shout *Deo laudes*.[3]

In a sermon delivered at Carthage at the end of 403 Saint Augustine had much to say about the history of the Donatist schism.[4] He mentioned the appeal of the Donatists Rogatianus and Pontius to the apostate Julian,[5] and discussed the judgements relating to Caecilianus at the onset of the schism, and the action before Zenophilus.[6] Mention of the Maximianist schism led him to read in full the conciliar letter of the Maximianist synod of Cabarsussa, and to comment upon it.[7] The Donatists had undermined their whole case against the Catholics by receiving back to their communion the Maximianists who submitted.[8] In the sermon following this one, and completing the analysis of the psalm, Saint Augustine mentions that he has already quoted at length from documents relevant to the schism, and does not renew this line of attack, but pleads for the unity of the African Church in Christ.[9]

A fragment of an Easter-Monday sermon to the newly baptized impresses on them the unity of the Church—which is one Bread, one Body—into which their baptism, confirmation and first communion have just grafted them.[10] The blessed sacrament of which they are now partakers is the symbol of their unity, and thus cannot be received by heretics.[11] In the course of a sermon on John v. 39–47, delivered at

[1] Aug. *Enarr. in Ps.* xcv, 5. [2] Ibid. xcv, 11.
[3] Ibid. cxxii, 6. [4] Aug. *Enarr.* II *in Ps.* xxxvi, 18–23.
[5] Cf. Aug. *Ep.* cv, 9; *C. Litt. Pet.* II, xcii, 97.
[6] See supra, p. 9, and the text in *P.L.* XLIII, 793 sq.
[7] Aug. *Enarr. in Ps.* xxxvi, 20; see pp. 32 sq. supra.
[8] Aug. *Enarr.* II *in Ps.* xxxvi, 22. [9] *Enarr.* III *in Ps.* xxxvi, 18–20.
[10] Aug. *Serm.* ccxxix.
[11] Ibid. ccxxix: 'postea ad aquam uenistis, et conspersi estis, et unum facti estis; accedente feruore Spiritus sancti cocti estis; et panis dominicus facti estis. ecce quod accepistis. quomodo ergo unum uidetis esse quod factum est, sic unum

Carthage, Saint Augustine quotes numerous Scriptural texts on the unity of the Church, and makes yet another appeal to the Donatists to seek the unity and peace of Christ.[1] One Easter sermon of this period[2] dwells on the charge of Christ to the Apostles after the Resurrection to preach the good news to the whole world;[3] and another, on the fishing recorded in John xxi, brings the preacher back to his favourite theme of the good and bad fish gathered into the same net, a type of the admixture of good and evil in the Church Militant.[4] An Ascension sermon insists that charity can only be preserved within the unity of the Church[5] and one delivered on Whitsun Eve, on the text Psalm cxl. 5, is specially directed against the Donatists.[6] Speaking of the gift of the Holy Spirit, then being commemorated, the preacher attacks the Donatist error that the Holy Spirit can only be conferred by the hands of holy men,[7] and shows that at times he is given without men's ministry at all, as in the outpouring on the day of Pentecost, and when he fell upon Cornelius, who had not even been baptized.[8] The gift of the Spirit to Cornelius foreshadows his outpouring through the ministry of the Church upon the Gentile world, and refutes the contention of the Donatists that none but holy men can confer his gifts.[9] Another Whit-Sunday sermon of the same period is an exposition of the unity of the Church, manifested by the gift of tongues which accompanied the effusion of the Holy Spirit.[10] He filled the Church, and shed abroad in our hearts the love of God, but those who are outside the Church cannot receive his gifts.[11] For this gift of the Spirit is distinct from incorporation into the Church by the sacrament of baptism; and, although it is admitted that heretics and schismatics possess baptism, yet, unless they come into the unity of the Church, they are destitute of the gifts of the Holy Spirit.[12] For disunity and dissension in the Church are

estote uos, diligendo uos, tenendo unam fidem, unam spem, indiuiduam caritatem. haeretici quando hoc accipiunt, testimonium contra se accipiunt; quia illi quaerunt diuisionem, cum panis iste indicet unitatem. sic et uinum in multis racemis fuit, et modo in unum est.' For this unity prefigured by bread and wine, cf. Cypr. *Ep.* LXIII, 13, LXXVI, 6; and Aug. *Serm.* CCLXXII.

[1] Aug. *Serm.* CXXIX.
[2] Ibid. CCXXXVIII.
[3] Luke xxiv. 47.
[4] Aug. *Serm.* CCXLIX.
[5] Ibid. CCLXV, ix, 10–x, 12.
[6] Ibid. CCLXVI.
[7] Ibid. CCLXVI, 3.
[8] Ibid. CCLXVI, 6.
[9] Ibid. CCLXVI, 7.
[10] Ibid. CCLXVIII.
[11] Ibid. CCLXVIII, 2.
[12] Ibid. CCLXIX, 2 (delivered at Whitsuntide during this period): 'nec inmerito recte intelligitur, quamuis ipsos baptismum Christi habere fateamur, haereticos non accipere uel schismaticos Spiritum Sanctum, nisi dum compagini adhaeserint unitatis per consortium caritatis.'

the fruits of uncharitableness, the manifestation of what Saint Paul calls the 'mind of the flesh'. Therefore the Donatists are summoned to share in the charity which alone engenders unity among brethren.[1] It is mere hypocrisy for the schismatic to celebrate the feast of the Holy Spirit when he refuses to let the charity of the Holy Spirit rule in his heart.[2]

The feast of the Nativity of Saint John Baptist, with its suggestion of the thought of Christ's baptism by Saint John, evokes another sermon against the Donatists on the ministry of Christian baptism.[3] Christ submitted to the baptism of John: what would a Donatist say if he had been counted worthy to baptize Christ?[4] But the Donatist not merely says, 'I baptize': he says, 'I make like myself who baptize the man whom I baptize', supporting his case with the text, 'A good tree bringeth forth good fruit, and a corrupt tree bringeth forth evil fruit'. This analogy is attacked, and its absurdity shown by applying it to the baptism of Christ.[5] The final blow is struck with the weapon of Saint John's own words, 'I baptize with water, but there cometh one after me...he shall baptize you with the Holy Ghost and with fire'.[6]

On the feast of Saint Peter and Saint Paul (29 June), the commission given to Saint Peter to feed the flock of Christ is contrasted with the attitude of the Donatists, who talk about their own flock, and not Christ's flock.[7]

4. *The period 405–411*

The next division of the struggle brings the culmination of the policy of active Catholic resistance, with State support, to the ravages of Donatism, and concludes with the definitive overthrow of the schism by the judgement of the imperial commissioner Marcellinus at the Conference of Carthage in June 411. Carthage was at peace after the edict of unity of 12 February 405; but the Roman administration proved too weak to eradicate Donatism in the provinces; and many of

[1] Ibid. CCLXIX, 3: 'respondemus eis: habetis baptismum Christi; uenite ut habeatis et Spiritum Christi.'
[2] Ibid. CCLXXI: 'quid enim eis prodest percipere auribus, quod cordibus respuunt; et eius diem celebrare, cuius lumen oderunt?'
[3] Ibid. CCXCII.
[4] Ibid. CCXCII, ii, 2: '...a Ioanne baptizatus est Christus. ubi sunt qui de ministerio baptismi arrogantia tumidae animositatis inflantur? ubi sunt uoces carentes humilitate, elatae superbia, Ego baptizo, ego baptizo? quid dixisses, si Christum baptizare meruisses?'
[5] Ibid. CCXCII, iv, 5: 'creaturam uocabis arborem, et fructum Creatorem?'
[6] Ibid. CCXCII, iv, 8.   [7] Ibid. CCXCV, v, 5.

the local magistrates were too impotent or too indifferent to enforce the law. The Donatist basilica at Hippo, for instance, which had been taken over by Saint Augustine on behalf of the Church, was regained by the schismatics, who rehallowed it by washing down the walls.[1] Their bishop, Proculeianus, returned;[2] and Circumcellion outrages were multiplied.[3] This time the Catholics, at the end of their patience, retaliated.[4] The priests of Hippo wrote to Ianuarius, the Donatist primate of Numidia, to demand that he should restrain the violence of his party,[5] but without effect.[6] On one occasion the Donatists baptized forty-eight Catholics again by force.[7] A Donatist bishop, Maximinus of Sinitum, submitted to the edict, and came over to the Church. He became an object of special Circumcellion hatred, and the Donatists engaged a town-crier to announce at Sinitum that anyone who went over with him to the Catholic Church would have his house burned down.[8] They even threatened to murder Saint Augustine if he would not cease his propaganda against them.[9]

Macrobius succeeded Proculeianus as Donatist bishop of Hippo, and entered the town to take possession of his see, escorted by a great procession of armed Circumcellions. They entered the basilica with him, but when he delivered a sermon urging restraint, they immediately left the town.[10] There were, however, many conversions to Catholicism, even among the Circumcellions,[11] and the tenants of numerous estates came over *en bloc*, including those of Festus, and of the proconsul Donatus.[12]

But in many parts of Numidia the Donatists were still strong enough to continue their persecution. At Milevis, for instance, they destroyed four basilicas;[13] at Bagai they set fire to the basilica, and burned the sacred books;[14] at Thibilis they forcibly rebaptized the Catholic bishop, who was ninety years of age;[15] at Rotaria they murdered the Catholic bishop;[16] and at Caesariana all kinds of outrages were perpetrated. But in some places the number of conversions to Catholicism was so great

---

[1] Aug. *Ep.* CVIII, v, 14.   [2] Ibid. LXXXVIII, 6.
[3] Aug. *C. Cresc.* III, xliii, 47, xlvii, 51; *Ep.* LXXXVIII, 1, 8.
[4] Aug. *Ep.* LXXXVIII, 9; CVIII, vi, 19.   [5] *Apud* Aug. *Ep.* LXXXVIII.
[6] Aug. *Ep.* CV, ii, 3, 4; CVIII, v, 14, vi, 18; CXI, 1.
[7] Ibid. CXI, 1.   [8] Ibid. CV, ii, 4.
[9] Ibid. CV, i, 1, v, 17.   [10] Ibid. CVIII, v, 14.
[11] Ibid. LXXXIII, 1; LXXXVIII, 9; LXXXIX, 7; XCIII, i, 1, 2, v, 18; XCVII, 4; CXII, 3; CLXXXV, vii, 29, 30.
[12] Ibid. LXXIX, 8; CXII, 3.
[13] *Gesta Coll. Carthag.* I, 139.   [14] Aug. *Breu. Coll.* II, 11, 23.
[15] *Gesta Coll. Carthag.* I, 188, 197.   [16] Ibid. I, 187.

that dioceses had to be subdivided; and among these was Milevis, now divided into the sees of Milevis and of Tucca.[1]

In 406 the Primianists made an appeal to the State, and on 30 January of that year an embassy sent by them to Ravenna asked the *praefectus praetorio* to adjudicate there between the petitioners and representatives of the Catholics; but he refused.[2] The eleventh Catholic synod of Carthage met in the *secretarium* of the Basilica of the Second Region on 13 June 407.[3] It ordered[4] that communities which returned as a whole from Donatism to the Church, and had bishops of their own, might keep them; but on the death of such bishops they might join another diocese. Bishops who came into the Church with their flocks before the edict of union of 408 might keep their sees, but those who returned afterwards must submit to the Catholic bishop in whose diocese they were. The same rule was to apply to all Church property and rights. A deputation was sent from this council to seek further imperial measures against the Donatists; and Honorius, in a constitution of 15 November 407, addressed to Porphyrius, proconsul of Africa, urged the suppression of the obstinate and the reception of those who would submit to the Church.[5]

In 408 the principal minister of state, Stilicho, died in disgrace, and was succeeded by Olympius. Stilicho had been a great opponent of the schismatics, and they now hoped for a change of policy. In this year two Catholic councils met at Carthage.[6] The former, on 16 June, was the twelfth of Carthage, and it decided to send delegates to the Emperor regarding the affair of the Donatists, and to ask him to confirm the laws already enacted against them. The thirteenth Council of Carthage, on 13 October, sent a similar request.[7] At the same time Saint Augustine wrote a personal letter to Olympius, the new minister, to emphasize this appeal.[8] The appeal produced several constitutions directed against the schism. On 11 November 408 the first of these proscribed the partisans of Gildo.[9] Another, of 24 November 408, addressed to the proconsul of Africa, Donatus, was directed against those who brawled at divine service.[10] By a law of 27 November 408, all heretical

[1] Ibid. I, 130, 131.
[2] Ibid. III, 141; Aug. *Brev. Coll.* III, iv sq.; *Ad Don. post coll.* xxv, 44; *Ep.* LXXXVIII, 10.
[3] Hefele, op. cit. vol. II, p. 442; Migne, op. cit. vol. I, p. 498.
[4] Canon 5 (*C.C.E.A.* 99).   [5] *C.Th.* XVI, v, 41.
[6] Hefele, op. cit. vol. II, p. 444; Migne, op. cit. vol. I, p. 501.
[7] *C.C.E.A.* between Canons 106 and 107.
[8] Aug. *Ep.* XCVII.
[9] *C.Th.* IX, xl, 19.   [10] Ibid. XVI, v, 44; Aug. *Ep.* C, 2.

assemblies were forbidden;[1] and on 13 January 409, punishments were prescribed for those who pillaged basilicas.[2] On 15 January and 26 June 409 further instructions followed, that orders already given were to be carried into effect, and that officials who neglected to do this were to be removed from office.[3] At this time the proconsul of Africa promulgated a severe edict concerning the application of all these laws, and Saint Augustine wrote to ask him to inflict some penalty less than death on the schismatics who resisted.[4]

But in 410 there was a sudden reversal of the imperial policy. The Count of Africa, Heraclianus, a man of cruel, avaricious and drunken habits,[5] received a constitution proclaiming liberty to all sects.[6] The schismatic bishop of Hippo, Macrobius, made another triumphal entry into the town, escorted by Circumcellions.[7] On 14 June 410 the fifteenth synod of Carthage met to consider the situation thus created.[8] It sent a message to the Emperor asking for the abrogation of his edict; and for the convocation of a general conference. The Emperor acceded to both these requests. A further imperial constitution again forbade heretical meetings of all kinds,[9] and the Emperor also ordered Marcellinus to go as commissioner to Carthage, and convoke and preside at a conference to discuss the whole question.[10]

During the rapidly moving events of these years Saint Augustine was intensifying his literary and pastoral campaign for unity. Unfortunately much of his work at this time has not survived. The first of these works was the *Probationum et testimoniorum contra Donatistas liber*.[11] Augustine published in 406 a catena of citations from ecclesiastical and State records, and from Scripture, to expose the errors of the Donatists. Some unknown Donatist wrote a criticism of this collection, and the work named in the *Retractations* was then written in answer to him, the catena already mentioned being annexed. This work was exhibited, as we have seen, on the walls of the recovered Donatist basilica at Hippo. It went right back in the history of the schism to the acquittal of Caecilianus. In the same year was published the one book *Contra Donatistam nescio quem*.[12] It is not clear what this contained, but

---

[1] *C.Th.* XVI, v, 45. [2] Ibid. XVI, ii, 31.
[3] Ibid. XVI, v, 46, 47. [4] Aug. *Ep.* C.
[5] Zos. V, 37; Orosius, VII, xlii, 10.
[6] *C.C.E.A.* 107; Aug. *Ep.* CVIII, vi, 18.
[7] Aug. *Ep.* CVIII, v, 14.
[8] *C.C.E.A.* after Canon 107. Hefele, op. cit. vol. II, p. 444; Migne, op. cit. vol. I, p. 501. [9] *C.Th.* XVI, v, 51 (25 August 410).
[10] Ibid. XVI, xi, 3 (14 October 410).
[11] Aug. *Retract.* II, xxvii. [12] Ibid. II, xxviii.

from the corrections supplied by the *Retractations* it is at least evident that it dealt, like the previous work, with the case of Caecilianus, and that Saint Cyprian was quoted in it. The next work to be written against the Donatists is also not extant. From its title it is clear that it refuted the Donatists on the ground of their treatment of the Maximianists. This *Admonitio Donatistarum de Maximianistis, liber unus*, was written in 409.[1] It was a short book, and confined itself to the matter of the Maximianist schism, and was written for popular reading.

The only surviving full-length work of the period on Donatism is the *De unico baptismo contra Petilianum ad Constantinum, liber unus*, of which the date is probably 410.[2] Constantine, a friend of Saint Augustine, had received from an unknown Donatist priest a work written by Petilianus, their bishop at Constantina, which he submitted to the Bishop of Hippo, with an urgent request that he would answer it. The answer received the same title as the Donatist pamphlet, namely, *De unico baptismo*. It is an exposition of holy baptism as the gift of Christ, and not of the man, perhaps sinful, by whose hands it is administered with Christ's authority. The use made by Petilianus of certain New Testament passages is corrected, and the authority of Saint Cyprian is considered. As elsewhere, Saint Cyprian is shown to have been wrong, and Stephen right; and the Donatist is reminded that, in spite of so severe a dissension on so important a subject—a subject, moreover, identical with the sacramental problem now at issue between Catholics and Donatists—no schism was consummated between Cyprian and Stephen, because they both had a firmer hold on the necessity of charity than the Donatists have.

In 410 there came from Saint Augustine's pen a further book on the Maximianist schism, *De Maximianistis contra Donatistas*, which has not survived.[3] Unlike the work of 409 it was a long and carefully written attack,[4] but it showed, as did the *Admonitio*, that the treatment of the Maximianists was sufficient of itself to undermine the entire Donatist theory.

The loss of four of these five works is a serious one, but it is partly compensated for by the extraordinary length and fullness of the letters written at this period, two of which resemble treatises. By these letters we are enabled to trace the course of Saint Augustine's part in the controversy during these active years. Of uncertain date, but somewhere between 405 and 411, is a letter to Emeritus, the

[1] Ibid. II, xxix.
[2] Ibid. II, xxxiv.   [3] Ibid. II, xxxv.
[4] Ibid. II, xxxv: 'non breuissimum sicut antea, sed grandem, multo diligentius.'

Donatist bishop of Caesarea in Mauretania, who was to be one of the seven Donatist *actores* at the great Conference.[1] Saint Augustine begins by paying tribute to the great erudition of Emeritus, and then attacks the Donatist teaching on the holiness of the Church. He prefers against his correspondent the charge of schism, on the ground that he remains in a sect separated from the Church by the action of his predecessors. The Maximianist schism is brought into the argument, and the appeal of the Catholics to the State is justified, as being necessary for the defence of Catholics against the private animosity of Donatists, by the example of Saint Paul, who appealed to the Emperor for protection against his enemies.[2] At the end of the letter Saint Augustine propounds once more the cardinal spiritual question between Catholics and schismatics: Which is the true Church?

Soon after this the priests of the diocese of Hippo sent to Ianuarius, Donatist bishop of Casae Nigrae and primate in Numidia, the letter expostulating with him with regard to the violence of the Circumcellions.[3] It was written on their behalf by Saint Augustine, and its date is 406. The priests recount the history of the schism from its inception to the acquittal of Caecilianus, and mention also specific cases of recent Circumcellion activities. They point out that Crispinus, the Donatist bishop of Calama, was condemned on a charge of heresy, and fined ten pounds of gold; but excused on the intervention of the Catholic bishops. But in spite of this act of charity, the persecution has been intensified.[4]

They ask for a cessation of violence, and for a conference to determine the theological issue. About the same time Saint Augustine wrote to the landowner Festus to draw his attention to the anti-Donatist laws, and to press for his application of them in Numidia, where the Donatists still raged, and where his own tenants were still Donatists.[5] Festus was urged to study the history of the schism by reading the relevant documents, and to send a representative to see the Bishop of Hippo and learn the facts of the situation.

In 408 Saint Augustine wrote two official letters to imperial officials. In November he wrote the letter to the new minister Olympius, reinforcing the appeal made to the Emperor by the synod of Carthage of

---

[1] Aug. *Ep.* LXXXVII.   [2] Acts xxiii. 21.
[3] Aug. *Ep.* LXXXVIII. See supra, p. 61.
[4] Ibid. LXXXVIII, 8: '(armati uestri) uiuunt ut latrones, moriuntur ut circumcelliones, honorantur ut martyres; et tamen nec latrones aliquando audiuimus eos quos depraedati sunt excaecasse.'
[5] Aug. *Ep.* LXXXIX.

13 October, and asking Olympius to take action immediately in view of the gravity of the situation in Africa.[1] After 24 November in the same year, Augustine addressed a letter to the proconsul of Africa, Donatus, congratulating him on his friendly disposition towards the Church, and asking that the Donatists might be restrained without the imposition of the death penalty.[2]

Probably in 408 the long letter to Vincentius, bishop of the tiny Rogatist schism at Cartenna, was also written.[3] Saint Augustine reminds him of their former acquaintance at Carthage during the lifetime of Rogatus, the originator of the schism.[4] He goes on to defend the policy of State coercion.[5] Force may be rightly or wrongfully used: everything depends upon the end in view. If that end is the reformation of sinners whose obstinacy must be broken down, then the use of force is justified. If, on the other hand, force is used for unrighteous ends, it ceases to be justified.[6] Saint Augustine admits that his earlier view was that persuasion was the only weapon available for a Christian, but remarks that he has been brought to his present opinion by the evidence of results. For not merely single Donatists, but whole communities, have been converted by the fear of the laws against the schismatics. An example ever before his eyes is his own city of Hippo, formerly practically entirely Donatist, but now thoroughly converted. Many Donatists would have come over to the Church before, had it not been for terror at the violence of their own partisans; but now the way had been thrown open, and they had been eager to take advantage of it. Others had been made to realize for the first time the true gravity of schism, which they had simply inherited without thought from their fathers.[7] But schism is not merely wrong because it is proscribed by imperial authority: it is contrary to the mind of Christ, who prayed that his Church might be one, and who commanded his disciples to preach to all nations. The Church therefore is catholic and not national.[8] And with the testimony of Scripture the writings of Christian Fathers are in accord. Of these patristic writers no man held a loftier conception of Catholic unity than Saint Cyprian, whose authority the Donatists are so fond of quoting in support of their own views.[9] The epistle concludes with an appeal to the Rogatists to return to the fold of the Church: they share Catholic baptism, and other sacraments, and they

[1] Ibid. xcvii. See supra, p. 62.   [2] Ibid. c.
[3] Ibid. xciii.   [4] Ibid. xciii, i, 1.
[5] Ibid. xciii, i, 3–v, 19 et passim.   [6] Ibid. xciii, ii, 4–8.
[7] Ibid. xciii, v, 16–19.   [8] Ibid. xciii, vi, 20–ix, 24.
[9] Ibid. xciii, x, 35–44.

believe the Catholic creed; let them submit to the judgement of the Catholic Church and join the Catholic unity.[1]

At the beginning of the next year a similar appeal was made by Saint Augustine in a pastoral letter addressed to the Donatists in general.[2] After urging the need of unity, and treating again of the charge of *traditio* brought against the Church,[3] he justified the appeal which had been made to the Emperor. That appeal was only necessitated by the persecution of Catholics organized in the Donatist interest, and it was an appeal primarily for protection against that persecution, of which numerous examples are then quoted.[4] The early history of the controversy is once more recapitulated;[5] and the remainder of the letter is concerned with the theological issue as it affects schism and the sacraments.[6]

Saint Augustine sent an answer at the end of 409 to the priest Victorianus, who had asked for a long letter of consolation on account of the persecutions which the Church in Europe, and especially in Spain and Gaul, was suffering by reason of the barbarian invasions.[7] The Bishop sympathizes with the sufferings of these churches, and recommends patience in time of adversity, but wonders if the barbarians are any more cruel than the Circumcellions who rage in Africa.[8]

A letter to the former proconsul of Africa, Donatus, written at the end of 409 or in early 410, praises the excellence of his administration as proconsul, and expresses the Bishop's hope that he will bring over to Catholicism all his tenants in the Numidian districts of Sinitum and Hippo.[9]

In one of these two years, 409 or 410, a severe protest was addressed by Saint Augustine to Macrobius, the Donatist bishop in his town, who had proposed to rebaptize one of the Catholic subdeacons of the town.[10] This letter was delivered to Macrobius by Maximus and Theodorus, who reported that Macrobius refused to read it, and answered, 'I am bound to receive those who come to me, and to give them the faith for which they have asked'. When they had asked him for a statement about the Maximianists who had not been rebaptized by Primianus when received back into his schism, he replied that it was not for him,

[1] Ibid. XCIII, xi, 46–xiii, 53.
[2] Ibid. CV.
[3] Ibid. CV, i, 1, 2.
[4] Ibid. CV, ii, 3–7.
[5] Ibid. CV, ii, 8–10.
[6] Ibid. CV, iii, 11–v, 17.
[7] Ibid. CXI.
[8] Ibid. CXI, 1: 'ecce in regione nostra Hipponensi, quoniam eam barbari non attigerunt, clericorum Donatistarum atque Circumcellionum latrocinia sic uastant ecclesias, ut barbarorum fortasse facta mitiora sint.'
[9] Ibid. CXII.
[10] Ibid. CVI.

a bishop newly consecrated, to question the action of his superior, but that it was his intention to maintain the usual custom of rebaptism.[1] This churlish reply elicited from Saint Augustine a long letter expounding the history of the Maximianist schism, discussing the authority of Saint Cyprian as it concerned rebaptism, and complaining of the attacks of the Circumcellions, and of the disruptive effects of the schism on family and business relations.[2]

In 411, and before the Conference, Aurelius, Bishop of Carthage, and all the Catholic bishops of Africa, addressed two letters to Marcellinus, the imperial commissioner designated by the Emperor to conduct the Conference on reunion.[3] They expressed themselves ready to agree to the arrangements provisionally made for the Conference, and to submit to the decision of Marcellinus, whether favourable to them or not. If the Donatists can prove their case, the Catholics will put their sees at their disposal: if the Donatists lose their case, they will be received into the Church on the same terms as they themselves imposed on their Maximianist converts.[4] For the sole desire of the party of Aurelius is the unity of the Catholic Church as set forth in Scripture. The Donatists betray their lack of confidence in their own case by their conduct towards the Maximianists.[5]

The sermons delivered at this time touch certain points of the controversy with the Donatists. Thus in a sermon on the feast of the Twenty Martyrs of Tarsus (6 June), the sacrifice of real martyrs in a righteous cause is contrasted with the pseudo-martyrdoms so avidly sought by the Donatists.[6] Saint Augustine alludes to his favourite dictum, 'martyrem non facit poena sed causa', and uses his favourite illustration of the three crosses on Calvary, on which three men suffered the same penalty, but the cause in which Christ's suffering was offered distinguished his suffering from that of the thieves.

He comments on this same theme in a sermon on Psalm cxlv: 7, 'facientem iudicium iniuriam patientibus'.[7] Heretics and schismatics suffer rightly for their disobedience to lawfully constituted authority, and for their contumacy in schism. It is vain to cloak injury to men's spirits under the name of justice.[8]

[1] Ibid. cvii.
[2] Ibid. cviii.
[3] *Apud* Aug. *Ep.* cxxviii, cxxix.
[4] Aug. *Ep.* cxxviii.
[5] Ibid. cxxix.
[6] Aug. *Serm.* cccxlv, 2.
[7] Aug. *Enarr. in Ps.* cxlv, 15.
[8] Ibid. cxlv, 16: 'fratres carissimi, et quae est quae patitur iniuriam, nisi ecclesia catholica, quae tanta ista perpetitur? inter tot scandala haereticorum gemit: uidet per malas suasiones et fraudes rapi de gremio suo infirmos, paruulos pertrahi per nescio quae secreta malarum speluncarum, rebaptizari, exsufflari in

At the end of 405 the verse of Psalm cxlix, 'Let Israel rejoice in him that made him', prompts the reflexion that in baptism a man is made the child of God, not in Arius, nor in Donatus, nor in Caecilianus, nor in Proculeianus (the Donatist bishop of Hippo), nor in Augustine, but in Christ.[1]

The catholicity of the Church, and the rightness of the appeal to the State, are discussed in a sermon of 406.[2] The next sermon on the Donatist question which can be dated is Sermon XLVI, preached in the middle of 410, on the shepherds of Ezekiel xxxiv. Heretics and schismatics are the wandering sheep of the Church;[3] and they are found in the Church over all the world, but, unlike the Church, no heresy or schism is world-wide.[4] But they have one common source, which is pride, and the uncharitableness which it engenders. The sermon finishes with a justification of the Catholic appeal for adjudication.[5] The next sermon is of the same date, and on the same text, and also directed against Donatism.[6] It condemns the Donatists for anticipating the Last Judgement[7] by separating wheat from tares before the harvest, and segregating sheep from goats before the Great Shepherd appears. On the Feast of Saint Peter and Saint Paul in the same summer Saint Augustine had much to say in his sermon on the need of patience in time of adversity, and in his peroration pleaded for the charitable reception of converted Donatists.[8] He had occasion also to blame the congregation for clamouring for the ejection of such a penitent.[9] On the Feast of the Epiphany in one of these years just before the Conference, Saint Augustine remarked that it was no wonder that the Donatists refused to observe this feast (which they rejected as being of recent introduction) because they did not love unity, which was prefigured by the adoration of the Gentiles, and were not in communion with the churches of those Eastern regions whence came the Magi to visit the infant Christ.[10]

Saint Augustine had arrived at Carthage by the middle of May in 411 in preparation for the great Conference, and two of the sermons delivered there in the time before the Conference are extant. They do not discuss the problems at issue, but indicate the spirit in which the Catholic laity is to approach the Conference. The former, preached

eis Christum, occidi in eis non mortale illud suum quo homines sunt, sed illud quo in aeternum uicturi sunt. suadetur homini dicere, Non sum christianus, et iustitia uocatur.'

[1] Ibid. CXLIX, 4.
[2] Aug. Serm. II in Ps. CI, 8, 9.
[3] Aug. Serm. XLVI, viii, 17.
[4] Ibid. XLVI, viii, 18.
[5] Ibid. XLVI, xvii, 41.
[6] Ibid. XLVII.
[7] Ibid. XLVII, v, 6, x, 16–18.
[8] Ibid. CCXCVI.
[9] Ibid. CCXCVI, xi, 12.
[10] Ibid. CCII, ii, 2.

SAINT AUGUSTINE AND THE DONATIST CONTROVERSY

between 15 and 20 May, is an eulogy of peace.[1] The faithful are urged to seek peace, and to pray for it.[2] Peace is the fruit of love;[3] and love will be ready to seek those who have gone astray, as have the Donatists.[4] Animosity arising from past sufferings must be put away,[5] and the people must prepare themselves after Whitsuntide with prayer, fasting and almsgiving.[6] At the end of May, just before the Conference, which opened on 1 June, was delivered the second sermon, likewise on peace and charity.[7] The aim of the Catholic bishops in their work of the next few days is the restoration of peace to the stricken African Church.[8] For this purpose the Donatists are lovingly invited to share in the Church's unity,[9] in the inheritance of the saints throughout the earth. Our faith must be stayed on God, and not on men,[10] and charity among men can alone bring peace.[11] It is in this spirit that Saint Augustine and his fellow-bishops come to the judgement of Marcellinus,[12] and the people are urged to forward their purpose by abstaining from violent incursions into the place of meeting,[13] and to assist by their prayers.[14]

5. *The Conference of Carthage*, 411

Thus with the watchword of peace upon his lips the great architect of Christian unity in Africa came to the consummation of his protracted campaign against the schism. The imperial commissioner Marcellinus, tribune and notary, a Catholic, and a friend of Saint Augustine,[15] convoked the Conference for 1 June 411, in the magnificent Thermae Gargilianae in Carthage, the capital of Africa.[16] He promised to restore

[1] Ibid. CCCLVII. [2] Ibid. CCCLVII, 1. [3] Ibid. CCCLVII, 2.
[4] Ibid. CCCLVII, 3. [5] Ibid. CCCLVII, 4. [6] Ibid. CCCLVII, 5.
[7] Ibid. CCCLVIII.
[8] Ibid. CCCLVIII, 1: 'curam nostram pro uobis et pro inimicis nostris et uestris, et pro salute omnium, pro quiete, pro pace communi, pro unitate quam Dominus iussit, Dominus diligit, adiuuent preces Sanctitatis uestrae, ut de illa identidem et ad uos loquamur et uobiscum gaudeamus.'
[9] Ibid. CCCLVIII, 2. [10] Ibid. CCCLVIII, 3. [11] Ibid. CCCLVIII, 4.
[12] Ibid. CCCLVIII, 5.
[13] Ibid. CCCLVIII, 6: 'ad collationis locum nullus uestrum irruat, fratres mei.'
[14] Ibid. CCCLVIII, 6: '...per nomen ipsius Domini, per auctorem pacis, plantatorem pacis, dilectorem pacis, oramus uos, ut eum pacifice oretis, pacifice deprecemini, et memineritis esse filii eius, a quo dictum est, Beati pacifici, quoniam filii Dei uocabuntur.'
[15] To Marcellinus the *De ciuitate Dei* and the *De spiritu et littera* were subsequently dedicated.
[16] Migne, op. cit. vol. I, p. 501; Monceaux, op. cit. vol. IV, ch. iv; vol. VI passim; W. J. Sparrow Simpson, *S. Augustine and African Church Divisions* (London, 1910), ch. x. Primary sources: *Gesta Coll. Carthag.* in *P.L.* XI, 1223 sq.; Aug. *Breu. Coll.* in *P.L.* XLIII, 613 sq.

their churches to the schismatic bishops who agreed to attend,[1] and, as long as the cause should be *sub iudice*, to suspend all penalties and seizures of churches inflicted upon the schismatics; and promised them safe conduct to Carthage. He expressed himself willing to accept a schismatic coadjutor on the bench, but the Donatists were unwilling to nominate one. The Maximianists were excluded: only the Primianists were invited, and they were present in large numbers at his request.[2] This invitation was conveyed to the Donatist leader Primianus by the municipal magistrates at Carthage in the spring of 411, when he was summoned and officially informed of the edict of Marcellinus of 19 January 411, calling the Conference for 1 June.[3] The Donatist bishops gathered on 18 May, and made a solemn entry in procession into the city.[4] Then from 25 May to 7 June Primianus presided at a Donatist council which conducted the arrangement and presentation of their case at the Conference. This council met in the principal cathedral basilica of the Donatists, the Theoprepia.[5] During this time, the Catholic bishops had been assembling quietly, and they also held a preparatory council for the week before the Conference, and during the week of the Conference. The procedure was to be thus: seven disputants, or *actores*, were to be appointed by each side, to conduct the case before the commissioner. Seven assessors of each party were to prepare matter for these *actores*, and on each side four clerks were to be appointed to make a verbatim report for subsequent publication. The agreed minutes of the proceedings have come down to us in large part as the *Gesta Collationis Carthaginensis*.[6] These officials were chosen by the respective party councils; and for the Catholics the *actores* were the Bishops of Carthage, Aurelius; of Tagaste, Alypius; of Hippo, Augustine; of Culusi, Vincentius; of Constantina, Fortunatus; of Sicca, Fortunatianus; and of Calama, Possidius: and for the Donatists Primianus of Carthage, Petilianus of Constantina, Emeritus of Caesarea, Protasius of Thubunae, Montanus of Zama, Gaudentius of Thamugadi, and Adeodatus of Milevis.[7] There were 286 Catholic bishops present in all, 120 absent and 64 sees vacant; and of the Donatists 279 bishops present, and about the same number of absentees and vacant sees.[8]

---

[1] *Gesta Coll. Carthag.* I, 5; Aug. *Breu. Coll.* I, 2.
[2] Aug. *Ad Don. post coll.* XXIV, 41.
[3] *Gesta Coll. Carthag.* I, 5; II, 50; Aug. *Breu. Coll.* I, 2; II, 3; *Ad Don. post coll.* XXIV, 41.
[4] Aug. *Ad Don. post coll.* XXV, 43.   [5] *Gesta Coll. Carthag.* III, 5.
[6] Printed in Migne, *P.L.* XI, 1223 sq.   [7] *Gesta Coll. Carthag.* I, 148.
[8] Ibid. I, 213–17; Aug. *Breu. Coll.* I, 14; *Ad Don. post coll.* XXIV, 41.

To trace the proceedings in detail would be a task of unparalleled wearisomeness, owing to the prolixity of the Donatist obstruction; and it will suffice to outline the course of the debates. The first session was held on 1 June; and the Catholics sent their eighteen chosen representatives, whereas the Donatists appeared in full force. The day was occupied in tedious formalities. The imperial rescript summoning the Conference was first read;[1] and then the edict of Marcellinus fixing the date of the Conference.[2] Thirdly, another edict of the commissioner was read, fixing the time and place of the meeting.[3] The Donatists then protested against the restriction of the meeting to the chosen representatives, and demanded that all the bishops should be present.[4] The Catholics accepted these arrangements, and promised to abide by the decision of the judge, and resign their sees if they should lose their case.[5] The commissioner then read the letters he had received from both parties.[6] A heated discussion ensued on the question of representation at the Conference,[7] and there were many Donatist complaints and obstructions.[8] They then asked that the matter should be argued on the basis of Scriptural quotations and not on matters of law.[9] The Catholic representatives submitted the mandate they had received from their council, which contained a short exposition of their whole case, composed on an historical basis, with citations from relevant documents.[10] The commissioner ordered the signatures appended to this document to be read; but the Donatists claimed that some of the signatures were not genuine, but had been dishonestly interpolated.[11] They succeeded in having all the Catholic bishops brought in to answer to their names and to be identified.[12] Marcellinus then proposed that the Conference should sit for the rest of the proceedings; but when the Donatists resisted this proposal, the assembly remained standing for the rest of the day.[13]

The Donatist mandate was next read, and, at the request of the Catholics, the list of the Donatist bishops, to which they answered. When the names were called, it was discovered that some were not present who were said to have signed; and in fact, one of them, Quoduultdeus, had died on the way. When the Catholics inquired how he could have signed in this case, the Donatists were at a loss for an answer, but eventually said that he had gone home after signing, and died on the return journey. But this falsity was exposed, and they would not agree to affirm it on oath. The names totalled 286 Catholic and 279

[1] Aug. *Breu. Coll.* I, 1.   [2] Ibid. I, 2.   [3] Ibid. I, 3.
[4] Ibid. I, 4.   [5] Ibid. I, 5.   [6] Ibid. I, 6.   [7] Ibid. I, 7.
[8] Ibid. I, 8.   [9] Ibid. I, 9.   [10] Ibid. I, 10.   [11] Ibid. I, 11.
[12] Ibid. I, 12.   [13] Ibid. I, 13.

Donatist bishops, the Donatist figure including the man who died on the way, and certain others who had signed, and then gone home. All the 286 Catholics were present in the Baths. When the lists were thus confirmed by both parties, the day was drawing to a close, and Marcellinus adjourned the Conference till the next day but one.[1]

On 3 June only the eighteen representatives of each party were admitted. The judge invited them to be seated, and the Catholics took their seats, but the Donatists would not do so, for it was written, 'non sedi cum concilio uanitatis'.[2] Marcellinus said that he would therefore adjudicate standing, and the Conference rose, and remained all the session on its feet.[3] On 2 June the Donatists had asked for a copy of the Catholic mandate, and this matter was first raised at the session of 3 June, and their request read, together with the affirmative answer of the commissioner.[4] Further obstruction followed from the Donatists, concerned with the lists of bishops present, and with the taking of minutes. The Catholics, at the end of their patience, asked for an adjournment of six days to allow the report of 1 June to be edited and published, and subscribed by the schismatics. This was granted.

Before the next session these minutes had been published, and at last the real business of the Conference was reached on 8 June. The Donatists were still intent on obstructing the proceedings, and drew from Saint Augustine, who had spoken little in the first two days, the protest: 'How much is done in order that nothing may be done!' The schismatics quarrelled about the use in the imperial rescripts of the word 'Catholic' as applied to the party of Aurelius on the ground that it prejudged the question at issue. Marcellinus said that it must be applied to those to whom the Emperor had applied it, and that the Donatists should devote their attention to proving their main point, which, if justified, would establish their right to the exclusive use of the title 'Catholic'.[5] The Catholics claimed that they were Catholic by reason of their being in communion with the universal Church; and the Donatists said on their side that 'Catholic' refers not to universality of local extension, but to sacramental integrity, which they claimed for their own party. After a long and time-wasting wrangle over this,[6] the Catholics succeeded in bringing the discussion to the historical problem of the case of Caecilianus.[7] Saint Augustine took a great part in this argument, and the next move of the schismatics was to attack his personal character, and the alleged irregularity of his consecration by

[1] Ibid. I, 14.   [2] Ps. xxvi. 4.   [3] Aug. *Breu. Coll.* II, 1.
[4] Ibid. II, 2.   [5] Ibid. III, iii, 3.
[6] Ibid. III, iv, 4, 5.   [7] Ibid. III, v, 6–vii, 8.

Megalius. Possidius came to the rescue of his friend, and said that in any case the Church did not stand or fall by Augustine's character.[1] At last the crucial question of the nature of the Church, and of its admixture of good and evil, was broached.[2] After an exhaustive discussion of this topic, the commissioner said he had heard enough, and would give his decision on it in delivering his judgement. He would now hear argument on the cause of the original schism. Both sides resisted this, and asked for an immediate judgement on the previous question; but Marcellinus would not yield.[3] However, the persistence of the Donatists succeeded in introducing the irrelevant topic of religious persecution, and they lodged several complaints before they were called to order.[4] The source of the schism was then argued, and the Donatists failed to prove that Caecilianus was a *traditor*. Documents were produced on both sides, and questioned by the opposing party; but at last the Catholics contrived to have the documents read which related to the Donatist appeal to Constantine and its rejection.[5] After considerable discussion of the synods of those days just after the persecution,[6] the commissioner ordered the final judgement of Constantine to be read.[7] Other correspondence of Constantine relevant to the case of Caecilianus was then discussed at length.[8] The Donatist arguments on historical and theological grounds were now thoroughly undermined; and, as they were unable to bring forward any fresh evidence, the Catholics asked that judgement might now be given. The commissioner adjourned the Conference for a short time, and the same day called the representatives in again, and gave judgement for the Catholics.[9] He reported the judgement to the Emperor;[10] and on 26 June 411 caused to be posted in Carthage a notice proscribing the Donatists.[11] It stated that they had failed to prove the guilt of Caecilianus, and that even if they had done so, his guilt would not have defiled the Church, or justified schism from the Church. The final judgement of Constantine had been in favour of Caecilianus. Donatist conventicles were therefore to be suppressed everywhere, and their churches without any delay handed over to the Catholics unless they came over to the Catholic Church as whole communities, in which case they might keep them. Those who refused to submit would be liable to the penalties

[1] Ibid. III, vii, 9. [2] Ibid. III, viii, 10–x, 20.
[3] Ibid. III, xi, 21. [4] Ibid. III, xi, 22, 23.
[5] Ibid. III, xii, 24–xvi, 28. [6] Ibid. III, xvi, 29–xviii, 36.
[7] Ibid. III, xix, 37. [8] Ibid. III, xx, 38–xxiv, 42.
[9] Ibid. III, xxv, 43. [10] *Gesta Coll. Carthag.* I, 4; III, 29.
[11] This notice, under the incorrect title of *Sententia Cognitoris*, is printed at the end of the *Gesta Coll. Carthag.* in *P.L.* XI, 1223 sq. and in *P.L.* XLIII, 840, 841.

already provided by the law. Every Donatist bishop must now return to his city and submit to the Catholic Church, or be dispossessed. Owners of estates on which Circumcellions reside must extirpate them, or the estates would be confiscated.

The Donatists appealed to the Emperor Honorius from this judgement,[1] and began a campaign of sermons and pamphlets.[2] But the judgement of Marcellinus was upheld by a constitution, or edict of unity, of 30 January 412, which confirmed all the laws of repression against the Donatists.[3]

The Donatists were not slow to complain that the Catholics had used unfairly against them the weapon of an appeal to the State, and there is little doubt that, if this appeal had not been made, Donatism would have flourished for much longer in Africa, and, with the weakening of imperial administration, might well have tormented the land until Christianity itself was reduced to impotence there by the onset of the Arab invasion of the seventh century. It would have taken much longer to do by argument and by patient endurance of Donatist persecution what was achieved very speedily by the enforcement of the judgement of Marcellinus. The action of the Catholic bishops in submitting a spiritual question to lay adjudication may be open to criticism as an unworthy method. For truth will ultimately prevail, and that by its own compelling force, and it is often a sign of weakness for its upholders to seek adventitious support. It is clear from the *Retractations*, written nearly twenty years after the victory had been won, that Saint Augustine himself had felt all these doubts acutely. From the beginning of his campaign he had hoped by the power of love and of sound argument to bring in the erring sheep of the fold. But it is clear also that what had brought him over to the opinion of his colleagues, who even before 400 pressed for an appeal to the civil power, was the continued violence of the Circumcellions. The appeal in the first place was a just one for protection against malicious attacks on persons and property. When the enforcement of the law against such attacks was frustrated by the indifference or incapacity of local magistrates and officials, it became necessary to appeal to the Emperor for an authoritative pronouncement upon the questions at issue between the Church and the schismatics, and for the enforcement of such a decision when given. It is evident to all who read the report of the Conference of Carthage that the

---

[1] Possid. *Vita Aug.* xv; Aug. *Ad Don. post coll.* xii, 16.
[2] Possid. *Vita Aug.* xvi; Aug. *Ep.* cxli, i, 12; *Retract.* ii, lxvi; *Breu. Coll.* iii, xviii, 36; *Ad Don. post coll.* i, 1; iv, 6; xi, 15; xii, 16; xiii, 17; etc.
[3] *C.Th.* xvi, v, 52.

Donatists were given every opportunity of presenting their case, and that the commissioner, although himself a Catholic (though not an African), was rather to be blamed for allowing so much latitude to Donatist obstruction and stupidity than condemned for giving rein to any bias against them. Their dishonest proceedings, some of which we have noticed in tracing the order of the Conference, and the complete lack of cogent evidence to support the case they advanced, either on historical or on theological grounds, both vindicate the judgement pronounced by Marcellinus.

It must also be remembered that, as far as Saint Augustine's part in the controversy is concerned, this appeal to independent judgement is never allowed to supersede the rational appeal to individual schismatics, and to the Donatist church in general, to forsake schism, and to embrace Catholic unity. The end which he set before himself was the end that a faithful pastor of souls must always have imprinted on his mind: it was (if the words of the English ordinal may be quoted in this connexion) to bring all who were committed to his charge 'unto that agreement in the faith and knowledge of God, and to that ripeness and perfectness of age in Christ, that there be no place left among (them) either for error in religion or for viciousness in life'. That was the tenor of all Saint Augustine's ministry, and all his writing: there is not one of his writings from the smallest to the greatest, after his ordination, which was not evoked directly or indirectly by the demands of his pastorate, for the instruction of the faithful, for the combating of error, for the propagation of the truth. In that unwearying toil for the salvation of the souls entrusted to his charge, the Conference of Carthage took its place. It remained for him to enforce the lessons of the Conference, and to apply them to his diocese and in Africa generally. To this end his remaining work on the Donatist schism is directed.

6. *After the Conference*

The Catholics took care to reap the fruits of the victory in their propaganda. Many of the bishops caused copies of the *Gesta Collationis* to be exhibited, and during the next Lent they were read in churches at divine service at Carthage, Constantina, Tagaste, Hippo, and in other districts.[1] Saint Augustine undertook the preparation of a convenient précis of the *Gesta* which should be easier to read than the wearisome full text. It was numbered on the same plan as the *Gesta*, for convenience of reference, entitled *Breuiculus Collationis*, and published by the end of 411.[2] The imperial authorities enforced the decision of

[1] Aug. *Gesta cum Emer.* 4. [2] Aug. *Retract.* II, xxxix; *Breu. Coll.* praef.

Marcellinus, and the Donatist churches were handed over. They succeeded in burning down their basilica in Carthage after it had been taken from them.[1] Their bishops and clergy were dispossessed and fined, and their property was confiscated.[2] When the fear of the Circumcellions was in part removed, many of the Donatist laity were glad to return to the Church, and in some places their numbers were so great as to necessitate the division of dioceses. Saint Augustine's own diocese was divided, and a bishopric of Fussala founded.[3] But in certain country districts, especially in Numidia, Circumcellionism continued strong and violent, and there were further attacks on Catholics. Two priests of Hippo, Restitutus and Innocentius, were mutilated, losing an eye and a finger each, and murdered.[4]

When the Donatist appeal from the judgement of Marcellinus failed, and the final edict of unity was promulgated on 30 January 412,[5] the way was left open for the gradual elimination of Donatist power in Africa. The Catholic bishops of Numidia assembled in council on 14 June 412, to discuss the problems of the great reunion. But if the Donatists could not succeed in reversing the decision of 411, they at least contrived to wreak their vengeance upon Marcellinus. In 413 he was falsely denounced, with his brother Apringius, to the authorities, for having assisted in the revolt of Count Heraclian; and they were both imprisoned. Saint Augustine, who was in Carthage at the time, solemnly asserted their innocence before the Count of Africa, Marinus, and secured his leave to appeal to the Emperor Honorius. Before the answer came from Ravenna, Marcellinus and Apringius were secretly executed on 13 September.[6]

In the next year the Emperor ordered the proconsul of Africa, Iulianus, to take all civil rights from the pertinacious schismatics, to deport their bishops and clergy, and confiscate any remaining churches.[7] The death of Marcellinus was not to be taken as abrogating the sentence pronounced by him.[8] On 25 August 415 the Emperor again ordered the enforcement of the edict of unity against the schismatics;[9] and in

[1] Aug. *C. Gaud.* I, vi, 7.
[2] *C. Th.* XVI, v, 52–8, vi, 6; Aug. *Ep.* CLXXXV, ix, 36; *C. Gaud.* I, vi, 7, xvi, 17, xxxvii, 50 sq.; *In Ioan. Evang. tract.* VI, 25.
[3] Aug. *Ep.* CCIX, 2.
[4] Aug. *Ep.* CXXXIII, 1; CXXXIV, 2; CXXXIX, 1, 2; CLXXXV, vi, 50; *Gesta cum Emer.* 9; Possid. *Vita Aug.* XV.
[5] *C. Th.* XVI, v, 52.
[6] Aug. *Ep.* CLI, 3–9; Hieron. *Adv. Pelag.* III, 19; Orosius, *H.L.* VII, 42.
[7] *C. Th.* XVI, v, 54 (17 June 414).
[8] Ibid. XVI, v, 55 (30 August 414). [9] Ibid. XVI, v, 56 (25 August 415).

the same year enacted a constitution against those who practised rebaptism.[1] These were the last laws of Honorius against the Donatists; but in 425 Valentinian III ordered his officials to proscribe all heresies,[2] to turn all heretics and schismatics out of the towns,[3] to restore churches to the Catholics, and to prevent rebaptism and the giving of legacies to heretics.[4]

A Catholic council met in Byzacium on 24 February 418.[5] It ordered that schismatics were to be reconciled to the Church by the imposition of hands. The Council of Carthage on 1 May in the same year, a general African council, meeting in the *secretarium* of the Basilica of Faustus, and numbering not less than two hundred bishops, enacted several canons against the Donatist menace.[6] Reference is made in Canon 9[7] to the provision of the council of 407 concerning Donatist bishops who returned to the Church, and brought with them their whole flock.[8] But now, as many disputes have arisen and do arise among the bishops for this cause, it is resolved that if in any place a Donatist and a Catholic community have existed side by side, and belonged to different dioceses, both shall be made over to the diocese to which the Catholic section belonged, whether the conversion took place before or after the publication of the imperial decrees. Further, it was decided that if a Donatist bishop had himself become Catholic, the two bishops should divide equally between them the two communities now reunited, so that one portion of the towns should belong to one, and the other to the other bishop.[9] The bishop who had been longer in office was to make the division, but the other would have the choice. If there was only one township of this description, then it was to belong to whichever see was nearest to it; but if there were two sees equally near, the people were to decide it by a majority of votes. If the votes were equal, the elder bishop had the preference. If, however, the towns to which both parties belonged were of unequal number, so that they could not be equally divided, the remaining one should be dealt with as was prescribed above, in the preceding canon, with respect to a single town. Canons 11–16[10] regulate smaller matters concerning reunion. The next

[1] Ibid. XVI, v, 58 (6 November 415).
[2] Ibid. XVI, v, 63 (6 July or 4 August 425).
[3] Ibid. XVI, v, 64 (6 August 425).
[4] Ibid. XVI, v, 65 (30 May 428).
[5] Ferrandus, *Breuiatio Canonum* (Voelli & Iustelli), p. 174.
[6] Hefele, op. cit. vol. II, p. 458; Migne, op. cit. vol. I, p. 514.
[7] *C.C.E.A.* Canon 117. [8] Supra, p. 62.
[9] *C.C.E.A.* Canon 118 (Canon 10 of this council).
[10] *C.C.E.A.* Canons 119–24.

Council of Carthage, which met in the same church a year later, on 25 May 419, confirmed the previously enacted canons of the African synods, which were collected into the corpus which is now known as the *Codex Canonum Ecclesiae Africanae*.[1] These included the canons already enacted against the Donatists.[2]

In the *De fide et operibus* of 412, Saint Augustine returned once more to the Donatist error on baptism, and reiterated his teaching on the admixture of good and evil in the Church.[3] About the same time he wrote a pastoral to the Donatists on the present situation, entitled *Ad Donatistas post collationem*.[4] It was a long and careful work, designed to prevent further seduction of the Donatist laity by their leaders. It covered the whole question at issue: the suggestion that Marcellinus had been bribed by the Catholics, the universality of the Church, its admixture of good and evil in this present world, the authority of Saint Cyprian in the matter of Church unity, the origins of the Donatist schism, and the alleged *traditio* of Caecilianus; and finally the exercise of discipline by the Church. Saint Augustine pressed home strongly the evasion practised by the Donatist representatives at the Conference.[5] And the work concluded with an appeal to the dissidents to embrace the unity of the Catholic Church.[6] The same ground was covered by

---

[1] Hefele, op. cit. vol. II, pp. 467 sq.

[2] Viz. *C.C.E.A.* Canons 27, 47, 48, 57, 61–9, 85, 91–4, 99, 106, 107, 117–19, 123, 124.

[3] Aug. *De fid. et op.* II, 3–V, 7.

[4] Aug. *Retract.* II, xl.

[5] Aug. *Ad Don. post coll.* xxv, 43: 'congregantur ex uniuersa Africa tot episcopi, ingrediuntur Carthaginem, cum tanta speciosi agminis pompa, ut tam magnae ciuitatis oculos in se intentionemque conuertant. qui loquantur pro omnibus eliguntur ab omnibus, locus etiam re tanta dignus in urbe media procuratur, utrique conueniunt, iudex praesto est, tabulae patent, suspensa omnium corda exitum tantae conlationis expectant. tunc a lectissimis et disertissimis uiris, quantis uiribus agi debuit aliquid, tantis agitur ut agatur nihil.'

[6] Ibid. xxxv, 58: 'nocte causa finita est, sed ut nox finiretur erroris: nocte dicta sententia est, sed fulgens lumine ueritatis...scimus quam multi uestrum et forte omnes aut paene omnes dicere soleatis: "o si in unum locum conuenirent, o si aliquando conferrent, atque illis disputantibus ueritas appareret." ecce factum est, ecce conuicta est falsitas, ecce apparuit ueritas. quid adhuc fugitur unitas, quid adhuc contemnitur caritas? quid nobis opus est per nomina hominum diuidi? qui nos creauit unus est deus, qui nos redemit unus est Christus, qui nos consociare debet unus est spiritus. iam nomen Domini honoretur et appareat uobis in iucunditate, ut agnoscatis fratres uestros in ipsius unitate. iam in prosecutionibus episcoporum uestrorum qui nos separabat error est uictus: aliquando in cordibus uestris uincatur et diabolus, et gregi suo collecto atque pacato sit propitius qui hoc praecepit Christus.'

the conciliar letter addressed to the Donatists by the Numidian bishops assembled at Cirta on 14 June 412,[1] of which the redaction is acknowledged by Saint Augustine himself.[2]

We have lost the next work he wrote against the Donatists, the *Ad Emeritum episcopum Donatistarum post collationem*, which seems to have been written about 416.[3] Emeritus had been one of the *actores* at the Conference; and Augustine wrote to remind him of the case which the Catholics had there put forward and established. Emeritus remained obstinate, as we shall see later.

The *Retractations* also mention the letter *De correctione Donatistarum*, now printed among the epistles.[4] It was written at the beginning of 417 to Boniface, tribune and later Count of Africa, and urged the stringent application of the law in the case of recalcitrant Donatists. Saint Augustine reminds Boniface in his letter that the Donatists are free from the Arian heresy, but are schismatics from the Church.[5] He justifies the coercive policy adopted by the Catholics, and asks Boniface to borrow a copy of the *Breuiculus Collationis* from Bishop Optatus, or, if he does not possess one, from the church of Sitifi.[6] The Maximianist schism is mentioned as undermining the Donatist cause.[7] Saint Augustine confesses his earlier doubts about the use of State coercion, and attributes it to the divine providence that the pacific policy of the earlier days had failed, and the Catholic bishops had been forced back on the only method which would effectually appeal to the Donatist mentality, the method of compulsion.[8] The Emperor decided not to leave the Donatists to perish in schism, but to bring them within the fold of the Church, and because of his laws many have in fact returned.[9] The policy has thus been amply justified by its results,[10] and the Donatist clergy have been able to retain their rank on their return to the Church.[11] It remains only to finish the work, and for this task the co-operation of Boniface is requested.[12]

The little treatise on Patience, written about 418, has some echoes of the Donatist controversy. It contrasts true patience with the action of those who prefer suicide to reunion,[13] and shows that the patience of schismatics under tribulation is vitiated by their lack of charity in resisting Catholic unity.[14]

[1] *Apud.* Aug. *Ep.* CXLI.
[2] Aug. *Retract.* II, xl.
[3] Ibid. II, xlvi.
[4] Aug. *Ep.* CLXXXV; *Retract.* II, xlviii.
[5] Aug. *Ep.* CLXXXV, i, 1.
[6] Ibid. CLXXXV, ii, 6.
[7] Ibid. CLXXXV, iv, 17.
[8] Ibid. CLXXXV, vii, 25–8.
[9] Ibid. CLXXXV, vii, 29–viii, 32.
[10] Ibid. CLXXXV, ix, 36.
[11] Ibid. CLXXXV, x, 45, 46.
[12] Ibid. CLXXXV, xi, 48–51.
[13] Aug. *De patientia*, XIII, 10.
[14] Ibid. XXVI, 23.

In 418 also Saint Augustine visited Caesarea in the western province of Mauretania, where his friend Deuterius was bishop, with a view to conferring with the Donatists there. Their bishop, Emeritus, a native of Caesarea, who had ruled the Donatist church there as bishop since about 385, had been one of the seven Donatists who led their case at the Conference of Carthage. Emeritus, who was out of town, returned while Saint Augustine was there, and they met in the street on 18 September 418. Augustine invited him to come with him into the Catholic basilica to talk the question over. He did so, and a crowd soon assembled in the church, and Saint Augustine addressed them in a sermon still extant, entitled *Sermo ad Caesariensis ecclesiae plebem*.[1] The congregation was urged to pray for the conversion of Emeritus, and Emeritus invited to share in Catholic unity. He sat in silence, while the people cried, 'aut hic aut nusquam'.[2] Saint Augustine in his sermon said that salvation and charity were only to be found within the Church, and that no faith, not even that which moves a man to face martyrdom, is of any use outside the Church's unity.[3] The irrelevance of the cause of Caecilianus was urged, and the bad record of the Donatists in the matter of persecution stressed.[4] 'The congregation has cried, "Here or nowhere": I pray that it may be here', concluded Saint Augustine.[5]

Two days later, on 20 September 418, a further and more formal conference was held in the church. The Bishop of Caesarea, Deuterius, presided, and all the clergy of the town were present, with certain visiting bishops, including Augustine and Emeritus, Alypius of Tagaste, Possidius of Calama, Rusticus of Cartenna, and Palladius of Tigabis. Reporters were also there, and took minutes of the proceedings.[6] Saint Augustine first addressed the congregation, and related his meeting two days previously with Emeritus, when he had spoken about peace and charity and the unity of the Church. He had failed to win Emeritus, but did not despair.[7] Now he invited Emeritus to justify his accusation that Marcellinus had been corrupted; but Emeritus would not enter into the question.[8] Saint Augustine then recapitulated the results of the Conference, and asked Deuterius to follow the example of Carthage, Tagaste, Constantina, and Hippo, in having the *Gesta* read publicly in church during Lent.[9] Alypius then read the letter addressed by the Catholic bishops to Marcellinus before the Conference, which expressed their willingness to abide by his decision.[10] Saint Augustine interrupted

---

[1] Aug. *Retract.* II, li.
[2] Aug. *Serm. ad Caes. eccl. pleb.* 1.
[3] Ibid. 6. [4] Ibid. 7. [5] Ibid. 9.
[6] Aug. *Gesta cum Emer.* 1; *Retract.* II, li. [7] Aug. *Gesta cum Emer.* 1.
[8] Ibid. 2, 3. [9] Ibid. 4. [10] *Apud* Aug. *Ep.* CXXVIII, 1–3.

this reading to make comments on certain points,[1] and, when it was finished, he made a full statement on the schism of the Maximianists.[2] At the conclusion of the address, Emeritus remained unmoved,[3] but soon afterwards he left the town.

The tribune and notary Dulcitius was engaged in 420 in an energetic campaign in Africa for the final suppression of the Donatists according to the imperial constitutions. In the course of this campaign he wrote a strong letter to Gaudentius, the Donatist bishop at Thamugadi, which had ever been a great Donatist stronghold, summoning him to submit to the imperial judgement, and dissuading him from assembling his flock in the church, and burning it down over their heads, as he had threatened to do. Gaudentius sent two letters, one short and one long, refusing to submit; and Dulcitius forwarded them to Saint Augustine, with the request that he would reply to them. This he did in the work *Contra Gaudentium* I, which evoked a letter from Gaudentius to Augustine, which in turn was answered by him in his second book *Contra Gaudentium*.[4]

The first of these two books states the circumstances of its publication,[5] answers the letters of Gaudentius point by point, and remonstrates with him for rebelling against the unification of the Church.[6] The rightfulness of compulsion in spiritual matters is discussed,[7] and the Donatist addiction to suicide reprobated.[8] Finally, Gaudentius is invited to embrace the unity of the Catholic Church, and advised, if he decides to send a reply, to take into consideration the facts about Maximianism which Saint Augustine put before his brother bishop Emeritus.[9] Book II is Saint Augustine's reply to a letter received from Gaudentius in answer to his challenge.[10] In that reply he had cited Saint Cyprian on the necessity of holiness to the Church, and this argument is first answered.[11] But it really demands no answer, for the reception of the Maximianists shows that the Donatists do not really believe their own case.[12] And Saint Cyprian is the last man whom they should quote, for he had a passionate belief in charity, and therefore in the unity of the Church, which is foreign to the Donatists.[13] The compulsion applied to them by the Emperor has a purely corrective object: it is to lead them by fear to love, to establish earthly peace by which men may be led to

[1] Aug. *Gesta cum Emer.* 5–7.   [2] Ibid. 8–12.   [3] Ibid. 12.
[4] Aug. *Retract.* II, lix; *C. Gaud.* I, i, 1.   [5] Aug. *C. Gaud.* I, i, 1.
[6] Ibid. I, xi, 12–xiv, 15.   [7] Ibid. I, xix, 20–xxv, 28.
[8] Ibid. I, xxvi, 29–xxxvi, 46.   [9] Ibid. I, xxxvii, 47–xxxix, 54.
[10] Ibid. II, i, 1.   [11] Ibid. II, ii, 2–vi, 6.
[12] Ibid. II, vii, 7–viii, 8.   [13] Ibid. II, viii, 9–x, 11.

know the peace of eternal salvation.¹ And therefore, in conclusion, Gaudentius is exhorted to return to the Church.² We do not know what happened, whether he returned, which seems unlikely, or, if not, whether he carried out his threat.

The work against Gaudentius is the last of Saint Augustine's anti-Donatist works. The battle was now practically won; and in his remaining writings, of the last ten years of his life, there are only casual references to the controversy. In the work *De anima et eius origine*, addressed to Vincentius Victor, Saint Augustine congratulates him on returning to the Church from the Rogatist schism, but wonders why he should retain the name 'Vincentius', which he had taken in honour of the principal Rogatist bishop.³ The judgement of Miltiades, in the case of Caecilianus, is mentioned in the *Contra Iulianum*.⁴ In the same work⁵ the validity of the appeal to the State is established by reference to the happy results of the Conference of Carthage; and the terror of the Circumcellions is graphically described.⁶ The Donatists are here coupled with the Manichaeans as the enemies of the Christianity of Africa.⁷ The escape of Saint Augustine from the Donatist ambush, mentioned by Possidius,⁸ is recalled in the *Enchiridion*, written in 421.⁹ Donatism is included in the heresies described in the work of 428;¹⁰ and in his last unfinished work against Julian, the Pelagian controversialist is reminded of the felicitous results of a policy of State coercion against the Donatists.¹¹

Much is said in the letters and sermons of Saint Augustine's last twenty years concerning the overthrow of Donatism. The first of these letters was written to Marcellinus at the end of 411.¹² Saint Augustine has heard of the conviction of a number of Circumcellions for the murder of the Hipponensian priests Restitutus and Innocentius; and he asks

¹ Ibid. II, xii, 13: 'proinde cum regibus ea, quae secundum deum sunt, religioso timore iubentibus quisquis obtemperat, a timore incipiens et ad dilectionem proficiens a domino accipit pacem, non sicut pacem dat saeculum, quoniam saeculum pacem dat propter temporalem utilitatem, dominus autem propter aeternam salutem.'
² Ibid. II, xiii, 14.
³ Aug. *De anima et eius origine*, II, ii, 2.
⁴ Aug. *C. Iulianum*, I, iii, 7. ⁵ Ibid. III, i, 5.
⁶ Ibid. III, i, 5: 'illorum... furor occupauerat Africam totam, nec praedicari a Catholicis ueritatem contra suum patiebantur errorem, uiolentis aggressionibus, latrocinationibus, itinerum obsidionibus, rapinis, ignibus, caedibus multa uastantes, cuncta terrentes.'
⁷ Ibid. III, cvii, 31. ⁸ Possid. *Vita Aug.* XII.
⁹ Aug. *Enchir.* XVII, 5. ¹⁰ Aug. *De haeres.* LXIX.
¹¹ Aug. *Op. imp. c. Iulian.* I, x. ¹² Aug. *Ep.* CXXXIII.

Marcellinus to punish them severely, but not to inflict the death penalty. At the same time he wrote to Apringius, the proconsul of Africa, and brother of Marcellinus, interceding for mercy towards these same offenders.[1] In May of the next year he wrote again to Marcellinus, to ask him that the *Gesta Collationis* which were shortly to be published might be exhibited in a public place for the people to read. It was also hoped that they would be read to the people in church. In this letter he again asked Marcellinus not to impose the death penalty upon Donatists who still resisted.[2] The conciliar letter of the Council of Cirta of 14 June 412, which was drawn up by Saint Augustine, is the next in chronological order.[3] During 412 he wrote two letters to converted Donatists. The first was to those who had come over at Constantina,[4] where the whole church, clergy as well as laity, had submitted. The letter was therefore addressed to all grades in the church. Saint Augustine ascribed to God the conquering of men's obstinacy by the power of truth,[5] and welcomed the converts to the unity of the Church.[6] The other was to the priests Saturninus and Euphrates, and other clergy who had returned with them.[7] The Bishop welcomed them to their ministry in the Catholic Church, and bade them not to be perturbed by the mixture of evil with good in the Church. He wrote also in 412 to Donatus, a Donatist priest of Mutugenna in the diocese of Hippo, who was not pleased at his compulsory unification with the Church.[8] He tells Donatus that the Donatists are being compelled to come into the Church solely for their own good.[9] And none can doubt that persecution may sometimes rightly be used for good ends. Many a man has been consecrated bishop against his will;[10] Saint Paul was restrained from persecuting the Church; the children of Israel were brought up out of Egypt against their will; and compulsion for any good end is an exemplification of that legitimate principle of authority by which fathers chastise their children.[11] How much better is it to save schismatics from punishment in eternal flames![12] Now that the case has been finally judged at Carthage[13] the Church must bring in her wandering souls from the highways and hedges into the wedding-feast of the Church's unity, as the Master commanded when he said, 'compelle intrare'.[14]

Between 413 and 420 several letters were written to imperial officials

[1] Ibid. CXXXIV.
[2] Ibid. CXXXIX.
[3] Supra, p. 80.
[4] Aug. *Ep.* CXLIV.
[5] Ibid. CXLIV, 1.
[6] Ibid. CXLIV, 2.
[7] Ibid. CXLI.
[8] Ibid. CXLII.
[9] Ibid. CXLIII, 1.
[10] Ibid. CXLIII, 2.
[11] Ibid. CXLIII, 3.
[12] Ibid. CXLIII, 4–6.
[13] Ibid. CXLIII, 7–9.
[14] Ibid. CXLIII, 10.

on questions relating to the suppression of the schism. The earliest of these was sent at the end of 413 to Caecilianus, the governor of Numidia, about the murder of Marcellinus and Apringius, which Caecilianus had related in a letter to Augustine.[1] Augustine describes the arrest of the brothers, the appeal to the Court, and the death inflicted on them by Marinus, the Count of Africa, before any order could come from the Emperor. A year later an interesting letter was written to Macedonius, Vicar of Africa, concerning the peace of earth and the peace of heaven. Augustine praises Macedonius for his recognition of the close relation between them displayed in his suppression of the Donatists during his vicariate.[2] The epistle of early 417 to Boniface, the tribune, has been mentioned among the treatises of this period on account of its length and importance, and of its inclusion in the *Retractations*.[3] The last of this series of letters was written about 420 to the tribune Dulcitius, congratulating him on his activities in the suppression of Donatism.[4] It is the desire of the writer, as of all Catholic bishops, that the African Church shall be reunited; and they are confident that they have taken the right course in asking for State support in this policy. For if kings of the earth are right in restraining murder, adultery, and such crimes, how much more are they right in putting an end to schism, which is sacrilege![5]

At the beginning of 423 Saint Augustine had occasion to write to the new Bishop of Rome, Caelestinus, elected at the end of 422, about the appeal of Antonius, Bishop of Fussala, to the Roman see from a sentence of deposition pronounced against him.[6] In his letter Augustine relates the circumstances of the division of the see of Hippo by the creation of a new see of Fussala. The division had been necessitated by the wholesale conversion of Donatists after the second edict of unity. Before the edict there had hardly been a Catholic in Fussala, but when all the Donatists had been converted there, its distance from the cathedral (forty miles) made it necessary to have a bishop there. Such a bishop must be able to speak Punic, as Latin was little understood at Fussala. Saint Augustine chose a priest with this and other qualifications, and asked Siluanus, Primate of Numidia, to come and consecrate him.

[1] Ibid. CLI.
[2] Ibid. CLV, 17 et passim.
[3] See p. 80 supra.
[4] Aug. *Ep.* CCIV.
[5] Ibid. CCIV, 4: 'docuimus etiam liberum arbitrium sic homini datum, ut tamen et diuinis legibus et humanis recentissime grauium supplicia constituta sint peccatorum; et pertinere ad religiosos reges terrae non solum adulteria uel homicidia uel huiusmodi alia flagitia seu facinora uerum etiam sacrilegia seueritate congrua cohibere.'
[6] Ibid. CCIX.

When Siluanus had arrived, and all was ready, the candidate suddenly refused to accept the office; and rather than trouble such an old man as Siluanus with a second journey, Saint Augustine designated Antonius, a young reader trained in his own community, for the office of Bishop of Fussala. The episcopate of Antonius was not a success, and some grave charges were made against him in his diocese. He was therefore deposed, and had now appealed to the Bishop of Rome.

The last letter of Saint Augustine on Donatism was sent about 423 to the converted Donatist nun Felicia.[1] In it the Bishop urged her not to forsake the Church because she was distressed at scandals which arose among its members; for the Church will not be perfectly holy until the Last Judgement shall have separated the wicked from among the righteous.

The first sermon of Saint Augustine after the Conference in which reference was made to Donatism was eirenic, like the two preached at Carthage at the end of May in preparation for the Conference.[2] It was concerned with the bearing of one another's burdens, which is the manifestation of Christian charity, and at the end the preacher turned to the situation in the latter part of 411.[3] The toleration of evil in the Church did not include consenting to the evil deeds of men, which may be corrected; but did imply the striking of a balance between discipline and toleration.[4] This was illustrated by the unjust prosecution of Caecilianus, and his acquittal, and also in the treatment of the Maximianist schismatics by the main body of the Donatist sect,[5] which in itself furnished the condemnation of Donatism.[6] The case against Donatism had been proved at the Conference; and it remained for the Catholic laity to show forbearance and patience towards the erring schismatics.[7] Shortly afterwards, and probably in the early part of 412, a sermon on *concordia fratrum* is directed similarly to the pacification of the Church.[8] Such is the desire of the Catholics;[9] and even if the guilt of Caecilianus had been proved, it would still form no basis for the uncharitableness of divisions within the Church.[10] Uncharitableness, however, is not the desire of all Donatists, for many have returned to the Church.[11]

[1] Ibid. CCVIII.
[2] Aug. *Serm.* CLXIV.
[3] Ibid. CLXIV, vii, 10–x, 15.
[4] Ibid. CLXIV, vii, 11.
[5] Ibid. CLXIV, viii, 12.
[6] Ibid. CLXIV, ix, 13.
[7] Ibid. CLXIV, x, 15.
[8] Aug. *Serm.* CCCLIX.
[9] Ibid. CCCLIX, 5.
[10] Ibid. CCCLIX, 5, 6, especially 6: 'nec iustitia Caeciliani coronat ecclesiam, nec culpa Caeciliani damnat ecclesiam.'
[11] Ibid. CCCLIX, 7: 'habemus eos sanos et gaudentes nobiscum in ecclesia.'

About the same time (412) Saint Augustine, speaking of the judgement of Solomon between the two harlots, warned his flock that in correcting hypocrisy the danger of schism is to be avoided,[1] since schism is a sword which divides the weaker members of Christ's Body.[2] In a sermon on the forgiveness of sins,[3] he dwelt on forgiveness as being the gift of Christ: sins are forgiven by the Holy Ghost, not by the priest who pronounces God's absolution.[4] Similarly in baptism the cleansing proceeds from the grace of God, and not from the merits of the minister.[5] It is still, evidently, necessary to combat the widespread Donatist theory of the sacraments. Another Donatist fallacy attacked at the same time is their claim that the true Church is confined to Africa.[6] This last sermon concludes with an eloquent appeal for unity.[7]

A sermon delivered between 412 and 420 in the Basilica Restituta at Carthage on the parable of the great supper mentions in conclusion the divine command to bring men in from the highways and hedges.[8] The highways represent the Gentiles, the hedges the heretics and schismatics, for hedges are divisions.

Of this period also is a commentary on Psalm cxlvii, in which the verse 'who maketh peace in thy borders' gives the preacher a chance to reiterate the longing of the African Church for peace, and to comment that peace is only found in the Church, and is not possessed by heretics and schismatics.[9] Moreover, it is a peace which is world-wide, and cannot be confined to Africa, or to any one local church. But for the Church on earth peace can never be perfect: it will only be so in the incorruptible joy of the heavenly Jerusalem,[10] where all the saints will be at unity and peace.[11]

---

[1] Ibid. x, 4.
[2] Ibid. x, 8.
[3] Ibid. xcix, preached about 412.
[4] Ibid. xcix, ix, 9.
[5] Ibid. xcix, xiii, 13.
[6] Ibid. cxxxviii, ix, 9; x, 10.
[7] Ibid. cxxxviii, x, 10: 'hortor uos, obsecro uos per sanctitatem talium nuptiarum, amate hanc ecclesiam, estote in tali ecclesia, estote talis ecclesia; amate pastorem bonum, uirum tam pulchrum, neminem fallentem, neminem perire cupientem. orate et pro dispersis ouibus; ueniant et ipsi, agnoscant et ipsi, ament et ipsi; ut sit unus grex et unus pastor.'
[8] Ibid. cxii, vii, 8: 'uenerunt de plateis et uicis gentes; ueniant de sepibus haeretici, hic inueniunt pacem. nam qui construunt sepes, diuisiones quaerunt. trahantur a sepibus, euellantur ab spinis. in sepibus haeserunt, cogi nolunt. uoluntate, inquiunt, nostra intramus. non hoc Dominus imperauit: coge, inquit, intrare.'
[9] Aug. *Enarr. in Ps.* cxlvii, 16.
[10] Ibid. cxlvii, 20.
[11] Ibid. cxlvii, 28: 'ibi laudabimus, omnes unus in uno ad unum erimus, quia deinceps multi dispersi non erimus.'

A sermon on Psalm lxvii can be referred to the year 415.[1] In it the 'congregatio taurorum inter uaccas populorum' is explained as meaning the heretics and schismatics among the faithful in the Church.[2] The schismatics cited are the Donatists and Luciferians, and their cardinal error is described as being the fallacy that evil men will defile the sacraments of the Church. But the kingdoms of the earth are to be ascribed to God, and not to such men.[3]

In a course of tractates on the Gospel and first Epistle General of Saint John, preached about 416 at the end of Lent and at Eastertide, Saint Augustine took occasion to warn his flock still further against Donatist errors.[4] The chief of these errors is that which maintains that baptism is the gift of the minister rather than of Christ.[5] There is a clear distinction between baptizing by power, which is the act of Christ, and by ministry, which is the act of the human agent;[6] but in any case there is only one baptism for the remission of sins in the Church.[7] And it is Christ's will that his Church should be one.[8] The bond of unity is charity, without which all other virtues are as stubble.[9] Surprisingly little reference is made to the appeal to imperial authority, which occupies so much of Saint Augustine's correspondence and writing at this time, and there are only two passing references to it in this series of tractates.[10]

At Easter, probably also in 416, ten tractates were preached on the first Epistle General of Saint John, and the Apostle's insistence on the virtue of love towards God and towards the brethren leads the preacher to dwell on schism as the negation of love, inflaming Christians with hatred against one another.[11] The man who goes out of the Church, which is the Body of Christ, ceases to be numbered amongst the members of Christ,[12] and joins the party of antichrist.[13] But this is precisely what the Donatists have done: by leaving the Church they have cut themselves off not only from African but from transmarine Christians.[14] The Donatists have become accustomed to defend this action by saying

[1] Ibid. LXVII.
[2] Ibid. LXVII, 39.
[3] Ibid. LXVII, 40.
[4] Aug. *In Ioan. Evang. tract.* IV–XII; *In Ep. Ioan. tract.* I–III, VI, X.
[5] Aug. *In Ioan. Evang. tract.* IV, 9, 16; V, 6, 7, 9, 11, 13, 16, 17; VI, 8, 11, 12; VII, 4; XI, 12, 13; XII, 9.
[6] Ibid. V, 6; VII, 4.
[7] Ibid. VI, 8.
[8] Ibid. VI, 22.
[9] Ibid. VI, 20, 21, 26; VII, 3; X, 5.
[10] Ibid. VI, 25; XI, 13.
[11] Aug. *In Ep. Ioan. tract.* I–III, VI, X.
[12] Ibid. I, 12; II, 9; III, 4, 5; VI, 2; X, 6.
[13] Ibid. III, 7–9.
[14] Ibid. II, 3.

that the whole Church in communion with the *traditor* Caecilianus has forsaken its holiness; and yet when the Maximianists separated from their sect they readmitted them on their submission.[1]

Further sermons on Saint John's Gospel were preached after Easter in the same year. In one of them baptism is again discussed,[2] and reference is once more made to charity as the bond of ecclesiastical unity,[3] and the test by which false prophets may be discerned.[4] In another, on Christ as the good shepherd, faithful and unfaithful shepherds are contrasted, and the Lord's injunction concerning one flock and one shepherd is mentioned.[5] Saint Augustine does not dwell on this, but says that he has often spoken of it previously.[6]

About 417 he preached a sermon against the Manichaeans on the text I John iv. 1–3; and charged them with error concerning the Incarnation.[7] He said that they could not proceed from God, according to the Johannine canon, since they denied that Jesus Christ was come in the flesh. But, he added, not all even who profess this faith are of God. Among other instances of such people the Donatists are included, and the discussion of this broader question is deferred until the next day, as time is short.[8] When he returns to this question on the next day[9] he says that various groups of heretics and schismatics confess that Jesus Christ has appeared in the flesh, among them the Arians, Eunomians, Sabellians, Photinians, Donatists and Pelagians.[10] The doctrine of the Incarnation held by these sects is then considered in more detail; and when the preacher speaks of the Donatist view, he says that most Donatists are orthodox on the matter, but that some incline to Arian views, saying that though the Son is consubstantial with the Father, yet he is not equal. But, objects Saint Augustine, if he is not the Christ, then he cannot truly be said to have come in the flesh.[11]

A number of other sermons and of commentaries on psalms make incidental reference to Donatism, and appear to have been preached before 420, but cannot be assigned to any particular period or date. The ejection of Hagar and Ishmael is referred to heretics and schismatics in a fragmentary sermon. Such men are by baptism born of the seed

---

[1] Ibid. II, 13.
[2] Aug. *In Ioan. Evang. tract.* XIII, 4–11.
[3] Ibid. XIII, 15, 16.
[4] Ibid. XIII, 17.
[5] Ibid. XLVII, 3, 4.
[6] Ibid. XLVII, 4: 'de uno autem ouili et uno pastore iam quidem assidue soletis audire: multum enim commendauimus unum ouile, praedicantes unitatem, ut per Christum omnes oues ingrederentur, et Donatum nulla sequeretur.'
[7] Aug. *Serm.* CLXXXII.
[8] Ibid. CLXXXII, vii, 7.
[9] Ibid. CLXXXIII.
[10] Ibid. CLXXXIII, i, 1.
[11] Ibid. CLXXXIII, v, 9.

of Abraham, but they are not of the Church, and do not inherit eternal life because of their arrogant self-exclusion from the fellowship of the Church.[1] Similarly the differing inheritances of Jacob and Esau lead to a discussion of the visible and invisible Church.[2] Those who are not spiritually of the Church share indeed in the same sacraments with those who are, but can only be segregated at the last day.[3] They are like the tares among the wheat, which are not to be separated until the time of harvest.[4] In the meantime, men are not to forsake the Church's unity because they are unwilling to tolerate the evil men in the Church.[5] On the other hand, those who are openly in heresy and schism are manifestly outside the Church even now.[6] Schismatics smite with the sword, and so perish by the sword: they leave the Church because they lack charity, and then, as the Donatists have done, they split into fragments themselves.[7]

In a sermon preached just before Easter on the struggle of Jacob with the angel, Saint Augustine reminds the flock how often he has spoken to them about the necessity of this bearing with evil men in the Church, and imitating only those who are holy.[8]

The praise of the holy woman at the end of the Book of the Proverbs[9] is applied to the Church, and a contrast is drawn between the precious stone, such as was Saint Cyprian, which remains part of God's edifice, and the precious stone, such as was Donatus, which refuses to form part of that building.[10] Similarly the holy mount of God[11] is likened to the Church, which has grown as a mountain until it has filled the earth. Those who would confine that mountain to Africa have seriously erred,[12] for the inheritance of Christ is world-wide and not limited to Africa.[13]

Preaching on the sin of blasphemy against the Holy Ghost, Saint Augustine insists that heresies and schisms do not subvert the kingdom of Christ, or destroy its fundamental unity in him,[14] but simply exclude their propagators from it. This is the Cyprianic doctrine in its purest form, and, taken by itself, does not square with the subtlety of the preacher's general doctrine of schism. Moreover, later in the same

[1] Ibid. III.
[2] Ibid. IV, xi, 11, xii, 12.
[3] Ibid. IV, xxviii, 31.
[4] Aug. *Enarr. in Ps.* LXIX, 9; CXXXVIII, 26, 27.
[5] Ibid. CXXXVIII, 29, 31.
[6] Aug. *Serm.* IV, xxx, 33.
[7] Ibid. IV, xxxi, 34.
[8] Ibid. V, 1–3.
[9] Prov. xxxi. 10–31.
[10] Aug. *Serm.* XXXVII, iii, 3.
[11] Isa. lvii. 13.
[12] Aug. *Serm.* XLV, 7.
[13] Aug. *Enarr. in Ps.* XXX, *serm.* II, 14; *in Ps.* XLIX, 3; *in Ps.* LXXXV, 14.
[14] Aug. *Serm.* LXXI, ii, 4.

sermon, he admits the possibility of repentance and reconciliation even for schismatics.[1] But such repentance can only be effective if they join themselves to the unity of the Church, outside which there is no remission of sins,[2] and no gift of the Holy Spirit.[3] What is more, those who wilfully and with an impenitent heart resist the unity of the Church, are guilty of the blasphemy against the Holy Ghost which has no remission.[4] For unity is the fruit of charity, and of the fear of God.[5] They stand therefore convicted of spiritual levity who are outside the Church because they have been brought up in schism, and never stopped to consider what it implies.[6] Schism is the fruit of pride, and unity of true humility.[7]

A sermon preached at Carthage in the Basilica Restituta on the parable of the wedding feast of the king's son, in which the necessary wedding garment is interpreted as meaning charity, is also directed against the Donatists.[8] Some are found worthy to share in that feast, which is the Church of Christ, and some unworthy, for they have not thought it worth while to provide themselves with the vesture of charity, which is the bond of unity.[9]

Again, Christ himself refused on one occasion to be a judge and a divider; but the Donatists have not hesitated to take it upon themselves to divide the inheritance of Christ, which is the Church;[10] and to put Donatus in the place of Christ as the supreme object of worship.[11] Schism is therefore seen to be the work of those who do not put their trust in God,[12] but in men, such as the great Donatus.[13] These men may be great, but we are not on their account to divide the Church and household of God,[14] still less to baptize Christ's faithful as if they were yet heathens.[15]

A further sermon on true and false prophets again leads back to the schism.[16] Saint Augustine begins with the need of unity between Christ

[1] Ibid. LXXI, xiii, 21: 'schismaticus est hodie: quid si cras amplectatur catholicam pacem?'
[2] Ibid. LXXI, xvii, 28, xx, 33.   [3] Ibid. LXXI, xviii, 30, xix, 32.
[4] Aug. Serm. LXXI, xxii, 36, xxiii, 37: 'unum ergo suffugium est, ne sit irremissibilis blasphemia, ut cor impoenitens caueatur; nec aliter poenitentia prodesse credatur nisi ut teneatur ecclesia, ubi remissio peccatorum datur, et societas Spiritus in pacis uinculo custoditur.'
[5] Aug. Enarr. II in Ps. XVIII, 6, 10; Enarr. II in Ps. XXX, serm. I, 3, serm. II, 1.
[6] Aug. Enarr. in Ps. XXX, serm. II, 8.   [7] Aug. Enarr. in Ps. XXXIII, serm. II, 7.
[8] Aug. Serm. XC.
[9] Ibid. XC, 5, 6.   [10] Ibid. CVII, ii, 3.
[11] Ibid. CXCVII, 4.   [12] Aug. Enarr. II in Ps. XXV, 6.
[13] Ibid. XXX, serm. II, 12.   [14] Ibid. LXXV, 7, 8.
[15] Ibid. XXXIX, 1.   [16] Aug. Serm. CXXXVII.

as the Head and the Church as his Body.¹ Such unity is violated by the false shepherds who creep and intrude into the fold some other way. Among these the Donatists are pre-eminent; they cannot come into the sheepfold by Christ, who is the door, for they have not the requisite humility, but must climb in some other way and steal the sheep.²

For, in short, the Church is the inheritance of Christ, and the native land of his children;³ and to separate oneself from this inheritance is the sin of schism:⁴ 'non est dimittenda unitas, non est praecidenda ecclesia Dei.'⁵

¹ Ibid. CXXXVII, i, 1, ii, 2. ² Ibid. CXXXVII, x, 12.
³ Aug. *Enarr. in Ps.* CXIX, 6, 7. ⁴ Ibid. LXXXV, 19; LXXXVIII, 14.
⁵ Ibid. CXIX, 9.

CHAPTER IV

SAINT AUGUSTINE'S DOCTRINE OF THE CHURCH

1. *The doctrine of the Church and Ministry before Saint Augustine*

This protracted warfare against schism in the African Church compelled Saint Augustine to consider afresh the true nature of the one holy catholic apostolic Church of Christ. He had to justify his claim that the communion which he served was the Catholic Church of Africa; he had to discover the ground of his rejection of the Donatist claims in the charity which is the bond of Catholic unity; he had to make smooth the way of return for the Donatists to the Church; and in defending the use of compulsion by the Church, he had to examine the relations of Church and State. In so doing he made contributions so far-reaching and so subtle to the doctrine of the Church and of its ministry and sacraments, that the discussion of them, though vitally necessary to our inquiry, is a matter of no small difficulty. Before it is approached, it is needful to ask what main views of the nature of the Church, and of its relation to schism and heresy, had been commonly held in the centuries before Saint Augustine.

What is the Church? The very title by which from New Testament times it has been designated will give us the clue. The first Christians called it ἡ ἐκκλησία, the word used in the Septuagint to designate the people of God, the congregation of the children of Israel. If the Church has an earthly founder, that founder is Abraham, from whom the history of Israel as a people is commonly dated. To the seed of Abraham the divine promises were made; and Saint Paul, 'an Hebrew of the Hebrews', claimed that at the Crucifixion, when all had forsaken Christ and fled, that *ecclesia* was reduced to one, and he is the faithful remnant, all that is left of Israel.[1] But on him, in the power of his Resurrection, the new Israel, the inheritor of all the promises made to the old Israel, has been built. For the Church of Christ are claimed all the privileges of Israel under the old Covenant, and the Church, now to be gathered in from every nation, will be, like Israel, the people and *ecclesia* of God.[2]

[1] Gal. iii, especially *v.* 16; Rom. ix–xi, especially xi. 5.
[2] See T. A. Lacey, *Unity and Schism*, Bishop Paddock Lectures, 1917 (London, 1917), Lecture 1; H. B. Swete, *The Holy Catholic Church* (London, 1916), pt. 1, ch. i; F. J. A. Hort, *The Christian Ecclesia* (London, 1897); H. B. Swete (ed.),

On this thought depends fundamentally every idea of Christian unity. There can be only one Israel, only one people of God, only one Body of Christ. The gravity of schism, and its inherent irrationality and inconsistency with true Christianity, are seen immediately when we stand face to face with the original ideal.

And yet from the earliest days fissiparous tendencies begin to appear, the fruit of human pride and uncharitableness. Sections split off, and go out of communion with their fellow-Christians; and it begins to be necessary to have some standard by which to decide whether a community or an individual is within or without the fellowship of Christ's Church. In the fourth century the compilers of the Nicene Creed found it necessary to include in their document some more stringent definition of the Church than had been used hitherto in the baptismal Creed. They described the Church as being one, holy, catholic and apostolic. It must have unity within itself and with its Lord; it must be holy, in that it is the Body of Christ, and its sacraments are a means of the sanctification of souls; it must be catholic, universally extended, and not confined to any one part of the world; and it must be apostolic, teaching the doctrine of the Apostles, and having a ministry recognized as deriving its authority from Christ through the Apostles. Down to the fifth century these notes of the Church were admitted by all Christians; the schismatics only differed from the true Church in the interpretation of them, not over the need for having them. All were agreed in holding that wherever the true Church is to be found it, and it only, can dispense the living water of God's grace to his people. The modern error of regarding 'churches' in the light of voluntary associations of like-minded people is entirely foreign to the mind of the first five centuries: men still believed then in the divine authority of the One Visible Church.

How, then, was a man to know which was the true Church? At the beginning of the second century Saint Ignatius makes the bishop the centre of this ecclesiastical unity.[1] The true Church in any particular place is that body which is in communion with the bishop. The diocese is the microcosm of the whole Church; and what Christ, as the head of the Body, is to the Church, that also is the bishop to the church he serves. Ignatius knows nothing of any distinction between a Visible and an Invisible Church. The unity he demands is visible, and easily

Early History of the Church and the Ministry (London, 1921), ch. 1: A. J. Mason, 'Early conceptions of the Church'.

[1] Texts illustrating S. Ignatius's doctrine of the Church and the episcopate are printed in Appendix 1 of T. A. Lacey, op. cit. pp. 161–7.

discerned. Succession of bishops to the Apostles is not stressed; but the idea of a bishop wielding in his diocese the plenary authority of Christ, which we are to meet later in Saint Cyprian, is the centre of his thought, and he is the first to give expression to this theory.[1]

Two generations later Saint Irenaeus is facing a situation in which erroneous teaching is far more widespread. For him therefore the bishop is rather the custodian of the doctrine and faith of the Apostles. The Church, he teaches, must shun 'heretics and evil-thinkers, self-pleasing and self-satisfied schismatics, hypocrites actuated by love of money or of reputation'.[2] It follows that bishops who prove themselves unworthy of their office by such errors of life and thought must be excluded from their ministry. Saint Cyprian later followed Irenaeus in this view, in spite of the exalted opinion he held of the episcopal authority and dignity; and in Irenaeus also we find the foreshadowing of the condemnation later to be emphasized by Saint Augustine of schism as the manifestation of uncharitableness.[3] The episcopate, which for Saint Ignatius had been the centre of ecclesiastical unity, is for Saint Irenaeus primarily the custodian of the apostolic *depositum*; and in the episcopate the Church extended throughout all the world has one and the same faith, derived from the Apostles of Christ.[4]

Similarly, Tertullian maintains that the test of truth is to be sought ultimately in the agreement of those churches which can claim to have received their teaching from Christ through an apostolic founder.[5] To him is due the thought so deeply imprinted in the mind of his great disciple Saint Cyprian, and mentioned also by Saint Augustine, that the man who has not the Church for his mother cannot have God for his Father.[6] It is only through the Church that we become the adopted

---

[1] On the teaching of Ignatius, see J. F. Bethune-Baker, *Introduction to the Early History of Christian Doctrine*, 4th ed. (London, 1929), pp. 357–9; Swete, *Early History of the Church and the Ministry*, pp. 113, 114, 229; J. B. Lightfoot, *The Christian Ministry* (London, 1901), pp. 83–90.

[2] C. H. Turner, in Swete, op. cit. p. 125.

[3] Iren. *Adu. haer.* III, xxiv, 1: 'ubi ecclesia, ibi et Spiritus Dei; et ubi Spiritus Dei, illic ecclesia et omnis gratia.'

[4] See Swete, op. cit. pp. 45–7, 104–8, 120–7, 200, 201; Bethune-Baker, op. cit. pp. 359, 360; Lightfoot, op. cit. pp. 90, 91.

[5] Tert. *De praescr. haeret.* XXXII; *De orat.* II.

[6] Tert. *De orat.* II: 'dicendo autem Patrem, Deum quoque cognominamus. appellatio ista et pietatis et potestatis est. item in Patre Filius inuocatur. "ego enim", inquit, "et Pater unum sumus." ne mater quidem ecclesia praeteritur, si quidem in filio et patre mater recognoscitur, de qua constat et patris et filii nomen.' *De bapt.* VI: 'cum autem sub tribus [sc. Sanctam Trinitatem], et testatio fidei, et sponsio salutis pignerentur, necessario adiicitur ecclesiae mentio; quoniam ubi

sons of God. Therefore heretics, who do not believe in the same God or the same Christ as Christians do, have no power to minister any of the sacraments of Christ. In Christ's Church the bishop is the fountain of order and the guardian of discipline.[1]

For the earliest Western Fathers, then, the Church's unity is founded upon its function as the Body of Christ, and in doctrine and discipline this unity is recognizable in subjection to the one episcopate and in acceptance of the apostolic faith. These beliefs were to be pushed to their logical extreme by Saint Cyprian in the middle of the third century, and his teaching is of the greatest importance for the discussion of the Donatist controversy, for in the fourth century he had become the African Father κατ' ἐξοχήν and the Donatist theologians, as patriotic Africans, made their appeal to him in the first instance. Saint Jerome tells us that Cyprian regarded Tertullian as his master, and that every day he studied Tertullian's works, calling for them with the words, 'Da magistrum'.[2] When we remember that Saint Cyprian was trained as a lawyer, and soon after his conversion raised first to the presbyterate and then to the episcopate at Carthage, it is not surprising to find that he was no original theologian, but imitated a good deal of the thought and reproduced much of the language of Tertullian; and that, being not merely a lawyer but an African, he preferred the clear-cut definitions of Western theology to the profundities of the more metaphysical thought of the East. His writings are practical and devotional; he was no theological pioneer, but was held in reverent and thankful remembrance by African Christians as a great bishop who finally laid down his life for the faith. We must now examine what Saint Cyprian taught concerning the nature of the Church and the basis of its unity.[3]

The Nicene Creed professes the Christian belief in one holy

tres, id est Pater et Filius et Spiritus Sanctus, ibi ecclesia, quae trium corpus est.' Cypr. *De unit.* VI: 'habere iam non potest Deum patrem, qui ecclesiam non habet matrem.' Aug. *C. Litt. Pet.* III, 10: 'Deum patrem et eius ecclesiam matrem habere.'

[1] See Bethune-Baker, op. cit. pp. 360–2; Swete, op. cit. pp. 35, 37, 38, 47, 48, 127–9, 134, 201, 221–4.

[2] Hieron. *De uir. illustr.* 53.

[3] On Cyprian's doctrine of the Church, see E. W. Benson, *Cyprian, his Life, his Times, his Work* (London, 1897); A. Harnack, *History of Dogma* (E.T.) (London, 1896), vol. II, pp. 84–93, 165–8; J. F. Bethune-Baker, op. cit. pp. 363–6; H. B. Swete, op. cit. pp. 217–62 (J. H. Bernard, 'The Cyprianic Doctrine of the Ministry'), and pp. 36, 38, 125, 130, 131, 140, 143, 181, 182, 185, 188, 195, 202, 229, 232, 241 n., 360, 361, 383, 384; T. A. Lacey, op. cit. pp. 34–40; T. G. Jalland, *The Church and the Papacy*, Bampton Lectures, 1942 (London, 1944), pp. 66, 97, 141 n., 159–78, 261, 279, 356; J. B. Lightfoot, op. cit. pp. 91–7.

catholic apostolic Church; and for Saint Cyprian this unity of the Body of Christ is clearly demonstrated to be the will of our Lord not only by the stress laid upon it in his great high-priestly intercession of the night of his Passion,[1] but also by the fact that the divine promise of the indefectibility of the Church was first given to one man, Saint Peter,[2] and then later to the other Apostles.[3] Moreover, after the Resurrection, Saint Peter was himself charged to feed the flock of Christ.[4] Since this unity is the will of God, nobody who is outside it can be considered sure of salvation; and so we have the clear principle enunciated from the earliest works of Cyprian onwards, the phrase which has for centuries been used as the succinct statement of his view, 'extra ecclesiam nulla salus'.[5] The form of the Creed used in Saint Cyprian's day in the African baptismal service guides his thought on the exclusiveness of the Church. The candidate was asked, 'credis in uitam aeternam et remissionem peccatorum per sanctam ecclesiam?'[6] For the House of God is one, and outside it none can be safe. In the old law he who would not obey the priest was slain with the temporal sword: to be cast out of the Church now, for disobedience to the bishops, is to be slain with the spiritual sword.[7]

[1] John xvii.   [2] Matt. xvi. 18.
[3] Matt. xviii. 18. Cypr. *Ep.* XLIII, 5: 'Deus unus est et Christus unus, et una ecclesia et cathedra una super Petrum Domini uoce fundata. aliud altare constitui aut sacerdotium nouum fieri praeter unum altare et unum sacerdotium non potest. quisquis alibi collegerit, spargit'; ibid. XLV, 3: 'hoc enim uel maxime, frater, et laboramus et laborare debemus, ut unitatem a Domino et per apostolos nobis successoribus traditam quantum possumus obtinere curemus.'
[4] Cypr. *De unit.* IV, 3: 'hoc erant utique et ceteri apostoli, quod fuit Petrus, pari consortio praediti, et honoris et potestatis, sed exordium ab unitate proficiscitur, ut ecclesia Christi una monstretur. quam unam ecclesiam etiam in cantico canticorum Spiritus Sanctus ex persona Domini designat et dicit: Una est columba mea, perfecta mea, una est matri suae, electa genetrici suae.' See John xxi. 15–17.
[5] In Cypr. *Ep.* LXXIII, 21 (to Iubaianus) we have it thus stated: 'salus extra ecclesiam non est.' In *De unit.* IV, 3 it is thus expanded: 'hanc ecclesiae unitatem qui non tenet, tenere se fidem credit? qui ecclesiae renititur et resistit, in ecclesia se esse confidit? quando et beatus apostolus Paulus hoc idem doceat et sacramentum unitatis ostendat dicens: Unum corpus, et unus spiritus, una spes uocationis uestrae, unus Dominus, una fides, unum baptisma, unus Deus?'
[6] Cypr. *Ep.* LXX, 2.
[7] Ibid. IV, LXIX; *De unit.* XXIII, 21: 'Deus unus est et Christus unus, et una ecclesia eius et fides una, et plebs in solidam corporis unitatis concordiae glutino copulata. scindi unitas non potest, nec corpus unum discidio compaginis separari, diuulsis laceratione uisceribus in frusta discerpi. quidquid a matrice discesserit, seorsum uiuere et spirare non poterit, substantiam salutis amittit.' T. A. Lacey, op. cit. p. 192, says: 'According to Cyprian schism does not divide the Church, which is essentially indivisible; but schismatics pass altogether outside the Church.'

Of this visible unity the bishop, for Saint Cyprian as well as for Saint Ignatius, is the focal point. In every diocese is seen the microcosm of the whole Church of God; the diocese is a self-contained unity, capable of administering the word and sacraments according to the ordinance of Christ, and within its borders the bishop is the vicegerent of Christ.[1] To set up a schismatic bishop in opposition to the chief pastor of any diocese is to rend the unity of the Church.[2] For this reason one of the principal duties of bishops is to use all means in their power to maintain unity,[3] and to enforce discipline among the flock, though not without consultation with their clergy and laity.[4] This authority of the bishop in respect of his own flock was established by Cyprian in practice by his victory in the conflict with the confessors and presbyters of Carthage who favoured a liberal policy, which would have thrown Cyprian's diocesan arrangements into confusion, towards the lapsed in the Decian persecution. But Cyprian held his view earlier than this: it was settled in his mind before any controversy arose; and to the end of his life he never modified it.[5]

As this controversy over the lapsed had resulted in the final definition of the bishop's supremacy in his own diocese, so the later controversy concerning heretical baptism was to provide the occasion of the establishment of the Cyprianic view of a bishop's relationship to the whole Church. For there was a parallel between the diocese and the Church: what the bishop is to his own diocese, the united episcopate is to the whole Church. What, then, if the bishops should not be unanimous on some question of doctrine or administration? The eighty-seven bishops who, on 1 September 256, attended at Carthage Saint Cyprian's seventh

[1] Cypr. *Ep.* LXXIII, 11: 'nos diuino permissu rigamus sitientem Dei populum, nos custodimus terminos uitalium fontium' (it is interesting to notice the phrase 'diuino permissu' surviving in the style of the modern English bishop); *Ep.* LXVI, 8; and *Ep.* IV (one of the earliest).

[2] Cypr. *Ep.* XLVI, 1 (to dissident confessors): 'grauat me atque contristat intolerabilis perculsi et paene prostrati pectoris maestitia praestringit, cum uos illic comperissem contra Dei dispositionem, contra euangelicam legem, contra institutionis catholicae unitatem alium episcopum fieri consensisse, id est, quod nec fas est nec licet fieri, ecclesiam alteram institui, Christi membra discerpi, dominici gregis animum et corpus enim discissa aemulatione lacerari'; *Ep.* LXIX, 6.

[3] *De unit.* v, 4: 'quam unitatem firmiter tenere et uindicare debemus, maxime episcopi qui in ecclesia praesidemus, ut episcopatum quoque ipsum unum atque indiuisum probemus.'

[4] Cypr. *Ep.* XVII, 1: 'praesentibus et iudicantibus uobis (i.e. plebe); *Ep.* XXXVIII, 1 (concerning ordination): 'solemus uos ante consulere et mores ac merita singulorum communi consilio ponderare.'

[5] E. W. Benson, op. cit. pp. 39, 40.

council (the third on baptism), and who came from the provinces of Africa, Numidia and Mauretania to give their judgement, in the presence of a vast concourse of presbyters, deacons and laity, on this vital question, and whose judgements have been preserved for us by Saint Augustine, who answered them in detail,[1] were unanimous, but Saint Cyprian, in his presidential remarks at the council, so often quoted by Augustine for their depth of charity and their passionate love for unity, lays down the principle that a bishop is entitled to hold his own opinion, even on so grave a matter, and to administer his diocese accordingly, though he may be the only bishop to hold such a view.[2] The bishops must decide these questions for themselves, for 'they have no power of delegation: Christ constituted them to govern, not to appoint governors'.[3] This seems to be directed against those who would follow the Roman custom of the admission of heretics on the ground that it was the custom of the *ecclesia principalis*. Although the Bishop of Rome has a primacy of honour, a *principalitas*, as it has come to be called,[4] yet his decision has no overriding authority. Saint Cyprian is careful to allow Stephen, Bishop of Rome, with whom he bitterly disagreed on the question of rebaptism, perfect liberty to administer the diocese of Rome according to his own view.[5] In another epistle Cyprian reminds a Mauretanian bishop that Saint Peter, when disputing with Saint Paul, the co-founder of the Roman Church, on the matter of circumcising converts, did not lay any claim to primacy, as Stephen was in fact doing at the time of the letter.[6] As Bishop of Carthage, Cyprian convenes and presides over the African synods in his own town (no doubt partly because of the political and administrative importance of Carthage, and of its convenience as a centre for such gatherings) but does not claim that his opinion is more important

[1] Aug. *De bapt.* VI and VII.
[2] Cypr. *Sent. episc. praef.* in Aug. *De bapt.* VI, vi, 9: '...superest ut de hac ipsa re singuli quid sentiamus proferamus, neminem iudicantes aut a iure communionis aliquem si diuersum senserit amouentes. neque enim quisquam nostrum episcopum se episcoporum constituit aut tyrannico terrore ad obsequendi necessitatem suos adigit, quando habeat omnis episcopus pro licentia libertatis et potestatis suae arbitrium proprium tamque iudicari ab alio non possit quam nec ipse potest alterum iudicare. sed expectemus uniuersi iudicium domini nostri Iesu Christi, qui unus et solus habet potestatem et praeponendi nos in ecclesiae suae gubernatione et de actu nostro iudicandi.' Cypr. *Ep.* LXXII, 3.
[3] Benson, op. cit. p. 193.
[4] Ibid. pp. 537–40, Appendix on *principalis ecclesia*.
[5] Cypr. *Ep.* LXXII, 3.
[6] Cypr. *Ep.* LXXI, 3. See Excursus to this Chapter, on Cyprian's view of the Roman primacy.

than that of a bishop from some obscure town in the ends of Mauretania.¹

This rigid theory of episcopacy, says Archbishop Benson, was not created by Saint Cyprian to solve his practical problems; 'it was far older than Cyprian, although in him it was lit and fired by that sense of love and feeling after unity which seemed to Augustine the most special characteristic of the man'.² For the unity of the Church is the manifestation of charity.³

The violation of this unity and charity is the sin of schism. To separate oneself from the divinely ordained unity is to renounce Christ, to bear arms against his Church, to militate against the disposition of God. It is to do something at once illicit and destitute of all authority.⁴ It constitutes spiritual whoredom, which will separate a man from God and exclude him from eternal salvation.⁵ The man who initiates schism rends the seamless robe of Christ.⁶ Schism does not indeed divide the Church, which is essentially indivisible, but it separates its authors from

¹ Aug. *De bapt.* VI, vi, 9.
² Benson, op. cit. p. 191. See Aug. *C. Ep. Parm.* III, ii, 9; *C. Cresc.* II, xxxiii, 42 (quoting Cypr. *De unit.* v), xxxiv, 43 (quoting Cypr. *Ep.* LIV, 3); III, ii, 2 (quoting Cypr. *Sent. episc. praef.*); *De bapt.* III, iii, 5 (quoting the same).
³ Aug. *De bapt.* IV, xvii, 24 (quoting Cypr. *Ep.* LXXIII, 21).
⁴ Cypr. *De unit.* XVII, 15: 'auersandus est talis atque fugiendus, quisquis fuerit ab ecclesia separatus. peruersus est huiusmodi et peccat et est a semetipso damnatus. an esse sibi cum Christo uidetur, qui aduersus sacerdotes Christi facit, qui se a clero eius et plebis societate secernit? arma ille contra ecclesiam portat, contra Dei dispositionem repugnat. hostis altaris, aduersus sacrificium Christi rebellis, pro fide perfidus, pro religione sacrilegus, inobsequens seruus, filius impius, frater inimicus contemptis episcopis et Dei sacerdotibus derelictis constituere audet aliud altare, precem alteram illicitis uocibus facere, dominicae hostiae ueritatem per falsa sacrificia profanare nec scire, quoniam qui contra ordinationem Dei nititur, ob temeritatis audaciam diuina animaduersione punitur.'
Ibid. VIII, 7, 8: 'nec alia ulla credentibus praeter unam ecclesiam domus est. hanc domum, hoc unanimitatis hospitium designat et denuntiat Spiritus Sanctus in psalmis dicens: Deus qui inhabitare facit unanimes in domo. in domo Dei, in ecclesia Christi unanimes habitant, concordes et simplices perseuerant.'
⁵ Ibid. VI, 5: 'adulterari non potest sponsa Christi, incorrupta est et pudica. unam domum nouit, unius cubiculi sanctitatem casto pudore custodit. haec nos Deo seruat, haec filios regno, quos generauit, assignat. quisquis ab ecclesia segregatus adulterae iungitur, a promissis ecclesiae separatur, nec perueniet ad Christi praemia, qui relinquit ecclesiam Christi. alienus est, profanus est, hostis est. habere non potest Deum patrem, qui ecclesiam non habet matrem. si potuit euadere quisquam, qui extra arcam Noe fuit, et qui extra ecclesiam foris fuerit, euadit...hanc unitatem qui non tenet, non tenet Dei legem, non tenet Patris et Filii fidem, uitam non tenet et salutem.'
⁶ Ibid. VII, 6.

DOCTRINE OF THE CHURCH

the Church, and puts them in the position of apostates. These are natural and inevitable judgements according to the rigid view of unity held by Saint Cyprian. For him schism is the mark of pride, selfishness and partisan feeling, just as unity is the outcome and manifestation of charity.[1] It was to remain for Saint Augustine to add the coping-stone to this fabric of doctrine, and to stigmatize schism as essentially sacrilegious.[2] Saint Cyprian illustrates his view from Scripture by reference to the seamless robe of Christ[3] of which mention has already been made, to the words of the Psalmist who describes God as 'making men to dwell of one mind in an house',[4] to the mission of the Holy Ghost in the form of a dove, the creature of peace, at Christ's baptism,[5] and finally to the choice of bread and wine as outward signs of the blessed sacrament, signifying by the compacting of many grains of wheat into bread, and the compression of the juice of many grapes into wine, the unity of the Church of Christ.[6]

Saint Cyprian was forced by the schism of Novatian at Rome to consider not only the unity of the Church, but also the application of his doctrine of unity to the problem of the second note of the Church, that of holiness. Against those who would separate from the Church because its holiness is not yet complete, he quotes, in a passage of his letter to the confessors on their return[7] (cited no fewer than three times by Augustine),[8] the parable of the wheat and tares,[9] and Saint Paul's

---

[1] Cypr. *De zelo et liuore*, VI (quoted by Aug. *De bapt.* IV, viii): 'hinc [sc. a zelo] Dominicae pacis uinculum rumpitur, hinc caritas fraterna uiolatur, hinc adulteratur ueritas, unitas scinditur, ad haereses atque ad schismata prosilitur, dum obtrectatur sacerdotibus, dum episcopis inuidetur.'

Ep. III, 3: 'haec sunt enim initia haereticorum et ortus atque conatus schismaticorum male cogitantium, ut sibi placeant, ut praepositum superbo tumore contemnant, sic de ecclesia receditur, sic altare profanum foris conlocatur, sic contra pacem Christi et ordinationem atque unitatem Dei rebellatur.'

[2] See infra, pp. 115, 116. [3] Cypr. *De unit.* VII, 6. See John xix. 23.

[4] Cypr. *De unit.* VIII, 7; *De orat. dom.* XXIII; *Ep.* LXIX, 5. He uses the old African version of Ps. lxviii. 6, 'unanimes in domo'. The later rendering of the Vulgate was 'unius moris in domo'.

[5] Cypr. *De unit.* IX, 8 (see Mark i. 10): 'idcirco et in columba uenit Spiritus Sanctus, simplex animal et laetum, non felle amarum, non morsibus saeuum, non unguium laceratione uiolentum, hospitia humana diligere, unius domus consortium nosse, cum generant simul filios edere, cum commeant, uolatibus inuicem cohaerere, communi conuersatione uitam suam degere, oris osculo, concordiam pacis agnoscere, legem circa omnia unanimitatis implere.'

[6] Cypr. *Ep.* LXIX, 5. [7] Ibid. LIV, 3.

[8] Aug. *Ep.* CVIII, 10; *C. Cresc.* II, 43; *C. Gaud.* II, 3. See also *C. Cresc.* II, xxxviii, 48.

[9] Matt. xiii. 24–30, 36–43.

image of the vessels unto honour and dishonour,[1] as applying to the condition of the Church Militant. Wheat and tares must remain together until the final harvest; the worthless vessels must not be smashed by human hands; and thus the separation of good and evil in the Church must, in spite of the impatience of man, await the time appointed by God. Saint Cyprian's was the first exposition of these passages of Scripture as presenting the type of the conditions of Church society; but it is easy to see how natural it was for Saint Augustine to take this presentation as the basis of his answer to the Donatist challenge and claim to holiness.

The Decian persecution, at its height at Carthage about the same time as the schism of Novatian at Rome, that is about 250, brought to the fore the question of martyrdom. Novatian is spoken of by Cyprian as a distinguished confessor.[2] What was to be the Church's answer to the claim of such a man to the crown of martyrdom, if, while a schismatic, he were called upon to die for the faith? Saint Cyprian applied the principle of ecclesiastical unity which has been outlined, and answered that those who lapsed under the stress of persecution might be reconciled by the imposition of hands; but that those who by schism had already severed themselves from the Church could lay no claim to the martyr's glory if they should die.[3] Unity is paramount: a man outside the unity has not charity, and so hates his brother, and he that hates his brother is a murderer.[4] For such a man death is not the crown of the martyr's glory, but the penalty of perfidy.[5] Nothing could be a closer

[1] II Tim. ii. 20.   [2] Cypr. *De unit.* XVII, XX, XXI.
[3] Cypr. *De lapsis*, VIII et passim; *Ep.* LIX, 13; *De unit.* XIX, 17: 'et cum lapsus semel peccauerit, ille quotidie peccat. postremo lapsus martyrium postmodum consecutus potest regni promissa percipere; ille si extra ecclesiam fuerit occisus, ad ecclesiae non potest praemia peruenire.' See Benson, op. cit. pp. 60–101.
[4] Cypr. *De orat. dom.* XXIV.
[5] Cypr. *De unit.* XIV, 12: 'tales etiamsi occisi in confessione nominis fuerint, macula ista nec sanguine abluitur; inexpiabilis et grauis culpa discordiae nec passione purgatur. esse martyr non potest, qui in ecclesia non est; ad regnum peruenire non poterit, qui eam, quae regnatura est, dereliquit. pacem nobis Christus dedit, concordes atque unanimes esse praecepit, dilectionis et caritatis foedera incorrupta atque inuiolata seruari mandauit: exhibere se non potest martyrem, qui fraternam non tenuit caritatem. docet hoc et contestatur Paulus apostolus dicens: Et si habuero fidem...caritas nunquam excidit (I Cor. xiii. 2–5, 7, 8). numquam, inquit, excidit caritas. haec enim semper in regno erit, haec in aeternum fraternitatis sibi cohaerentis unitate durabit...cum Deo manere non possunt, qui esse in ecclesia unanimes noluerunt. ardeant licet flammis et ignibus traditi uel obiecti bestiis animas suas ponant, non erit illa fidei corona, sed poena perfidiae, nec religiosae uirtutis exitus gloriosus, sed desperationis interitus. occidi talis potest, coronari non potest.' See also *Ep.* LV, 17; LX, 4.

parallel in thought than Cyprian's 'occidi talis potest, non coronari' and Augustine's 'martyres ueros non facit poena sed causa'.[1]

Saint Cyprian invests the Christian bishop with all the powers entrusted to the high priest under the old dispensation.[2] Hence the lapsed or schismatic bishop is prohibited from all sacred functions (and especially from offering the Eucharist) by the Mosaic statute against uncleanness, and his communicants are similarly tainted with his sin.[3] He has, moreover, cut himself off from the holy people. Saint Cyprian reminds his opponents (as Saint Augustine was later to remind the Donatists) that the punishment for the schismatics of the Old Testament, Korah, Dathan, and Abiram, was that they should be engulfed alive by the earth.[4] There is for Saint Cyprian no distinction between invalid and irregular ministrations: every sacrament can be conferred only within the Church, and if the minister has severed himself from the Church by heresy, schism, or unworthiness of life, then he has nothing that he can confer.[5] The Donatists founded their whole schism upon a rigid application of this principle in their own favour, and Augustine discovered his answer to them in enforcing the distinction between invalidity and irregularity.

Such is the clear-cut and rigid conception of ecclesiastical unity which Saint Cyprian bequeathed to the Church. Its advantages are obvious. It provides a ready standard by which the validity of ministrations may be judged, and it bears witness to the fervour with which Saint Cyprian, like other doctors of the primitive Church, believed in the Church as the sole fountain of divine grace. It is stringently logical to hold that only within the fold of Christ can the sheep be fed; and the Cyprianic scheme avoids all the difficulties of application inherent in the more subtle doctrine of Saint Augustine. Strong in theory, however, it was quite likely in practice, as Canon Lacey has pointed out,[6] to lead to schism through disagreement between groups of bishops. So long as all bishops were agreed on vital matters, the scheme would work. It is true that Saint Cyprian, at the council of September 256, allowed the

[1] Cypr. *De unit.* XIV, 12; Aug. *Ep.* LXXXIX, 2.
[2] Note that Cyprian constantly uses *sacerdos* of bishops, and *presbyter* of priests.
[3] Cypr. *Ep.* LXV, 2; LXVII, 1, 9; Benson, op. cit. pp. 33, 34. This equation of the Christian bishop with the Jewish priest appealed very strongly to the Donatists.
[4] Cypr. *De unit.* XVIII, 16; *Ep.* LXXIII, 8: 'quod supplicium manet eos qui alienam aquam baptismo inferunt falso, ut diuina censura ulciscatur et uindicet id haereticos contra ecclesiam gerere quod non nisi soli licet ecclesiae.'
[5] Swete, op. cit. pp. 232, 233.
[6] T. A. Lacey, op. cit. pp. 26–48; Appendix II, pp. 168 sqq.

possibility of certain African dioceses going their own way in the matter of rebaptism; but in fact none of them did so, and, had any done so, very inconvenient practical problems would have arisen. Cyprian feels very strongly, as we see from his letters on the subject, the great inconveniences of a divergent view at Rome; and he stresses the importance of episcopal unanimity on this and other matters.[1] If the Cyprianic doctrine would safeguard the Church against external schism by simply treating schismatics as apostates, it would provide no solution of the graver problem of groups of bishops divided against one another. It is scarcely an exaggeration to say that the Donatist schism could never have been healed if Saint Augustine and his contemporaries had stood firm upon the strict principles enunciated by Saint Cyprian.

Secondly, the insistence of Saint Cyprian on the complete autonomy of every bishop, and his entire liberty to administer his own diocese without reference to the remainder of the Church, is hard to justify. It was easy for him to say that his own judgement as Bishop of Carthage could not constrain the bishop of the smallest diocese in remote Mauretania, and that the sees of Carthage and of Rome could be administered on inconsistent principles with regard to baptism. In fact, primacies of honour, if not of jurisdiction, are bound to arise. Rome and Carthage, Alexandria and Constantinople, are but four cases of metropolitical sees acquiring an importance quite their own and establishing a *de facto* leadership in ecclesiastical politics, especially if their occupants are men of outstanding ability.

Thirdly, we must ask how far it was proper to invest the Christian episcopate with the authority of the Jewish priesthood. It may be felt that Saint Cyprian pressed his case too far in this matter, and that there is insufficient support for it in the little which the New Testament has to say concerning the Christian Ministry.

Saint Cyprian's practical contribution, therefore, to the early doctrine of the Church and Ministry lay not so much in the exaltation of the episcopate against the Papacy on the one hand, and the presbyterate on the other, as in the breadth of charity with which he propounded his views. Saint Augustine hardly ever mentions the teaching of Saint Cyprian without putting before the Donatist controversialists the charitableness of Cyprian's approach, or without praising the great African bishop in terms of admiration and affection. He never fails to render homage to Saint Cyprian, who, as Archbishop Benson well says, was tempted into the noble, and, alas, too fruitful error of arraying the Visible Church in attributes of the Church Invisible. But he said and showed how men

[1] Lightfoot, op. cit. p. 96.

DOCTRINE OF THE CHURCH

might gravely dissent without one wound to peace. He spoke a watchword of comprehension which, for lack of the charity which possessed him, we do not receive in the churches, although it must needs precede the unity we dream of.[1]

And Saint Cyprian's thought was summed by Saint Augustine, and 'rounded into one exact and perfect phrase'—*saluo iure communionis diuersa sentire*—on which Dr Benson comments: 'He means that schools of thought are not communions.'[2]

'I will learn,' exclaims Augustine, 'if I can, from Cyprian's writings, assisted by his prayers, with what peace and what consolation the Lord governed his Church through him';[3] and no higher praise can be bestowed upon Cyprian for his life's work for unity than the radiant phrase of Saint Gregory Nazianzen:

τὸ μεμνῆσθαι τοῦ ἀνδρὸς ἁγιασμός.[4]

The episcopal theory of ecclesiastical government taught by Saint Cyprian became standard in Africa until the time when Saint Optatus, Bishop of Milevis, prepared the way for Saint Augustine in his work on the Donatist schism published in the middle of the fourth century. But as far back as the days of Saint Cyprian, a hundred years earlier than this, an interesting adumbration of the theory of a Visible and Invisible Church which was destined to serve Saint Augustine so well in solving the disciplinary difficulty raised by Donatism appeared in the work of the anonymous author of the treatise on rebaptism.[5] Dr Benson identifies this work, so long preserved among the Cyprianic writings, with the epistle enclosed by Iubaianus in a letter to Cyprian.[6] This *Auctor de Rebaptismate*, arguing against the strict Cyprianic view that there is but one baptism, and that within the true Church, suggests that the operation of God cannot be so confined, and that his grace may flow even outside the Church.[7] It is only a suggestion, and he does not pursue it, or apparently realize its full value in the baptismal controversy. It remained for Saint Augustine to expand and enrich the thought that God has not bound his operations within the sacramental system of his Church.

---

[1] Benson, op. cit. p. 9.
[2] Ibid. p. 533.
[3] Aug. *De bapt.* v, xvii, 23; *Serm.* CCCXII, 6.
[4] Greg. Naz. *Or.* XXIV, vii.
[5] See Benson, op. cit. pp. 390–9, 416–21.
[6] Cypr. *Ep.* LXXIII, 4; Benson, op. cit. pp. 398, 399.
[7] *Auctor de Rebaptismate*, x: 'uirorum optime, reddamus et permittamus uirtutibus caelestibus uires suas, et dignationi diuinae maiestatis concedamus operationes proprias, et intelligentes quantum in ea sit emolumentum libenter ei adquiescamus.' See Benson, op. cit. pp. 416–18.

We have already noticed [1] the use which Saint Augustine made of the work of Saint Optatus in the historical background of his case against Donatism. But Optatus also provided the link between Saint Cyprian and Saint Augustine in the development of the doctrine of the Church, Ministry and sacraments. The special importance of the work of Optatus lies in the fact that he was the only Catholic Father before Augustine to examine these doctrines in the light of the Donatist challenge.

He more or less accepts the Cyprianic view of schism as being equivalent to apostasy. For Saint Cyprian there was no true schism at all, in the sense of a rent in the Body of Christ. Those who set up a church or altar or priesthood against the Catholic Church of Christ were to be compared with branches which cut themselves off from the tree through which they must necessarily derive their life. The tree still remains a tree; and the branch which is cut off withers and perishes: the tree itself—the Catholic Church—cannot be said in any true sense to be rent. In the very words used by Saint Cyprian, Saint Optatus says that schismatics are branches broken off from the vine, or a river severed from its source.[2] He condemns them, as Saint Cyprian had done, in the words of Jeremiah,[3] for leaving the fountain of living water, and digging for themselves cisterns which cannot hold water.[4] Like Saint Cyprian, he uses the text of the Song of Songs: 'una est dilecta mea, una est sponsa mea, una est columba mea.'[5]

Saint Augustine quotes the same passage of Jeremiah in two contexts,[6] but he is not prepared to go all the way with Saint Cyprian and Saint Optatus. The schismatics are not for him heretics (this distinction was made by Saint Optatus but not by Saint Cyprian), although he allows that inveterate schism may become heresy; and when schismatics are reconciled to the Church their baptism (and other sacraments) are not to be reiterated, but can revive, and for the first time become profitable to salvation.[7] This solution was made possible for Augustine by his

---

[1] Supra, pp. 24, 25.
[2] Opt. II, 9: 'intelligite uel sero uos esse filios impios, uos esse fractos ramos ab arbore, uos esse abscisos palmites a uite, uos riuum concisum a fonte. non enim potest origo esse riuus, qui paruus est et non de se nascitur, aut arbor a ramo concidi, cum arbor fundata suis radicibus haeret, et ramus, si fuerit exsectus, arescat.'
[3] Jer. ii. 13.
[4] Opt. IV, 9: 'dereliquerunt fontem aquae uiuae, et effossos ac detritos sibi fecerunt lacus.'
[5] Opt. II, 13. [6] Aug. De unit. eccl. XXV, 74; C. Ep. Parm. II, x, 20.
[7] Opt. I, 10: 'et cum...uos heredes traditorum et schismaticorum esse euidenter adpareat, satis te miror, frater Parmeniane, cum schismaticus sis

introduction into Western theology of a distinction between the irregularity and the invalidity of sacraments. Nevertheless, there are traces in his works of the old view of the disastrous spiritual effects of being in schism. Those men are children of the Devil, he says, who slay men by seducing them from the Church.[1] And this sacrilegious murder of a soul by schism is so much the more deadly by reason of the fact that men do not realize how much worse it is than the murder of the body.[2] Most striking of all is a passage in the work *Contra Faustum Manichaeum*, written about 400.[3]

But for Saint Optatus as well as for Saint Augustine schism is above all else the negation of charity: 'schisma...liuore nutritur, aemulatione et litibus roboratur.'[4] The mouth of schismatics is full of cursing and bitterness, and their feet are swift to shed blood.[5] They are reminded of Saint Paul's warning to the Corinthians[6] that self-sacrifice, even martyrdom, without charity, is useless in God's sight.[7] Saint Augustine also quotes this,[8] and for him schism is the work of the Devil,[9] and the expression of pride,[10] and of sacrilege,[11] for it divides the Body of Christ *nefaria separatione*. Christian charity can only flourish within the unity of the Christian Church.[12] Both Saint Optatus and Saint Augustine warn their opponents that the divine punishment for schism under the

schismaticos haereticis iungere uoluisse...quare paeniteat te talibus hominibus [sc. haereticis] etiam schismaticos adiunxisse: in te enim conuertisti sententiae gladium, cum existimas, quia alteros adpetebas, et non adtendisti inter schismaticos et haereticos quam sit magna distantia.' Cf. Aug. *Ep.* CXLI, 5.

[1] Aug. *C. Litt. Pet.* II, xiii: 'diaboli ergo filii sunt, qui homines ab ecclesia seducendo interficiunt.' See also ibid. II, xv.

[2] Aug. *C. Ep. Parm.* I, viii, 4: 'nam si sanguis exit de carne mortali, quisquis aspicit exhorrescit; si a pace Christi praecisae animae atque separatae in haeresis uel schismatis sacrilegio moriuntur, quia non uidetur, non plangitur, immo uero mors taetrior atque luctuosior, et, ut plane dixerim, uerior, iure consuetudinis deridetur....'

[3] Aug. *C. Faustum*, XII, xx: 'quod post dies quadraginta emissus coruus non est reuersus...significat homines immunditia cupiditatis teterrimos, et ob hoc ad ea quae foris sunt in hoc mundo nimis intentos, aut rebaptizari aut ab his quos praeter arcam, id est praeter ecclesiam, Baptismus occidit, seduci et teneri.'

[4] Opt. I, 11. [5] Opt. II, 25.
[6] I Cor. xiii. 3. [7] Opt. III, 8.
[8] Aug. *Ep.* CLXXXIII, 6; *De bapt.* I, ix, 12; *Ep.* CLXXXV, x, 43.
[9] Aug. *De bapt.* I, ii, 2: 'diabolica dissensio'.
[10] Aug. *Ps. c. part. Donati*, v. 116: 'sed superbia uos alligauit in cathedra pestilentiae.'
[11] Aug. *C. Ep. Parm.* II, xii, 25; *De bapt.* I, xi, 16; II, xii, 4; *C. Litt. Pet.* III, lviii; *Ep.* XLIII, viii, 21; LXI, 2; *Serm.* XC; CCLXV, ix, 11.
[12] Aug. *De unico bapt.* XV, 25: 'caritas ista non tenetur nisi in unitate ecclesiae.'

Old Covenant, as seen in the case of Korah, Dathan and Abiram, was that the offenders were swallowed up alive by the earth.[1] In Christian times schism results in the absurdity of erecting altar against altar, and of setting up bishop against bishop in the same see.[2]

How then is the true Church to be recognized? Saint Optatus proposes two tests: the possession of the Catholic sacraments[3] and the universal extension of the true Church throughout all the world, not confined to any one country, as it is on the Donatist thesis.[4] On either of these tests Donatism is seen not to be the true Church. The first of these lines of thought is not very strongly represented in Saint Augustine's works, but on the second he frequently lays emphasis.[5] The very fact of the division from Catholic unity is a proof that a body is not part of the true Church: 'securus iudicat orbis terrarum bonos non esse qui se diuidunt ab orbe terrarum in quacunque parte terrarum.'[6] For this cause he urged the Donatists to return to the only true fold.[7]

And, as there is but one Church, so there is but one episcopate. This unity of the episcopate is shown by communion with Saint Peter's chair at Rome,[8] and with the seven Churches of Asia which were addressed by the author of the Apocalypse.[9]

The Donatists were accustomed to defend their attitude by saying that they felt it their duty to separate themselves from the Church of the *traditores*, and to maintain a church whose members were holy and pure. Saint Optatus and Saint Augustine answer this by suggesting that such claim to holiness is forbidden by the words of the Lord's Prayer concerning forgiveness,[10] and by other texts, for instance I John i. 8;[11] and Saint Augustine says that if the Donatist church is pure, then it is better than the undivided Church of Saint Cyprian's day.[12]

---

[1] Opt. I, 21: 'tartareo carcere subito clausi ante sunt sepulti quam mortui'; Opt. V, 3; Aug. *Ep.* LXXXVII, 4; XCIII, ix, 28; *De bapt.* II, vi, 9.

[2] Opt. I, 15; Aug. *Ps. c. part. Donati, vv.* 24, 73, 109; *C. Ep. Parm.* II, v, 10; *C. Cresc.* IV, viii, 8; *Serm.* CCCLIX, 5.

[3] Opt. II, 1.

[4] Ibid. II, 1, 11; III, 9.

[5] E.g. Aug. *Ep.* XLIII, ix, 25; XCIII, vi, 20, ix, 28; *De unit. eccl.* VIII, 20–2; *C. Litt. Pet.* III, l, 62; *C. Ep. Parm.* II, i, 2, ii, 5.

[6] Aug. *C. Ep. Parm.* II, iv, 24.

[7] Aug. *C. Litt. Pet.* II, xcvii: 'corrigimini, redite ad hanc euidentissimam totius orbis unitatem.'

[8] Opt. I, 10; II, 2, 3; Aug. *Ep.* LIII, i, 2; *Ps. c. part. Donati, vv.* 229–31; *C. Cresc.* II, xxxvii, 46.

[9] Opt. II, 6; IV, 3; VI, 3; Aug. *C. Cresc.* II, xxxvii, 46; IV, xxv, 32.

[10] Opt. II, 20; Aug. *C. Ep. Parm.* II, x, 20.   [11] Opt. II, 20.

[12] Aug. *C. Ep. Parm.* III, ii, 8.

DOCTRINE OF THE CHURCH

In any case, it is not possible for human judgement to separate wheat from tares in this life; that must be left for the final judgement of Christ.[1]

This impossibility of pronouncing a final judgement on men implies that we must reject the Donatist thesis that sacraments derive their validity from the holiness of him by whose ministry they are conferred —'hoc munus baptismatis esse dantis non accipientis'. This maxim, says Saint Optatus, is true if it be applied to God, the giver of all sacramental grace, but not if applied to the human minister.[2] The part of the recipient is that he should receive in faith, and in baptism, which is administered not in the name of the minister, but of the Blessed Trinity, the gift is good—as being God's gift—whether the minister be good or evil.[3] Whoever plants and whoever waters, it is God who gives the increase.[4] The Donatists here relied on Saint Cyprian's teaching for their doctrine of the sacraments, and Saint Augustine feels it necessary to show why Saint Cyprian and others erred on this matter. It is because they failed to distinguish between the sacrament itself, which is the gift of God, and the use and effect of the sacrament, which depends upon the disposition of the man who receives it. Hence they erroneously concluded that because the effects—namely deliverance from sin and rectitude of heart—were not to be found with heretics and schismatics, therefore they possessed no sacrament.[5]

Saint Optatus goes further than this, and with Saint Cyprian teaches that schismatic sacraments have an actively defiling effect upon the recipient.[6] But Saint Augustine denies this. If the Church really perishes through the contamination of sinners, conveyed by the sacraments, then, he says, it would have perished already in the days of Saint Cyprian, through the schisms of that time; and there would in that case have been no Church left from which the Donatists could

---

[1] Opt. VII, 2; Aug. *Ep.* XXIII; XLIII, viii, 21; LXXVI, 2, 3; *Ps. c. part. Donati*, vv. 139, 183–94; *De unit. eccl.* XIV, 35; XVI, 43; *De unico bapt.* XVII, 12; *C. Ep. Parm.* I, vii, 12; *C. Cresc.* II, xxxiv, 43, xxxv, 44, xxxvi, 45; III, xxxv, 39, l, 55; IV, xxvi, 33, liv, 67, lxi, 74.

[2] Opt. v, 7.   [3] Opt. v, 7, 12.

[4] Opt. v, 7.

[5] Aug. *C. Cresc.* IV, xi, 14; III, v, 5; *Ep.* CV, iii, 12; LXXXIX, 5; XCIII, xi, 48; *Serm.* XCIX, xiii, 13; CCLXVI, 3; *De unit. eccl.* XXI, 58; *C. Litt. Pet.* II, cviii; III, xxxv, xlix; *C. Ep. Parm.* II, xiv, 32; III, xlii; and the whole of *De baptismo c. Donatistas* and *De unico baptismo*.

[6] Opt. IV, 6: 'audit ergo Deus iniurias non sibi debitas, et huiusmodi habitaculum deserit; et homo qui Deo plenus in ecclesiam intrauerat, egreditur uas inane'; ibid. v, 3: 'dum lauant, sordidant'; 'tales sunt, quos aut rebaptizatione aut poenitentia sauciastis.'

take their origin.¹ The evil do indeed receive the sacraments, but they do not receive the salvation which those sacraments are designed to confer.² Those who in ignorance receive sacraments from the Donatists are not indeed so deeply implicated in guilt as those who wilfully separate themselves from the true Church, but they do not escape the spiritual injury which is inflicted by the sacrilege of schism.³

An important Donatist charge refuted by both Saint Optatus and Saint Augustine was that it was improper for the Church to appeal to the State against the Donatists. They are both able to remind their Donatist opponents that it was they themselves who began this at the onset of the schism by appealing to Constantine.⁴ Saint Augustine further says that the appeal to the State is for the defence of Church property and the persons of ecclesiastics against the violent outrages of the Donatists (which are related by both Optatus and Augustine);⁵ and that it is part of the business of Christian rulers to repress schisms and heresies, which slay men's souls, with the same severity that they use against those acts of violence which slay men's bodies.⁶

We must now inquire how Saint Augustine amplified the existing teaching on Church, Ministry and sacraments in answer to his Donatist opponents.

EXCURSUS

SAINT CYPRIAN AND THE ROMAN PRIMACY

Dr Benson's exposition of the Cyprianic opinion on the primacy of Rome is here accepted, as such is undoubtedly the final doctrine of Cyprian on the matter. But his exposition of the notorious divergence of the two ancient texts of the fourth chapter and the beginning of the fifth chapter of the *De unitate* has been strongly challenged during the present century. The main authorities are as follows:

¹ Aug. *De bapt.* v, i, 1; and see the whole of *De bapt.* vi and vii, where the question is fully discussed.
² Ibid. vii, xxxiii, 65.
³ Ibid. i, v, 6: 'illi uero qui per ignorantiam ibi [sc. in parte Donati] baptizantur, arbitrantes ipsam esse ecclesiam Christi, in istorum quidem comparatione minus peccant, sacrilegio tamen schismatis uulnerantur non ideo non grauiter quod alii grauius.'
⁴ Opt. I, 22; Aug. *Ep.* CLXXXV, ii, 6; *C. Cresc.* III, xliv, 48; *C. Ep. Parm.* I, x, 16, xi, 17.
⁵ Aug. *Ep.* CV, ii, 3; CLXXXV, vii, 25; CCIV, 4.
⁶ Ibid. XCIII, v, 19: 'immo uero seruiant reges terrae Christo, etiam leges ferendo pro Christo'; ibid. CCIV, 4: 'docuimus...pertinere ad religiosos reges terrae, non solum adulteria...uerum etiam sacrilegia seueritate congrua cohibere.'

E. W. BENSON, *Cyprian, his Life, his Times, his Work* (London, 1897), pp. 200–21, 537–40, 544–52.

H. B. SWETE (ed.), *Early History of the Church and the Ministry* (London, 1921), Essay IV, J. H. Bernard, 'The Cyprianic Doctrine of the Ministry', pp. 250–3.

T. A. LACEY, *Unity and Schism*, Bishop Paddock Lectures, 1917 (London, 1917), pp. 168–96.

JOHN CHAPMAN, 'Les interpolations dans le traité de S. Cyprien sur l'Unité de l'Église', in *Revue Bénédictine* (Maredsous, 1902–3), pp. 246–54, 357–73 (1902); pp. 16–51 (1903); and in *Journal of Theological Studies* (London, 1902 3), pp. 103 23.

HUGO KOCH, 'Cyprian und der Römische Primat', in *Texte und Untersuchungen* (Leipzig, 1910), XXXV.

MAURICE BÉVENOT, 'Saint Cyprian's *De Unitate*, Chapter IV, in the light of the manuscripts', in *Analecta Gregoriana* (Rome, 1938), vol. XI, Series Facultatis Theologicae, Sectio B, N. 5.

T. G. JALLAND, *The Church and the Papacy*, Bampton Lectures, 1942 (London, 1944), pp. 161–78.

To these dissertations the reader may be referred for the details of the manuscript evidence, and of its interpretation. We are not competent to discuss them here, but the following considerations may be advanced. Certain manuscripts, although not the oldest, bear witness to a version of chapter IV of the *De unitate* which diverges widely from the received text. The *textus receptus* may be read in Hartel's edition in the Vienna Corpus,[1] and the interpolated text (called the 'Primacy text' because of its exaltation of the primacy of the see of Rome) in the edition of the Abbé Migne.[2] This Primacy text is very ancient, and was quoted as early as the sixth century (between 584 and 589) by Pelagius II. Dom Chapman and Father Bévenot hold that both versions came from Cyprian's own hand, though neither of them is able to cite any references earlier than that of Pelagius II, and though Dr Harnack refused to believe that the interpolated text could in any case be traced back earlier than the fourth century. But Chapman and Bévenot differ one from another, the former holding that the *textus receptus* is prior, and the interpolation later, the latter the reverse. Their sole argument for the Cyprianic authorship of both versions rests upon internal evidence, not entirely cogent. And the disagreement of those who argue solely from internal evidence is, as Dr Bernard has shown,[3] liable to be violent. Fr Bévenot sets out to establish the truth by a re-examination of the many available manuscripts. Yet he is unable to produce any evidence which would clearly establish the priority of the Primacy text which he holds; he merely assures us that its language is Cyprianic. That is exactly what a forger would have taken care to ensure. And moreover he confesses in the introduction to his paper[4] that he has been unable to collate some of the

---

[1] C.S.E.L. Cyprian, vol. III, pt. i.   [2] *P.L.* IV, 512 sq.
[3] Swete, op. cit. p. 252.   [4] Bévenot, op. cit. p. i.

manuscripts either personally or from photographs, and that 'for others time and other circumstances allowed him only to make the collation without studying the codices as a whole, or recording peculiarities of script, headings, incipits, etc. Unfortunately this is particularly true of the manuscripts in England.' But it happens that these manuscripts are of great importance,[1] and we are not entirely solaced by the writer's optimistic appendix to this confession, that he 'is convinced that further study will only provide confirmation of the main conclusions arrived at here on the origin of the different versions'. His enthusiasm for the cause that he has undertaken leads him later[2] to abuse Dr Benson for the virulence of his attack on the Roman forgeries. 'No one made more capital out of it than Archbishop Benson in his *Cyprian*....The duplicity, insincerity, hypocrisy of the Church of Rome in imposing forgeries on the world were laid bare in true pamphleteering style.' If Archbishop Benson's opinions were correct, it is clear that Roman Catholic scholars through the ages have had an obvious interest in perpetrating such forgeries, and the imposing list of such falsities officially encouraged or countenanced by the Roman see which was compiled by Dr Robertson[3] would be sufficient to make us wonder whether they would have hesitated to manipulate the text of Cyprian. The erudition of Chapman and Bévenot has been insufficient to undermine Dr Benson's view (which is also that of Dr Koch, himself a Roman Catholic scholar); and perhaps the best summary of the whole dispute is still that of Archbishop Bernard:[4] 'The difficulty of accepting the disputed or alternative text as Cyprian's is simply this, that *prima facie* its argument is quite unlike anything that Cyprian says elsewhere. At two points especially it has not the true Cyprianic ring. First, the argument that the significance of Matthew xvi. 18 depends on the fact that the Church is built on *one* man is absent, and in its place is substituted the wholly different argument that the Lord's words indicate a peculiar authority for Peter personally and for the see of Peter. It is one of the characteristics of Cyprian's exposition, often repeated, of the Lord's promise to Peter, that he does not take this line, and it is highly suspicious that such an exegesis should be found here, and here only, in the writings ascribed to him. And secondly, the assertion made at the close that whoever deserts the see of Peter deserts the Church of Christ, is an assertion which it would have been wholly inconsistent for Cyprian to have made at any stage in his career. His unchanging doctrine is that the unity of the Church is to be found in the consensus of the collective episcopate, and not necessarily in communion with the Roman See. Despite the care that has been taken by the author of the "interpolation" to use phrases of Cyprianic origin, the tenor of the argument is so unlike Cyprian's general teaching that internal evidence concurs with manuscript authority in rejecting the whole passage.'

[1] Benson, op. cit. pp. 548–52.
[2] Bévenot, op. cit. p. 4.
[3] A. Robertson, *Regnum Dei*, Bampton Lectures, 1901 (London, 1901), p. 232, n. 2.   [4] Swete, op. cit. pp. 252–3.

2. Saint Augustine on the Church and Ministry

The doctrinal aspect of the Donatist controversy may be said to turn upon the answer given to the question 'What is the true Church?', for the sacraments, about which there was much dispute, are Christ's: he instituted them, and they are administered through his Body the Church. The Church throughout the world is, in Saint Augustine's thought, the inheritance of Christ, and whosoever is not in communion with this inheritance disinherits himself. Whoso fights against this inheritance acknowledges himself a stranger to the household of God.[1] This was, of course, common ground to all Christians: their disputes were concerned with the problem where this one Church was to be found. Any body which could establish its claim to be that one Church automatically disinherited all other bodies. It will be most convenient to consider Saint Augustine's doctrine of the Church under the heads of its four notes, unity, holiness, catholicity and apostolicity; and then to contrast his theory with that of Saint Cyprian.[2]

(a) *Unity*

Christ prayed before his Passion that his Church might be one,[3] and therefore schism, the rending of that unity, is repugnant to him, and a crime in those who wilfully separate themselves from his Church, and set up their own judgement in opposition to the mind of that Church.[4] There is only one Christ, and only one Bride of Christ.[5] What is outside that unity is outside the Body of Christ. First of all the Church is the unity of the faith,[6] and breach of this leads to heresy.[7] Secondly, it is the unity of charity, the mutual love which binds its

---

[1] Aug. *Ep.* XLIII, ix, 25: 'huic haereditati qui non communicat...exhaeredatum se esse cognoscat. hanc haereditatem quisquis expugnat, alienum se esse a familia Dei satis indicat.'

[2] On Augustine's theory of the Church, see Thomas Specht, *Die Lehre von der Kirche nach dem h. Augustin* (Paderborn, 1892), especially pp. 268–82, 288–94, 294–313; Hermann Reuter, *Augustinische Studien* (Gotha, 1887), especially Studien III und V, pp. 106–52, 231–358; A. Harnack, *History of Dogma* (E.T.) (London, 1898), pp. 140–68; A. Robertson, *Regnum Dei* (London, 1901), pp. 194–205; J. Tixeront, *Histoire des Dogmes*, tome II, ch. X; Swete, *Early History of the Church and the Ministry* (London, 1921), passim.

[3] John xvii. 21, 23. [4] Aug. *Ep.* LXXXIX, 4, 6.

[5] Aug. *Enarr. in Ps.* LXXXVIII, serm. II, 14; *Serm.* CXCII, 2; *C. Faustum*, XV, 3.

[6] Aug. *De ciu. Dei*, XVIII, li, 1.

[7] Aug. *De util. cred.* 20, 21; *Ep.* CXVIII, v, 32: 'porro illi qui cum in unitate atque communione catholica non sint, christiano tamen nomine gloriantur, coguntur aduersari credentibus, et audent imperitos quasi ratione traducere, quando maxime cum ista medicina Dominus uenerit, ut fidem populis imperaret.'

members in one, and the rending of this unity is schism.¹ A man may indeed preserve his faith pure, and thus avoid heretical error, and yet offend against the unity of charity by being a schismatic.² This was the position of the Donatists.³ Hence the belief of Augustine is that the principle of Catholic unity is the Holy Spirit, who is also the bond of the unity of the Godhead in Trinity; and this unity of the Church is organic and not institutional, an unity of faith and hope and charity. Its bond is the *caritas unitatis*, without which no man can please God.⁴ Even martyrdom for the faith will not save a man who has rejected this unity.⁵

¹ Aug. *Serm.* CCLXV, vi, 7: 'in ueste illa (u. Joan. xix. 23, 24) unitas commendata est, in illa ueste caritas praedicata est, ipsa est, desuper texta. de terra est cupiditas, desuper caritas.'

² Aug. *C. Litt. Pet.* II, xiii, 30: 'quaerimus autem unde fuerit diabolus homicida ab initio; et inuenimus, quod primum hominem occiderit, non gladium stringendo, aut aliquam uim corporaliter inferendo; sed persuadendo peccatum, et a paradisi felicitate deiiciendo. quod tunc paradisus, hoc nunc ecclesia. diaboli ergo filii sunt qui homines ab ecclesia seducendo interficiunt. sicut ergo per uerba Dei nouimus ubi sit plantatus paradisus, sic per uerba Christi ubi sit ecclesia didicimus: per omnes, inquit, gentes, incipiens ab Ierusalem. ab isto uniuerso ad partem quamlibet quisquis separat hominem, ille diaboli filius et homicida conuincitur.'

³ Aug. *C. Cresc.* I, xxix, 34: 'non autem existimo quemquam ita desipere, ut credat ad ecclesiae pertinere unitatem eum qui non habet caritatem. sicut ergo Deus unus colitur ignoranter etiam extra ecclesiam, nec ideo non est ipse, et fides una habetur sine caritate etiam extra ecclesiam, nec ideo non est ipsa. unus enim Deus, una fides, unum baptisma, una incorrupta catholica ecclesia, non in qua sola unus Deus colitur, sed in qua sola unus Deus pie colitur, nec in qua sola una fides retinetur, sed in qua sola una fides cum caritate retinetur, nec in qua sola unus baptismus habetur, sed in qua sola unus baptismus salubriter habetur.' *C. Litt. Pet.* II, lxxvii, 172: 'caritas enim christiana nisi in unitate ecclesiae non potest custodiri, etsi baptismum et fidem teneatis.'

⁴ Aug. *De unit. eccl.* IV, 7: 'totus Christus caput et corpus est. caput unigenitus Dei Filius et corpus eius ecclesia, sponsus et sponsa, duo in carne una. quicumque de ipso capite ab Scripturis sanctis dissentiunt, etiamsi in omnibus locis inueniantur in quibus ecclesia designata est, non sunt in ecclesia. et rursus quicumque de ipso capite Scripturis sanctis consentiunt, et unitati ecclesiae non communicant, non sunt in ecclesia; quia de Christi corpore, quod est ecclesia, ab ipsius Christi testificatione dissentiunt...etiamsi per omnes terras inueniantur per quas est ecclesia, non utique sunt in ecclesia: quia ipsum caput ecclesiae non tenent, quod est Christus Iesus...item, quicumque credunt quidem quod Christus Iesus...in carne uenerit...sed tamen ab eius corpore, quod est ecclesia, ita dissentiunt, ut eorum communio non sit cum toto quacumque diffunditur, sed in aliqua parte separata inueniatur; manifestum est eos non esse in catholica ecclesia.' Aug. *De ciu. Dei*, XXI, 25; *De peccat. mer. et remiss.* I, 59; *Serm.* CCCLIV, 1.

⁵ Aug. *Ep.* CLXXIII, 6: 'foris ab ecclesia constitutus et separatus a compagine unitatis et uinculo caritatis aeterno supplicio punireris, etiamsi pro Christi nomine uiuus incenderis.'

Of this charity shown forth in unity schism is the antithesis: it rends the seamless robe of Christ.¹ Saint Augustine's charge against the Donatists is this: 'nos eis obiicimus furorem schismatis, rebaptizationis insaniam, ab hereditate Christi quae per omnes gentes diffusa est, nefariam separationem.'² These are strong words, the words of one who has the unity of the Church at heart, and feels the essential wickedness of schismatic exclusiveness.³ Schism is criminal because it is essentially sacrilegious, dividing the body of Christ *nefaria separatione*,⁴ and robbing God of his own children.⁵ It involves also the absurdity of erecting altar against altar,⁶ and of having two bishops in one see.⁷ Time and again Augustine warns his Donatist readers, as Optatus had done, of the punishment meted out under the Old Covenant to Korah, Dathan and Abiram for the same sin.⁸

Saint Augustine's approach to the question is thus deeper and more realistic than Saint Cyprian's: but how often does he turn aside from the course of his argument against the Donatists to praise Cyprian, and to exhort the Donatists to follow that love of unity which inspired him!⁹ For Augustine as for Cyprian, unity is the manifestation of charity¹⁰ and schism a sign of the service of the flesh, carnal-mindedness.¹¹ Brotherly love will indeed seek to correct the erring, but will not split the Body of Christ because that Body has not yet attained the perfection of its holiness.¹²

Saint Cyprian had taught that the sacraments of schismatics are not merely worthless, but actually sacrilegious, since they are an unreal

---

¹ Aug. *Serm.* CCLXV, vi, 7.   ² Aug. *Ep.* XLIII, viii, 21.

³ Aug. *De bapt.* V, ii, 2: 'diabolica dissensio'.

⁴ Aug. *Ep.* XLIII, viii, 21.

⁵ Ibid. LXXVI, 1: 'ut quid uos a totius orbis unitate nefario schismatis sacrilegio diuisistis?'; ibid. 2; ibid. CXLI, 5: '...hoc solo scelere quod a Christi unitate disiunctus est'; *De bapt.* I, xi, 16: 'nulli autem schismata facerent, si fraterno odio non excaecarentur.'

⁶ Aug. *Ps. c. part. Donati*, vv. 24, 73, 109; *C. Ep. Parm.* II, v, 10; *C. Cresc.* IV, viii, 8; cf. Opt. I, 15.

⁷ Aug. *Serm.* CCCLIX, 5.

⁸ Aug. *Ep.* XLIII, viii, 24; LI, 1; LXXXVII, 4; XCIII, ix, 28; CLXXXV, 43; *De bapt.* II, vi, 9; cf. Opt. I, 21; V, 3; and see Num. xvi. 31–5.

⁹ E.g. Aug. *C. Cresc.* II, xxxi, 39; *De bapt.* IV, viii, 11; V, ii, 2.

¹⁰ Aug. *De bapt.* I, ix, 12.

¹¹ Ibid. I, x, 14, xi, 16: 'audimus quippe Iohannem dicentem: Qui odit fratrem suum, in tenebris est usque adhuc. nulli autem schismata facerent, si fraterno odio non excaecarentur...an non est in schismate odium fraternum? quis hoc dixerit, cum et origo et pertinacia schismatis nulla sit alia nisi odium fratris?'; ibid. I, xvi, 23.

¹² Aug. *C. Ep. Parm.* III, ii, 9–16.

imitation of the real sacraments in the Church: to Saint Augustine himself, as we have seen, the schism itself is sacrilege. Schism could not have been sacrilege in Cyprian's eyes, for to break away from the Church is, in his view, to commit spiritual suicide, by severing oneself from the Body of Christ: it is pure apostasy. With Saint Augustine, on the other hand, schism is not thought of as automatically excluding a man from the Church, and leaving the Church as united as it was before: it is a true rending of the Body of Christ itself, and not only its authors, but the faithful part of the Church also, suffer by it. For this reason the only word which adequately describes it is 'sacrilege'. Augustine has better justification than Cyprian for applying to it the illustration of the rending of the seamless robe of Christ.[1] But even with Augustine there seems an echo of Cyprian's idea of spiritual suicide, for he says:

> si sanguis exit a carne mortali, quisquis aspicit exhorrescit; si a pace Christi praecisae animae atque separatae in haeresis uel schismatis sacrilegio moriuntur, quia non uidetur, non plangitur, immo uero mors taetrior atque luctuosior... nos corporum persecutores uocant, se animarum interfectores non uocant.[2]

One of Augustine's Donatist correspondents, Vincentius, chief bishop of the tiny Rogatist schism at Cartenna, is warned to save himself from the wrath which will come upon the obstinate and proud who harden themselves in schism. The promise of God is a blessing upon all nations of the earth:

> et benedicentur in ipso omnes tribus terrae; omnes gentes magnificabunt eum. benedictus Dominus Deus Israel, qui facit mirabilia solus; et benedictum nomen maiestatis eius in aeternum; et replebitur maiestate eius omnis terra.

And the Psalmist adds: 'fiat, fiat.' 'Et tu [sc. Vincentius] sedes Cartennis, et cum decem Rogatistis qui remansistis dicis: Non fiat, non fiat.'[3] More than this, not only is schism sacrilegious, but it is the sin against the Holy Ghost which has no forgiveness,[4] for no man can receive the Holy Ghost, or be a partaker of the divine love, who is not a member of the unity of Christ; for he may have faith, but outside the unity of Christ's Body it is impossible for him to possess charity.[5] Schism is the fruit of uncharitableness and hatred of the brethren, as unity is the

---

[1] Aug. *Serm.* CCLXV, 7.   [2] Aug. *C. Ep. Parm.* I, viii, 14.
[3] Aug. *Ep.* XCIII, 20; cf. Ps. lxxii. 17–19.
[4] Aug. *Ep.* CLXXXV, 48–50.
[5] Ibid. 51; *C. Cresc.* I, 34; *De unico bapt.* xv, 25: 'caritas ista non tenetur nisi in unitate ecclesiae.'

expression of brotherly love.[1] It is the outcome of pride, as unity is of humility.[2]

(b) *Holiness*

In the second note of the Church we touch the core of Donatist theology. The Body of Christ must be holy, on account of its intimate relation with him, and because it is indwelt by the sanctifying Spirit. It is only within the Church that individual Christians can attain personal holiness.[3] And yet they are not at present perfectly holy, although potentially so; or how could they continue to ask in the Lord's Prayer for forgiveness of their sins?[4] In God's house there are also vessels unto honour and vessels unto dishonour. The Church is a *corpus permixtum*, which must look forward to the last day for its perfection in holiness. The Donatists rejected this view of the holiness of the Church, and demanded an empirical sanctity here and now in every member of the true Church. As Cyprian had taught that the schismatic by his apostasy cuts himself off from the society of the faithful, so the Donatists, whose schism had arisen from the rigorist position adopted by some African Christians in the disciplinary problems raised by the last persecution, insisted that all members of the Church must be actually holy. But they warped this view, erroneous to begin with, by restricting the test of holiness to a mere assessment of a man's rectitude in the persecution of Diocletian. They attacked the clergy of the Catholic Church as being unholy, not because of any patent viciousness of life, but simply because they were held to be successors of those who had apostatized under Diocletian. They were *filii traditorum*, the Donatists said. We have seen that the Donatists were always unable to establish the guilt of Felix, the consecrator of Caecilianus, and that this subversion of their whole position at its very beginning had not hindered them from propagating their sect widely in Africa. But what was still more inconsistent with their principles was their approval of the Circumcellions, and their use of them; and the obvious and violent uncharitableness and cruelty with which they treated Catholic Christians. Unholiness of that kind was

[1] Aug. *De bapt.* I, ix, 12, x, 14, xi, 16, xvi, 23.
[2] Ibid. II, xii, 4: '...sine ullo tyfo sacrilegae superbiae, sine ulla inflata ceruice arrogantiae, sine ulla contentione liuidae inuidiae, cum sancta humilitate, cum pace catholica, cum caritate christiana'; *Ps. c. part. Donati*, v. 116: 'sed superbia uos ligauit in cathedra pestilentiae'; *C. Litt. Pet.* III, lviii: 'inmani separationis crimine maculamini.'
[3] Aug. *Serm.* IV, 11: 'omnes quotquot fuerunt sancti ad ipsam ecclesiam pertinent.'
[4] Aug. *C. Ep. Parm.* II, x, 20; cf. Opt. II, 20.

apparently no argument against a man's Christianity: the only crime that mattered was that of *traditio* in the persecution, and even that they were unable to prove against the Catholics.

In answer to such teaching Saint Augustine established the second note of the Church on a sound basis. It did not mean that all Christians were perfectly holy: it did mean that in the end all those who were not holy would be segregated with their father the Devil, although till the Judgement they must remain *congregationi sanctorum admixti*, as tares growing with the wheat until the time of the angelic harvest should come. Meanwhile the Church exercises her discipline (*correptio*) in the case of open and notorious evil-livers; and the occult sinner she leaves to the divine judgement.[1] But during this necessary interval of waiting, says Augustine, the good in the Church are not, as the Donatists held, contaminated by their admixture with the evil. The Church is always working for the sanctification of souls;[2] and, though it is a *corpus permixtum*, yet it has a fundamental bond of love.[3] The Church is not yet an *élite* of saints, as Donatism claimed to be: until the *consummatio saeculi* it will embrace both good and bad. But if the good are not contaminated by their association with the evil, no excuse is left for the rupture of the Church's unity over a question of discipline.[4] The *opus Dei* which is being constantly wrought out in the Church is the sanctification of souls, and to create schisms because this work is yet incomplete is merely to hinder its completion.[5] The Donatists are like tares which separate themselves from the wheat before the final harvest; for Christ said, 'The harvest is the end of the world', and not 'The harvest is the time of Donatus'.[6]

---

[1] Aug. *Serm.* LXXXVIII, xix, 22, xx, 23; CCXIV, 11; *Breu. Coll.* III, 20; *De bapt.* VII, li, 99.

[2] Aug. *De util. cred.* XXXV; *Enarr. in Ps.* LXXXIII, 7.

[3] Aug. *De bapt.* III, xix, 26: 'inuisibilis caritatis compago'; ibid. v, xxi, 29; *C. Litt. Pet.* II, cviii, 247: '(sacramenta) enim et in talibus sancta sunt, et in eis indigne tractantibus et sumentibus ad maius iudicium ualebunt. ipsi autem non sunt in ecclesiae compage, quae in membris Christi per connexum et contactum crescit in incrementum Dei.'

[4] Aug. *C. Ep. Parm.* I, i sq., iv, 6, xi, 12; II, i sq.; III, ii sq.; *C. Litt. Pet.* II, xx, 44, xxxii, 73; *De unit. eccl.* II, 2 sq.; *C. Cresc.* III, i, 2 sq.; IV, xviii, 21 sq.; *De unico bapt.* XV, 25 sq.; *Breu. Coll.* III, viii, 10, 11, ix, 15 sq.; *Ad Don. post Coll.* III, 3 sq.; XX, 28; XXVIII, 48 sq.

[5] Aug. *C. Cresc.* III, xxxv, 39: 'fugio paleam, ne hoc sim; non aream, ne nihil sim.'

[6] Aug. *Ep.* LXXVI, 2; see also *Ep.* XXIII; XLIII, viii, 21; LXXVI, 2, 3; *Ps. c. part. Donati*, vv. 139, 183–94; *De unit. eccl.* XIV, 35; XVI, 43; *De unico bapt.* XVII, 12; *C. Cresc.* II, xxxiv, 43, xxxv, 44, xxxvi, 45; III, l, 55; IV, xxvi, 33, liv, 67.

(c) *Catholicity*

The argument from catholicity used by Saint Augustine clinches the case he has been establishing concerning unity and sanctity. For the Church as an universal, world-wide polity is opposed to all particularist, nationalist tendencies. Because they believed that they alone possessed the holiness which is distinctive of the Church of Christ, the Donatists claimed that they were the only true Catholic Church, and that the party of Saint Augustine was in schism from that Church.[1] In answer Augustine ridicules the notion that the true Church can have perished from all the world, and from all the great sees of apostolic foundation, and remained only in Africa.[2] How is it possible that the tares should have filled the whole world, and the wheat remained only in Africa?[3] The churches of the East know nothing of this dispute at all: some of them have never even heard of the name of Donatus. How can they be contaminated, and excluded from the Catholic Church, by the supposed crimes of men on the other side of the world, about which they know nothing?[4] How can the deeds of Caecilianus have polluted whole nations who never heard of his name?[5] Yet the Rogatist bishop of Cartenna would no doubt assure us that, though the Gospel has been preached to the Indians and Persians, none of them can be cleansed from his sins unless he comes to Cartenna to receive the only true baptism.[6]

Moreover, not only does the Donatist case fail on the ground of its geographical limitations, but the term Catholic, as applied to the Church, means not only that it is spread over all the world, but also that it teaches the whole truth, and not, like the heretics, only a part of the truth.[7] If a man separates himself from the Church, and sets up a sect which he proclaims to be the only true and Catholic Church, how is he to be sure that the same has not happened before, and that the body from which he separates is not in reality the Catholic Church, but itself only a sect?[8] If the Donatist case is really so good, it ought

---

[1] *Gesta Coll. Carthag.* III, 102; Aug. *Breu. Coll.* III, 3; *Ep.* XCIII, vii, 23.

[2] Aug. *Ep.* XLIII, ix, 15; XLIX, 3; LII, 2; LXVI, 2; LXXXVI, 2; LXXXVII; XCIII, vi, 20, ix, 28; *De unit. eccl.* VIII, 20–2; *C. Litt. Pet.* III, 1, 62; *C. Ep. Parm.* II, i, 2, ii, 5; III, iv, 24. Cf. Opt. II, 1, 11; III, 9.

[3] Aug. *Ep.* LXXVI, 2; LXXXVII; CXLII, 2.

[4] Ibid. LXXXVII, 1, 2, 5, 6.

[5] Ibid. CXXIX, 2, 3: 'non autem inuenerunt aliquod testimonium diuinorum eloquiorum, ubi dictum est eam perituram de ceteris partibus mundi, et in sola Africa Donati parte mansuram'; ibid. 6.

[6] Ibid. XCIII, vii, 22.   [7] Ibid. XCIII, vii, 23.

[8] Ibid. XCIII, vii, 25.

to have been possible to prove it to the satisfaction of the churches across the sea.[1] For the whole Church must be right in detecting and excluding schismatics.[2]

(d) *Apostolicity*

Finally, Donatists can lay no claim to the possession of the fourth note of the Church, apostolicity. There is no Donatist name in the list of the Bishops of Rome, which is extant from Saint Peter down to Anastasius.[3] For Saint Peter is the representative not only of the Apostles, but of all Christians in general.[4] Nor can the Donatists trace their own succession back to the Apostles,[5] nor are they in communion with other apostolic sees besides Rome, in particular with the foundations of Saint John in Asia with which he communicated in his Apocalypse.[6] Yet with all such sees the Catholic Church in Africa is in communion. It is interesting to note that the case is not made to rest solely upon communion with Rome, but with other apostolic sees as well.

3. *Saint Augustine's development of the Doctrine of the Church*

Such is the outline of Saint Augustine's teaching on the notes of the Church as developed in answer to the challenge of the Donatists. But it is to be remembered that the Donatists had not evolved their rigid theory of the Church as the result of theological controversy. On the contrary, they had maintained it from the beginning of the schism in the early fourth century, and claimed that the Catholics were the innovators, and they themselves the inheritors of the classical African ecclesiology as established by Saint Cyprian. Thus their doctrine of the Church accorded admirably with their intense national devotion to things African. Of all their teaching this was the most influential point, because of the domination of Saint Cyprian's memory in the Africa of this date. Whatever might be said against Cyprian on the ground of

[1] Ibid. LII, 2.

[2] Aug. *C. Ep. Parm.* II, i, 2, ii, 5; III, iv, 24: 'quapropter securus iudicat orbis terrarum bonos non esse qui se diuidunt ab orbe terrarum in quacunque parte terrarum.'

[3] Aug. *Ep.* LIII, i, 2; *Ps. c. part. Donati*, vv. 229–31; *C. Cresc.* II, xxxvii, 46; cf. Opt. I, 10; II, 2, 3.

[4] Aug. *Ep.* LIII, i, 2: 'si enim ordo episcoporum sibi succedentium considerandus est, quanto certius et uere salubriter ab ipso Petro numeramus, cui totius ecclesiae figuram gerenti Dominus ait: Super hanc petram aedificabo ecclesiam meam, et portae inferorum non uincent eam. Petro enim successit Linus; Lino Clemens... Siricio Anastasius. in hoc ordine successionis nullus Donatista episcopus inuenitur.'

[5] Aug. *De ciu. Dei*, XX, 10.   [6] Aug. *C. Cresc.* II, xxxvii, 46; IV, xxv, 32.

the inadequacy of his doctrine—and what could be said was cogently expressed by Augustine—yet he was the great national martyr of Africa, who, as so many Donatists liked to claim for their own 'martyrs', had fallen in defence of the faith, and at the hands of the Roman power which was so detested by ardent African separatists like the partisans of Donatus. In Cyprian's martyrdom, for the Donatist mind, was seen the victory of light over darkness in that struggle in which they themselves felt proud to be still engaged. Moreover, this admiration for Cyprian was not confined to their party, but was common to all African Christians. Augustine was not insensible of the appeal of this attitude to the African mind, and he himself hardly ever mentions Cyprian without praising him for his steadfastness, charity and love of unity.[1] Nevertheless, he was able to find in Cyprian's life and writings the very answer which he needed against the Donatists. He could ask them why they were eager to justify their disciplinary doctrine of rebaptism and ecclesiastical exclusiveness by the word of Cyprian, but yet were unwilling to emulate the deep love of Catholic unity and peace which so manifestly inspired all the work of Cyprian.[2] Augustine was also able to remind them that Cyprian was the first to apply to the Church's holiness the parable of the wheat and tares, and Saint Paul's image of the house with its vessels unto honour and dishonour,[3] as showing us that it is wrong to split the Church because it is yet imperfect in holiness. These two passages, with Saint Cyprian's treatment of them, are quoted no fewer than three times by Augustine in the anti-Donatist treatises.[4] Their boast that their church is the true Church because it is holy, in contrast to the *corpus permixtum* of the Church of Augustine, is answered with the challenge: 'Let them maintain, if they can, that they have a better and purer church than the united Church of Cyprian's day.'[5]

But the chief answer of Saint Augustine to the Donatist claim to

[1] See, for example, Aug. *C. Cresc.* II, xxxi, 39; *De bapt.* III, i, 1.

[2] Aug. *C. Cresc.* II, xxi, 39: 'quid, quod etiam beati Cypriani mentionem facere audetis, uelut ille auctor sit uestrae diuisionis, tantus defensor catholicae unitatis et pacis? primo esto in ecclesia, quam constat tenuisse et praedicasse Cyprianum, et tunc aude uelut auctorem sententiae tuae nominare Cyprianum. primo imitare pietatem humilitatemque Cypriani, et tunc profer concilium Cypriani'; *De bapt.* IV, viii, 11; V, ii, 2.

[3] Matt. xiii. 24–30, 36–43; II Tim. ii. 20.

[4] Aug. *Ep.* CVIII, iii, 10; *C. Cresc.* II, xxxiv, 43; *C. Gaud.* II, iii, 3; see Cypr. *Ep.* LIV, 3 and Benson, op. cit. p. 174.

[5] Aug. *C. Ep. Parm.* III, ii, 8: 'dicant ergo, si possunt, meliorem se atque purgatiorem habere nunc ecclesiam, quam erat ipsa unitas beatissimi Cypriani temporibus.'

have the authority of Saint Cyprian is the whole of his work in seven books *De baptismo*, written, in fulfilment of a promise made in the treatise against the Epistle of Parmenianus,[1] to prove that nothing is a better case against Donatism than the words and actions of Cyprian.[2] Augustine is bound to admit that Cyprian did teach that baptism must be administered to all who came into the Church from heresy and schism; but he is able to show that both before Cyprian and after him, the judgement of the Church has concluded that his view was mistaken.[3] Moreover, nothing is more remarkable in the works of Cyprian than his constant insistence upon the right of every bishop to make his own decision, and to administer his own diocese accordingly, even though no bishop should agree with him. For Cyprian the unity of the Church is a far greater principle than any opinion, even on so grave a matter as rebaptism.[4] 'Suppose', says Augustine, 'that Cyprian had separated from the Church on this matter. How many followers would he not have had? Cyprianists would have been even more widespread than Donatists. But Cyprian was not a son of perdition, but of the peace of the Church, a lover of her unity, and a possessor of the divine gift of charity, without which any other gift is useless.'[5]

Thus Cyprian remained in communion with Stephen, Bishop of Rome, with whom he fundamentally disagreed on rebaptism,[6] because the peace of Christ ruled in their hearts: and Augustine picks on this passionate love of unity as the characteristic mark of Cyprian's life, and one in which the Donatists would do well to imitate him.[7]

In love of unity, therefore, Augustine is at one with Cyprian. And yet Cyprian's doctrine is not inclusive enough to satisfy Augustine's yearning to reunite the Church of Africa shattered by schism. If

[1] Ibid. II, xiv, 32. [2] Aug. *Retract.* II, xliv; *De bapt.* I, i, 1.
[3] Aug. *De bapt.* I, xviii, 28. On the baptismal question, see infra, Chapter VI.
[4] Cypr. *Ep.* LXVI, 8; LXXII, 3; LXXIII, 26; *De unit. eccl.* v et passim. Cypr. *Sent. episc. praefat.* is quoted by Aug. in *De bapt.* II, ii, 3, and in many other places.
[5] Aug. *De bapt.* I, xviii, 28: 'quod ergo ille uir sanctus de baptismo aliter sentiens quam se res habebat, quae postea pertractata et diligentissima consideratione firmata est, in catholica unitate permansit, et caritatis ubertate compensatum est et passionis falce purgatum'; ibid. II, ii, 3, iii, 4.
[6] Ibid. v, xxv, 36.
[7] Ibid. II, vii, 12; v, xvii, 22, 23: 'sed iam ad illa eloquia pacifica Cypriani, hoc est ad epistulae finem [Cypr. *Ep.* LXXIII, 26] omnibus consideratis pertractatisque peruentum est, quae me legentem et saepe repetentem non satiant. tanta in eis iucunditas fraterni amoris exhalat, tanta dulcedo caritatis exuberat'; VI, v, 8: 'tam multis autem sibi consentientibus quod cum ceteris diuersa sentientibus in unitate permansit, catholicae uniuersitatis sanctissimum uinculum non timore solitudinis sed pacis amore seruauit'; VII, l, 98.

schismatics are simply apostates, the way of return is easy, if they will submit. They must be baptized, as if they were for the first time entering the Church of God. But Augustine, as we shall see,[1] adheres to the general Western doctrine of his time that baptism, even if administered outside the Church's fold, is not invalid, though it may be irregular, and therefore cannot be repeated. There may be Christians, therefore, outside the Visible Church, and equally there may be within the Visible Church those who are not pure and loyal members, men who are of the body of the Church without being truly of its soul. Cyprian's theory was clear-cut, and he could decide easily whether a man was within or without the Church. Augustine's more subtle theory could give no such definitive answer to the problem.

For it must be remembered that Augustine had been led to Catholicism from the Manichaeism of his youth by way of Platonism. To the end of his life he viewed things persistently *sub specie aeternitatis*, and in his theological as much as in his philosophical thought it was always true to him that the phenomenal is but the pattern of the real laid up in heaven.[2] So it is when he is considering the nature of the Church and Body of Christ. On earth the Church, for all its glories (and it was those glories which in part had led Augustine to enter its fold),[3] is still necessarily imperfect, still but the image of the true Church in heaven, which is the fullness of him that filleth all in all. The perfection of the *societas caelestis* cannot be on earth. For here on earth the Church is a *corpus permixtum*, in which good and evil await the final separation. Entry into the Church is by baptism, and while Augustine accepts the classic doctrine of the Visible Church, the body of the baptized, dispersed throughout the world, as Cyprian had done,[4] and believes with African Christians in the remission of sins through the Holy Church,

---

[1] Chapter VI.   [2] See *Conf.* VII, ix; *De uita beata*, i, 4.
[3] H. Reuter, op. cit. p. 98: 'Die katholische Kirche nicht wie er dieselbe begrifflich konstruierte, sondern sie in ihrer von allem Lehrbegrifflichen unabhängigen Existenz, in der Grofsartigkeit ihrer Organisation, in der reichen Gliederung der Episkopate, mit ihrer die persönliche Selbstgewifsheit ersetzenden auktoritativen Tradition, mit ihrem alle Irrungen und Differenzen menschlichen Meinens aufhebenden, einheitlichen überlieferten Dogma, in der Pracht ihres mysteriösen Zeremoniells, der Fülle der Gnadenmittel war für den Mann....'
Trans. A. Robertson, op. cit. pp. 184-5: 'The grandeur of her organization, the ordered ranks of her episcopate, the authoritative tradition superseding individual inquiry, the uniformity of her dogma in the face of all error and variations of opinion, the majesty of her mysterious rites, the rich resources of her means of grace....' Aug. *C. Ep. Fund.* VI: 'ego uero euangelio non crederem, nisi me catholicae ecclesiae commoueret auctoritas.'
[4] See p. 98 supra.

yet there is never absent from his mind the thought of the Church which is not yet perfected, the communion of those who are holy and spiritual, the Lord's body and household, not yet finally gathered in from the highways of heresy and the hedges of schism.[1] The subject of the *De ciuitate Dei* is the most glorious City of God, whether dwelling as a stranger and pilgrim among the wicked in this temporal world, or whether in that stability of her eternal abode which now she expects with patience until righteousness turn again unto judgement.[2] Again, in reviewing the work *De baptismo* against the Donatists, Augustine cautions the reader that wherever in that work he has spoken of the Church not having spot or blemish, he refers not to the Church as she now is, but as she will be in her glorious consummation.[3] For now she has an admixture of evil men: the Visible Church contains those who are unworthy and who will be rooted out at the last. And from the *Confessions* (397) onwards, Augustine is developing the thought which was later to crystallize in the distinction between the *certus numerus* of those predestined and called to eternal salvation, and those who are not so elected, and who, though they may now be by baptism members of the Church, are no true part of the communion of the saints.[4] Therefore in his fully developed doctrine of the Church Visible and Invisible there are distinctions made of various kinds. There are in the Visible Church good men and bad men; there are the elect and the non-elect. But side by side with these distinctions there is the predestinarian distinction of the number, unalterably determined by the foreknowledge of God, of those who are predestined to eternal life, and those not so predestined. Of the predestined some are within the Visible Church, and some still without. The communion of saints, which is the Visible Church, will from time to time include sincere Christians who have not been selected out of the *massa damnata* of fallen mankind, and so this *communio sanctorum* is not always identical with the *numerus praedestinatorum*. Augustine is not in every case careful to make these

[1] Aug. *Ep.* CLXXXV, vi, 24: '...hi qui inueniuntur in uiis et in sepibus, id est in haeresibus et schismatibus, coguntur intrare; non quia coguntur reprehendant, sed quo cogantur, attendant. conuiuium Domini, unitas est corporis Christi, non solum in sacramento altaris, sed etiam in uinculo pacis.'

[2] Aug. *De ciu. Dei*, praef.: 'gloriosissimam ciuitatem Dei siue in hoc temporum cursu cum inter impios peregrinatur ex fide uiuens, siue in illa stabilitate sedis aeternae, quam nunc expectat per patientiam, quoadusque iustitia conuertatur in iudicium, deinceps adeptura per excellentiam uictoria ultima et pace perfecta.'

[3] Aug. *Retract.* II, xviii.

[4] See Aug. *De corrept. et grat.* XIII, 39–42, etc.; Robertson, op. cit. pp. 194–205; Reuter, op. cit. Studie II.

distinctions between the various groups mentioned, and confusion is therefore apt to arise in the doctrine of the Visible and the Invisible Church.[1] And more than that, he never synthesized his theories of the Church and of predestination, though he often assumes that all the predestined still on earth are incorporated into the visible communion of saints.[2] In reviewing his beliefs, therefore, we must be content to hold the two aspects in tension. Ultimately, as Dr Harnack saw,[3] 'the thought of predestination shatters every notion of the Church...and renders valueless all divine ordinances, the institution and means of salvation'. Perhaps it was only the fact that the later developments of Augustine's doctrine of predestination took place at a date after the settlement of the Donatist controversy, in the last ten years of his life, which made it possible for him to push the predestinarian theory so far without apparently realizing the impossibility of synthesizing it with his general doctrine of the Church.

This brief review of Saint Augustine's belief about the Church will show what profound complication his thought had introduced into the question. For Cyprian the matter was clearly and rigidly defined. He could say in a moment who was within and who without the Church. Augustine can decide that as far as it concerns the *communio externa*, but in the case of the *communio sanctorum*, in so far as it is identified with the *certus numerus praedestinatorum*, no man can make a decision: it rests with the inscrutable wisdom of God. There is no doubt that such teaching made possible the reception of Donatists back into the Church, which would have been impossible by any other theory such as Cyprian's (except by means of baptism, in which case return would have been unacceptable to the Donatists). And yet, side by side with his willingness to receive penitent Donatists, Augustine would have been the last man to minimize the gravity of schism. For Cyprian schism was apostasy. But for Augustine it was, as we have seen, sacrilege, which is worse, for it rends the very Body of Christ. Essential grace is lacking, according to Augustine, to all those outside the Church, and what is lacking is the crown of Christian virtues, without which all other virtues are as 'sounding brass and a tinkling cymbal', the grace of charity, the first of the Spirit's fruits.[4] Charity is the proper gift of

[1] See Reuter, op. cit. pp. 68, 69, 98–100; Aug. *Serm.* CCXIII, 7; CCXIV, 11; *Enarr. in Ps.* CXXVI, 3.
[2] See Robertson, op. cit. p. 197, n. 4.   [3] Harnack, op. cit. vol. v, p. 166.
[4] *Ep.* CLXXXV, xi, 48–50: 'hoc [sc. uerbum aduersus Spiritum sanctum] est autem duritia cordis usque ad finem huius uitae, qua homo recusat in unitate corporis Christi, quod uiuificat Spiritus sanctus, remissionem accipere peccatorum ...huic ergo dono gratiae Dei quicumque restiterit et repugnauerit, uel quoquo

Catholic unity and peace.¹ The man who is destitute of it, and separates himself from the unity of the Church, is sunk in the darkness of schism by losing the light of charity.² Until he repossesses charity, no other gift in baptism or in any other sacrament or means of grace is of any use, though they may be held in suspense, as it were, until, by virtue of his unity with the Body of Christ, they revive and become for the first time profitable to salvation.³ That is the appeal which Augustine makes to the separated Africans, and in all this wearisome controversy he longs continually for the peace of the City of God, reunited in the bond of charity.

We shall be, as it were, in a city—brethren, when I speak of it, I would fain speak on for ever, especially when offences multiply. Who would not long for that city whence no friend goes out, where no enemy enters, where there is no tempter, no stirrer of faction, no divider of the people of God, no harasser of the Church in the Devil's service?⁴

For the root and persistence of schism is nothing else than hatred of the brethren.⁵

modo fuerit ab eo alienus usque in finem huius temporalis uitae, non remittetur ei, neque in hoc saeculo neque in futuro; hoc scilicet tam grande peccatum, ut eo teneantur cuncta peccata...proinde ecclesia catholica sola corpus est Christi cuius ille caput est, saluator corporis sui. extra hoc corpus neminem uiuificat Spiritus sanctus, quia, sicut ipse dicit Apostolus: caritas Dei diffusa est in cordibus nostris per Spiritum sanctum qui datus est nobis: non est autem particeps diuinae caritatis, qui hostis est unitatis. non habent itaque Spiritum sanctum qui sunt extra ecclesiam; de illis quippe scriptum est: qui seipsos segregant, animales, Spiritum non habentes.'

¹ Aug. *De bapt.* III, xvi, 21: 'ipsa est enim caritas, quam non habent qui ab ecclesiae catholicae communione praecisi sunt: ac per hoc etiamsi linguis hominum et angelorum loquantur, si sciant omnia sacramenta et omnem scientiam, et si habeant omnem prophetiam, et omnem fidem, ita ut montes transferant, et distribuant omnia sua pauperibus, et tradant corpus suum ut ardeant, nihil eis prodest. non autem habent Dei caritatem qui ecclesiae non diligunt unitatem; ac per hoc recte intelligitur dici non accipi nisi in Catholica Spiritus sanctus... quodlibet haeretici et schismatici accipiant, caritas quae operit multitudinem peccatorum, proprium donum est catholicae unitatis et pacis.'

² Aug. *Ep.* CLXXXX, v, 47: 'in tenebris cecidit schismatis amisso lumine caritatis.'

³ Ibid. LXI; LXXXIX, 7; XCIII, xi, 46; *De bapt.* I, i, 2, etc.

⁴ Aug. *Enarr. in Ps.* LXXXIV, 10: 'erimus in quadam ciuitate: fratres, quando de illa loquor, finire nolo, et maxime quando scandala crebrescunt. quis non desideret illam ciuitatem, unde amicus non exit, quo inimicus non intrat, ubi nullus tentator est, nullus seditiosus, nullus diuidens populum Dei, nullus fatigans ecclesiam in ministerio diaboli?' Trans. J. Burnaby, *Amor Dei*, Hulsean Lectures, 1938 (London, 1938), p. 55.

⁵ Aug. *De bapt.* I, xi, 16: 'nulli autem schismata facerent, si fraterno odio non excaecarentur...an non est in schismate odium fraternum? quis hoc dixerit, cum et origo et pertinacia schismatis nulla sit alia nisi odium fratris?'

CHAPTER V

CHURCH AND STATE

1. *The development of Saint Augustine's theory of coercion*

An adequate discussion of Saint Augustine's teaching concerning the relations of Church and State, and between the *ciuitas aeterna* and the *ciuitas terrena*, would require a book of its own. Yet his belief on these questions was at any rate in part forged on the anvil of the Donatist controversy, and therefore, in view of its intrinsic importance to that controversy, cannot be left aside in this study. For the defeat of the schismatics Augustine and his fellow-bishops found themselves compelled to ask the support of the government, and we can trace clearly in his works a gradual hardening of his view on the coercion of religious dissidents by the authority of the civil power.

In the beginning he was firmly of opinion that no permanent good can result from using compulsion in matters of faith. If a man's faith is erroneous, then the only secure way of bringing him to the knowledge of the truth is by the power of cogent argument, and by the attraction of the majestic Catholic Church. It was by such a path that Augustine had himself been led to the faith of Christendom. When he went to Milan he heard the sermons of Saint Ambrose in the cathedral church. And he attended them not because he thought to find in the preacher a teacher of the truth, for he had despaired of finding any such man in the Church, but because he desired to hear a fine orator, and because also he had a high personal regard for Ambrose.[1] But he soon began to attend not only to the form but also to the content of the Bishop's preaching, and, gradually, by the study of the Epistles of Saint Paul and the life of Saint Antony, he was led to the moment of his conversion. He would not, he tells us, believe the Gospel, were it not for the authority of the Catholic Church.[2] Such was the way in which he in turn hoped to win Donatists back to the true fold. It had been the method of his approach to the Manichees,[3] and, when his view changed, he was always at such pains to defend the change that we feel that to the end of his life he was never entirely comfortable about the

---

[1] Aug. *Conf.* v, xiii.
[2] Aug. *C. Ep. Fund.* vi: 'ego uero euangelio non crederem, nisi me catholicae ecclesiae commoueret auctoritas.'
[3] J. N. Figgis, op. cit. pp. 56, 57.

use of coercion.¹ If a man is to be a good Christian, he must be so of his own free will, and therefore should be moved by argument and not coerced by force.² We notice accordingly that all his early letters to Donatists have a most conciliatory tone.³ He invited several of their bishops to have conferences with him in which the questions at issue could be amicably discussed. Among these bishops were Maximinus, bishop of Sinitum,⁴ Proculeianus, bishop of Hippo,⁵ and Fortunius, bishop of Thubursicum Numidarum.⁶ These meetings seem to have been held in public, because in late 397 or early 398 he writes that his meeting with Fortunius was spoiled by the disorder and noise of the crowd which assembled.⁷ The discussion lasted some hours,⁸ and ranged over the meaning of the true Church,⁹ the question of persecution,¹⁰ and the history of the schism.¹¹ Augustine wrote also in 398 to Honoratus, a Donatist bishop, of the difficulties of holding these public colloquies, and of his preference for conducting the discussion by letter.¹² We learn from a letter written a year or two later that he had an additional reason for preferring this procedure, namely that if a statement was once in writing, there was no danger of its being twisted to suit the Donatists.¹³

But about this time, as we have seen,¹⁴ Augustine first adumbrated the next stage of the development of his views on coercion. In the lost work *Contra partem Donati*, written in 397, he considered the possibility of appealing to the State, and rejected this course. When he reviews this work in the *Retractations*¹⁵ he says that he did so because he had not yet realized to what extent Donatist violence would proceed, or the fruitful results of a salutary discipline. In the next year (398), however, the *Contra Epistulam Parmeniani* shows an inclination of his opinion towards approval of such intervention by the State.¹⁶ Is it true, as the Donatists assert, that harmful and false religion is no concern of the civil power? That power proceeds against pagans on these grounds, and why, if it punishes poisoning and other works of the flesh mentioned in Galatians v. 19–21, should it not also punish and restrain hatred,

¹ Note especially Aug. *Ep.* XCIII and CLXXXV.
² Aug. *Ep.* XXXIV.
³ E.g. Aug. *Ep.* XXIII, XXXIII, XXXIV, XLIV.
⁴ Aug. *Ep.* XXIII.   ⁵ Ibid. XXXIII, XXXIV.
⁶ Ibid. XLIV.   ⁷ Ibid. XLIV, i, 1.
⁸ Ibid. XLIV, i, 2.   ⁹ Ibid. XLIV, ii, 3.
¹⁰ Ibid. XLIV, ii, 4, iv, 7, 8.   ¹¹ Ibid. XLIV, iii, 6.
¹² Ibid. XLIX, 1.   ¹³ Ibid. LI (A.D. 399 or 400).
¹⁴ Supra, pp. 42, 43.   ¹⁵ Aug. *Retract.* II, v.
¹⁶ Aug. *C. Ep. Parm.* I, viii–xiii.

CHURCH AND STATE

violence, emulations, wrath, strife, seditions and heresies, all of which are mentioned in the same context?[1] In many of the letters of this period[2] he urges Donatists to be reconciled to the Church, and expresses the willingness of the Church to receive them when penitent. Whenever he defends the use of compulsion, he never fails to stress the desire of Catholics for reunion, and their preparedness to receive penitent Donatists into communion. But between 398 and 405 he defends the Catholic appeal to the State as being necessary for the defence of the Church against Donatist aggression. For all the time the Circumcellions were raging, and in everything he writes he makes mention of the abominable tyranny they were exercising in the African provinces. The work of the Church was being impeded; her bishops and clergy were continually exposed to the cruelties and depredations of these rascals; Donatist laity who would have responded to the arguments of the Catholic bishops dare not do so for fear of the Circumcellions, who had a special grudge against any Donatists who were converted. The work of theological argument in bringing men to a right mind was being hindered; and to prevent this, and to enable the Church to dwell in peace (which is, after all, from the Christian standpoint one of the chief ends of human government),[3] Augustine and the bishops of the African councils moved gradually towards an appeal to the civil government for defence against the illegal violence of the Donatists. At this stage that was the limit of their appeal. How was it to be accomplished?

There was no law against schism, but there was a stringent enactment against heresy, imposing a fine of ten pounds of gold.[4] It had been suggested from time to time that the Donatists were heretical, and had Arian tendencies in their Trinitarian doctrine.[5] But on the whole it appears from Augustine's writings that they were for the most part

---

[1] Ibid. I, x, 16: 'illud quaero, cum manifeste enumeret Apostolus opera carnis, quae sunt, inquit, fornicationes, immunditiae, contentiones, aemulationes, animositates, dissensiones, haereses, inuidiae, ebrietates, comessationes et his similia; quid istis uideatur, ut crimen idololatriae putent iuste ab imperatoribus uindicari; aut si nec hoc uolunt, cur in ueneficos uigorem legum exerceri iuste fateantur; in haereticos autem atque impias dissensiones nolint fateri, cum in iisdem iniquitatis fructibus auctoritate apostolica numerentur. an forte nec talia potestates istae humanae constitutionis permittuntur curare?'

[2] E.g. Aug. Ep. LI, 3; LII, 4; LXI, 1, 2; LXXVI, 2.

[3] Aug. De ciu. Dei, XIX, xiii; cf. Collect for Trinity V: 'da nobis, quaesumus, Domine, ut et mundi cursus pacifice nobis tuo ordine dirigatur, et ecclesia tua tranquilla deuotione laetetur.'

[4] C.Th. XVI, vi, 4.

[5] Aug. Serm. CLXXXIII, v, 9; Ep. CLXXXV, i, 1; Hieron. De uir. illustr. 93.

orthodox in doctrine, though schismatical in practice.[1] There were, however, laws against the reiteration of baptism, a typical Donatist delinquency;[2] and these could therefore be used against them. But, better than this, the Emperor Honorius, in a rescript of 399 answering a complaint from the African Church,[3] ordered the application against the Donatists of the laws already existing against heretics, forbidding them to receive or to make donations or legacies.[4] This procedure was used in 403 against the Donatist priest Crispinus for leading an attack on Possidius, the Bishop of Calama; and he was fined ten pounds.[5] He appealed, but the sentence was upheld.[6] The Council of Carthage pursued this incident on 16 June 404 by a formal request to the Emperor to assimilate Donatism to heresy,[7] and the Emperor acceded in the edict of unity of 12 February 405.[8] This edict explicitly stated that the practice of second baptism had transformed a schism into an heresy, an idea possibly suggested by Augustine himself.[9]

So the second stage of development was an appeal for defence against outrages and persecution.[10] When dealing in the year 417 with this development, Saint Augustine says explicitly that the object was not that all Donatists should be fined under the edict, but that the power of prosecution should be available to the Church in those areas which suffered most severely from Circumcellion depredations. If the violence of Donatists could be curbed, there might be the possibility that they could be taught freely to apprehend Catholic truth. Thus nobody would be compelled to become a Catholic, 'ne falsos et simulatores catholicos haberemus'.[11] The action of Maximianus, Bishop of Bagai, is next adduced to illustrate the Catholic principle. He suffered a severe assault in his own church, which nearly resulted in his death. When he

---

[1] Opt. I, 10: 'et cum...uos haeredes traditorum et schismaticorum esse euidenter adpareat, satis te miror, frater Parmeniane, cum schismaticus sis, schismaticos haereticis iungere uoluisse...quare paeniteat te talibus hominibus [sc. haereticis] etiam schismaticos adiunxisse: in te enim conuertisti sententiae gladium cum aestimas, quia alteros adpetebas, et non adtendisti inter schismaticos et haereticos quam sit magna distantia.' Cf. Aug. Ep. XLIII, 1; LXI, 1; CXLI, 5; Enarr. in Ps. LIV, 16.
[2] Aug. De bapt. I, i, 2, etc.   [3] C. Th. XVI, v.
[4] Aug. C. Ep. Parm. I, xii, 19.   [5] Supra, p. 56.
[6] Aug. Ep. LXXXVIII, 7; CV, ii, 4; C. Cresc. III, xlvii, 51; Possid. Vita Aug. XII.
[7] C.C.E.A. 93.
[8] C. Th. XVI, vi, 4.   [9] Aug. Ep. LXVI, 1.
[10] These are described in Aug. Ep. LXXXVIII, 8; CXI, 1; CLXXXV, vii; Ps. c. part. Donati, vv. 144–55; C. Cresc. III, xlii, 46, xliii, 47, xlvi, 50, xlvii, 51, xlviii, 52; IV, xlix, 59–li, 61; Opt. II, 19–21.
[11] Aug. Ep. CLXXXV, vii, 25.

CHURCH AND STATE

recovered, he sought imperial protection, not for revenge, but for the safeguarding of the church committed to him. In this he was entirely right: had not Saint Paul himself on more than one occasion sought as a Roman citizen the protection of the State against his enemies and persecutors? And Saint Paul appealed to a pagan Emperor, but Maximianus to a Christian.[1]

But the edict of unity of 405 did not succeed in its purpose. The reiteration, in terms of ever-increasing severity, of many of the imperial laws at this time, indicates the ineffectiveness of much of this legislation.[2] The provincial governors and administrators had every temptation to corruption. They were in many cases far removed from Rome, for the Empire was probably the vastest area ever ruled from a single centre. Complaints of injustice from the provinces were long in being answered; and governors who were tempted to corruption could for long periods discharge their corrupt administration with impunity. And yet the government depended on them for application of its laws. This was particularly the case in the administration of laws against pagans and heretics. Not until 416 were pagans excluded from civil office.[3] To such governors the Emperor trusted in vain for the energetic application of laws against superstitions with which they themselves sympathized. It was not to be expected that they would understand or sympathize with the Church of Africa in its death-struggle against schismatics. That Church had made a formal complaint against slackness in administering laws against paganism.[4] But the Emperors were quite aware of this. Honorius and Arcadius had themselves castigated their own officials for their ineptitude in applying the law,[5] and in the same law made such negligence a capital offence. Theodosius had also attacked the same negligence in his own day.[6] 'The Emperor', says Professor Dill, 'was met by a dead weight of official resistance or negligence, which apparently rendered legislation almost nugatory. The provincial governor and his staff were often in sympathy, or in league, with the offenders.'[7] Hence to enact a law was one thing, to secure its stringent administration quite another.

So it was with the anti-Donatist struggle. It took years to bring matters to a head in the Conference of Carthage in 411; and years again

---

[1] Aug. *Ep.* CLXXXV, vii, 26-8.
[2] See Samuel Dill, *Roman Society in the last Century of the Western Empire* (London, 1910), pp. 266, 267.
[3] By *C.Th.* XVI, x, 21. [4] Aug. *Ep.* XCI, 8; cf. *Ep.* XCVII.
[5] E.g. *C.Th.* XVI, x, 13. [6] *C.Th.* XVI, x, 12.
[7] S. Dill, op. cit. pp. 37, 38; see also ibid. pp. 26, 266, 267.

to suppress the schismatics once and for all. In Africa the enforcement of the edict of 405 was not sufficient either to restrain the violence of the Circumcellions or to unite the Donatists to the Church. It is true that a number of them were converted, and that some basilicas were taken over by the Church. In some cases these were lost again. We have seen that the Donatist bishop of Hippo made a triumphal entry into his recovered basilica, which had been confiscated in 405.[1] All this continuing activity of the Donatists moved Saint Augustine to accede to the view of many of his fellow-bishops that compulsion must be used on a greater scale if peace was to be established in the African Church. He gave himself whole-heartedly to the policy of appealing to the State. The Council of Carthage of 13 June 407 appealed to Honorius for further imperial measures against the dissidents, and in reply a constitution ordered the suppression of obstinate Donatists, and the reception of those who would submit to the Church. The two councils of 408 (16 June and 13 October) made similar requests, and Saint Augustine supported this action with a personal letter to Olympius, the new minister of State.[2] Further legislation proved ineffective,[3] and it remained to ask that a formal conference should be convened under imperial authority to settle the dispute finally. This conference met in June 411 at Carthage, and decided in favour of the Catholic Church.

The spheres of influence of Church and State were largely distinct, but since the recognition of Christianity by Constantine there had been fairly considerable interaction in some matters. A bishop was well known locally, and, as he was politically independent, many were glad to submit to his adjudication in litigation, and he became the arbitrator in many disputes. Gradually this function became extended to various classes of litigation; and Constantine made an attempt to convert it into a regular form of expeditious procedure, which avoided the delays and vexations of the law.[4] The cheapness of this new procedure had brought it within reach of the poorer classes, and popularized it extensively. At the end of the fourth century episcopal adjudication suffered some restriction under Arcadius, but its facility and the moral weight attaching to the decisions of bishops remained, and attracted many litigants. We learn from Apollinaris Sidonius, Bishop of Auvergne,[5] from Saint Ambrose,[6] from Possidius,[7] and from Saint

[1] Supra, p. 61.   [2] Supra, pp. 62, 63.   [3] Supra, pp. 62, 63.
[4] *Constit. Sirmond.* XVII, 1; Sozomen, *H.E.* I, 9; Ambros. *Ep.* LXXXII, 1.
[5] Sidon. *Ep.* VI, 2, 4, 9, 10.   [6] Ambros. *Ep.* LXXXII, 1; *De officiis*, ii, 125, iii, 59.
[7] Possid. *Vita Aug.* XIX.

CHURCH AND STATE

Augustine[1] that the pressure of this work was very heavy, and impeded the more strictly pastoral duties of a bishop.[2] The great churchman was often a leader of society in temporal as well as spiritual matters. The regulation of the rights of sanctuary and the education of orphans were other matters usually committed to bishops. Considerable help was thus rendered by the Church to the civil power; and on her side the Church felt justified in asking the State for protection against the ravages of heretics and schismatics. No new question of principle was therefore involved in appealing to the government against the Donatists, more particularly as the appeal, so far as it concerned the Circumcellions, was an appeal for the defence of persons and property which lies with any citizen. The Donatist bitterness over such an appeal when it was made against their own interests—'quid imperatori cum ecclesia?'—was pure hypocrisy. Their fathers had been the first to make such an appeal.[3] In pointing this out, Augustine is but repeating the argument used by Optatus against the Donatists of his day, who asked 'quid christianis cum regibus, aut quid episcopis cum palatio?'[4]

Thus by the pressure of circumstances Augustine had been led to his final view on the suppression of schism by State authority. He rejected the Donatist contention that righteousness is established by the suffering of persecution. It was a curious blindness which enabled the Donatists to claim that they were holy because they were persecuted, when all the time they were using lawless violence against their opponents.

[1] Aug. *Serm.* CCCII, 19.
[2] See also S. Dill, op. cit. pp. 214, 215; F. Homes Dudden, *The Life and Times of Saint Ambrose* (Oxford, 1935), pp. 121, 122; *Cambridge Medieval History*, vol. I, p. 173.
[3] Aug. *Ep.* CLXXXV, ii, 6: 'et quod in nobis modo reprehendunt, ut decipiant imperitos, dicentes non debere christianos contra inimicos Christi aliquid a christianis imperatoribus postulare, ipsi priores fecerunt. quod etiam in collatione quam simul apud Carthaginem habuimus, negare non ausi sunt; immo uero et gloriari ausi sunt quod apud imperatorem maiores eorum criminaliter Caecilianum fuerint insecuti; insuper addentes mendacium, quod eum illic uicerint fecerintque damnari'; Aug. *C. Ep. Parm.* I, viii-xiii; *Ep.* XCIII, v, 19; *C. Cresc.* III, xliv, 48; *Ep.* CV, ii, 3; CCIV, 4: 'docuimus...pertinere ad religiosos reges terrae non solum adulteria...uerum etiam sacrilegia seueritate congrua cohibere'; *Ep.* CLXXXV, vii, 25. For Donatist complaints of persecution, see Opt. III, 3, 4; Aug. *C. Ep. Parm.* I, viii, 13 sq.; *C. Litt. Pet.* II, lxxxiv, 185, xcii, 202; *C. Cresc.* III, li, 57; *C. Gaud.* I, xiv, 20; *Ep.* XCIII, ii, 5. For Donatist appeals to the civil power, see Aug. *Ep.* LXXXVIII, 2; XCIII, iv, 12; CV, ii, 9; *C. Cresc.* III, lxi, 67; IV, iii, 3 sq.; *Breu. Coll.* III, vii, 24; *C. Litt. Pet.* II, lxxxiii, 184, xcii, 203, 205, xcvii, 224; *C. Ep. Parm.* I, x, 16; *Gesta cum Emer.* 9; *Ep.* CVIII, ii, 5; Opt. I, 22; II, 16–19; III, 3.
[4] Opt. I, 22.

They glorified with the honours of martyrdom those of their party who fell in rebellious battle against the civil power (which for them as Africans typified the forces of darkness), and yet they claimed that they should be left to tyrannize Africa at their pleasure, and that any restraint from the Roman government was mere persecution.[1] Augustine is able to answer this argument by showing with a wealth of Scriptural citations that the Church possesses an undoubted power of exercising *correptio* over its children, and that in fact the righteous have in the course of history often used force to establish righteousness. The Psalmist says: 'I will follow upon mine enemies and overtake them; neither will I turn again till I have destroyed them. I will smite them that they shall not be able to stand, but fall under my feet.'[2] The accusers of Daniel were rent by lions; the false prophets were ordered by Elijah to be slain.[3] Hezekiah had restrained idolatry by force; and Nebuchadnezzar ordered all men to tremble before the God of heaven.[4] The examples of religious compulsion adduced from the New Testament are curious: they include naturally enough the scourging of the Jews out of the Temple by Christ; but the conversion of Saul of Tarsus by the assault of a blinding light is quoted[5] and also the delivering of the moral offender at Corinth to Satan for the destruction of the flesh and the salvation of the soul.[6] These New Testament instances are not, of course, by any means as satisfactory for Augustine's purposes as those from the Old Testament; but in the parable of the great supper he finds material ready to his hand.[7] For that parable represented the exact procedure which was being used against the Donatists, first a loving invitation, and then compulsion of the unwilling guests. The *compelle intrare* of the parable thus becomes the classic text of Saint Augustine at this time against the Donatists.[8] So there are two methods of dealing with schismatics, the sermons of Catholic prelates, and the laws of Catholic princes. If the schismatics will not listen to the former, let them be compelled by the latter.[9] This argument, he suggests, has even more force now that the princes themselves are Christian. For before Constantine men saw the exemplification of Psalm ii. 2: 'The kings of the earth stand up, and the rulers take counsel together, against the Lord and against his anointed.' But since Constantine the true picture

---

[1] Aug. *Ep.* CLXXXV, ii, 10.
[2] Ps. xviii. 37, 38: quoted by Aug. *Ep.* CLXXXV, ii, 11.
[3] Aug. *Ep.* CLXXXV, ii, 7.   [4] Ibid. CLXXXV, vi, 19.
[5] Ibid. CLXXXV, vi, 22.   [6] I Cor. v.
[7] Luke xiv. 16–24.   [8] Aug. *Ep.* CLXXXV, vi, 24.
[9] Ibid. CLXXXV, ii, 8.

is that of verses 10 and 11 of the same psalm: 'Be wise now therefore, O ye kings; be learned, ye that are judges of the earth. Serve the Lord with fear, and rejoice unto him with reverence.' The kings serve Christ even by enacting laws on his behalf, for the unification of his Church, and the suppression of schism.[1] Certain moral offences are punishable by law: why then should schism, which is sacrilege, go unpunished?[2] Of course the ideal method is that of love, working through the agency of argument. But when men's obstinacy is too great for them to be susceptible to this procedure, it remains to use the method of discipline. Schismatics are the children of the Church, and, until they attain the full use of reason, must be governed by the method of the rod; and, as with children, 'he that spareth the rod hateth the child'.[3] We may indeed have to begin with fear, but perfect love will later cast out fear.[4]

Such is Augustine's final position in the matter. He recognizes that this method of discipline will not attain true ecclesiastical unity, which must always remain a matter of the heart. All that he claims for it is that it makes two valuable things possible. It ensures the peace of faithful Christians to serve God without fear, and, as far as the schismatics are concerned, it opens the way for reunion by theological arguments.[5] Thus in his mind compulsion and persuasion are never separated. When he reviews his policy he claims that by the action of the Catholics many Donatists who were so from convenience and upbringing have rejoiced that the way of return was thus made open to them.[6] It had attained the end which its authors set before themselves: and who can indict them when he considers that the alternative would have been to abandon the Donatists to the torture of the eternal flames of Hell for their sacrilege and sin against the Holy Ghost?[7] As it is, they have been gathered into the peace of the holy City of God, in which their clergy have retained their sacred office. 'Veniant: fiat pax in uirtute Ierusalem, quae uirtus caritas est; cui sanctae ciuitati dictum est, Fiat pax in uirtute tua, et abundantia in turribus tuis.'[8]

2. *The relations of Church and State*

The development of this argument about compulsion obviously touches very closely on the whole theory of Saint Augustine concerning

[1] Ibid. xcIII, v, 19.   [2] Ibid. CLXXXV, v, 20.
[3] Prov. xiii. 24; Aug. *Ep.* CLXXXV, vi, 21.
[4] Aug. *Ep.* CLXXXV, vi, 22. Additional references on the appeal to the State: *C. Ep. Parm.* I, viii, 13 sq.; *C. Litt. Pet.* II, xcii, 203 sq.; *Ep.* xcIII, v, 16 sq.
[5] Aug. *Ep.* CLXXXV, ii, 7.   [6] Ibid. CLXXXV, ii, 7, vii, 29, viii, 32.
[7] Ibid. CLXXXV, viii, 32, x, 43, 44.   [8] Ibid. CLXXXV, x, 46.

the relations of Church and State. It is beyond our task to describe this theory in detail; but the outline of it is part of the background necessary to the working out of the anti-Donatist campaign; and so may not be left entirely on one side.[1]

The recognition of the Church by Constantine raised the question of the relations of Church and State in an entirely new form. Previously the Church had been tolerated, but had possessed no civil rights as a body; or else it had been outlawed and persecuted. Now it became for the first time a recognized religion receiving encouragement from the civil power and possessing certain political rights. Its clergy enjoyed certain exemptions from taxation, and, if curials, from curial burdens and responsibilities. As we have seen in the last section, the Church in turn helped the State in certain branches of administration. New relationships were thus set up, and from the days of Constantine down to our own times tension has appeared at times between the Church and the State, which has involved churchmen, who are also inevitably citizens, in moral difficulties where reconciliation of duty to Church and to State has been necessary. The State has not always supported the Church, as it might have done, in the suppression of error: in fact sometimes it has favoured dissidents against Catholic faith and discipline. In the fourth century this may be illustrated by reference to the epic battle of Saint Athanasius against a particularly dangerous and obnoxious heresy connived at by the State. The protest publicly addressed by the Church of Alexandria to Constantius 'for the salvation of his immortal soul' is a landmark in fourth-century Church history.[2] The Church was beginning to tell the State what its duty was in religious matters, in which the Church rightly (on New Testament principles) claimed supreme authority, derived not from below but from Christ its head.[3]

In this resistance to the civil power, so far as it was the supporter of heresy, Saint Athanasius, the saviour of orthodoxy in his day and generation, is but the forerunner of a greater ecclesiastical statesman of the

[1] On Augustine's thought on Church and State, see A. Robertson, *Regnum Dei*, Bampton Lectures, 1901, pp. 206–16; J. E. C. Welldon (ed.), *S. Augustine's 'De ciuitate Dei'* (London, 1924), vol. II, App. A, pp. 647–51; H. Reuter, *Augustinische Studien*, Studie III, pp. 106–50; J. N. Figgis, *Political Aspects of S. Augustine's 'City of God'* (London, 1921), especially Lect. III, 'The State' (pp. 51–67), and Lect. IV, 'The Church' (pp. 68–80); N. H. Baynes, *The Political Ideas of S. Augustine's 'De ciuitate Dei'* (London, 1936); *A Monument to Saint Augustine* (London, 1934), ch. I, Christopher Dawson, 'S. Augustine and his age'.
[2] Athanasius, *Hist. Arian.* 81.
[3] On Athanasius, see W. Bright, *The Age of the Fathers* (London, 1903), vol. I.

West, Saint Ambrose of Milan.[1] The struggle between Church and State was to be fought out in a more decisive way, and in Ambrose the occasion found the man. His training fitted him admirably for the difficult role for which his unexpected consecration to Milan cast him. It was the training of an administrator. He could look at the difficulties and limitations of civil government from the inside: as a provincial governor he knew what could be done, and what could not be done. He may be allowed to have been sympathetic with the difficulties of the civil power in its relations with the spiritual power. If compromise between Church and State were the right course, no one could have mediated better than Saint Ambrose, combining, as he did, the mind of the administrator with the responsibilities of a bishop in the Church of God. That he was firmly opposed to compromise on vital matters is a strong argument that compromise was intolerable to the Christian conscience. As the leading ecclesiastical statesman of his day, Ambrose was implacably opposed to the claims of heretics and of pagans. The fact that they were supported by civil authorities made no difference to his insistence on sound principle. So he refused to hand over his basilica to the representatives of the Empress Justina, an Arian, and showed himself prepared to hold it even at the cost of his life.[2] His opposition to paganism was just as emphatic.[3] Against the claims of the State he also vindicated the liberty of bishops and priests to declare the will of God by the authority of their office,[4] and condemned civil interference in the selection of bishops.[5] On the other hand, he claimed for the bishops the right of intervening in civil matters where questions of moral and spiritual import were involved. On this ground he subjected the Emperor Theodosius to spiritual discipline, involving suspension from communion until he signified his penitence, for his responsibility for the massacre of the recalcitrant citizens of Thessalonica.[6] In so doing he claimed to be exercising the undoubted office of a bishop in upholding the moral law of Christ, and defending the cause of God. The success of this policy and the submission of the Emperor showed clearly that the Church had become a power in imperial affairs which could not be set at nought in the framing of civil policy.

Ambrose's general doctrine of the Church and State is that the two

[1] On S. Ambrose's doctrine of Church and State, see F. Homes Dudden, *The Life and Times of S. Ambrose* (Oxford, 1935), pp. 381–92, 499–501, 542–44; C. N. Cochrane, *Christianity and Classical Culture* (Oxford, 1940), pp. 346–51.
[2] Ambros. *Ep.* I, 20; Aug. *Conf.* IX, vii, 15.
[3] Ambros. *Ep.* I, 57.   [4] Ibid. I, 40.   [5] Ibid. I, 21.
[6] F. Homes Dudden, op. cit. pp. 381–92; C. N. Cochrane, op. cit. p. 349.

have largely independent spheres, and need not normally intermeddle. The cases where the Church may rightly intervene are those which have just been enumerated: for the defence of Christianity against heresy and paganism, and for the upholding of the moral law.[1] In general it is man's first duty to obey God, and follow the injunctions of his bishops; and then secondly to live in dutiful allegiance to the civil power lawfully constituted.

The theory of Ambrose (which it will be our next duty to contrast with that of Saint Augustine) may be summarized in the words of Canon Homes Dudden:[2]

Ambrose himself had no desire to exercise political power. He regarded the Church and the State as two independent authorities, each autonomous within its own sphere, but each rendering general support and assistance to the other. The Church offers prayers for the State: the State is the 'secular arm' which gives effect to the decisions of the Church. The spiritual and the temporal authorities collaborate. It is only when princes presume to act in contravention of the essential principles of morality and religion that the bishops are required 'in the cause of God' to interfere. In such cases God and the law of God must be preferred to the Emperor and imperial law.[3] This, in sum, was Ambrose's doctrine. It was elaborated in various ways—not always with improvement—by the Popes and jurists of the Middle Ages. But the foundation upon which rest the mediaeval theories of the relation between Church and State, with all their tremendous practical consequences in mediaeval history, was laid originally by Ambrose. It is for this reason that the historical importance of the great Bishop of Milan—the first assertor of the independence and authority of the Church—can hardly be exaggerated.

With this brief statement of the position of Saint Ambrose may be contrasted the theory of Saint Augustine on the relations of Church and State, deeply tinged as it is with his doctrine of original sin.[4] The chief source is of course the greatest of his works, the *De ciuitate Dei*, with its picture of the two contrasted societies. But this must be supplemented by reference to the anti-Donatist works, in which the relations of Church and State are raised by the pastoral problems with which the Bishop of Hippo was faced.[5]

[1] Ambros. *In Ps.* xxxvii, enarr. 43. See F. Homes Dudden, op. cit. p. 544.
[2] F. Homes Dudden, op. cit. pp. 500, 501.
[3] See Ambros. *Ep.* x, 12; xxi, 10; xl, 28; li, 17.
[4] Cf. J. N. Figgis, op. cit. p. 6: 'Much of the book [i.e. the *De ciuitate Dei*] is but an expansion of Augustine's doctrine of grace applied on the scale of world history.'
[5] Cf. H. Reuter, op. cit. p. 151: 'Man kann die Staatslehre Augustins nur mit äusserster Vorsicht und selbst dann nur vollständig aus den Lib. de Ciu. schöpfen. Sie ist korrekt nur unter Vergleichung anderer Schriften namentlich der anti-Donatistischen aufzubauen.'

Saint Augustine's statement of this urgent problem must be seen thrown into vivid relief against the dark background of the calamitous times in which it was his responsibility to serve God. The sack of Rome in 410 brought to a head the triumphant campaigns which Alaric had for some time been conducting in Europe; and nothing gave the world, Christian as well as pagan, a greater shock than the fall of the eternal city, the mistress of all civilization. It represented to men of all schools of thought the undermining of the solid basis on which society rested. The shock reverberated from west to east: Saint Jerome in his seclusion at Bethlehem was shaken at the terrible news that the city which had conquered the world now lay prostrate at the barbarian conqueror's feet.[1] For the Church itself had grown great under the aegis of the Roman power. It had been natural for Saint Optatus to say not many years before that the Church is in the State, that is, in the Roman Empire;[2] and most Christians must have thought that the civilization and peace which Rome ensured was the essential seed-plot of the Church of God. In 410 men suddenly realized that this basis of all civilized life was destroyed. The pagans were not slow to attribute to the enervating effects of Christianity the debilitation of the old Roman spirit of domination, and it was being commonly said that Rome had perished *temporibus christianis*. A flood of refugees poured into Carthage, and spread abroad in the African provinces such criticisms of Christianity. And in 413 Augustine undertook the great and needful task of answering them. In that year he began his great work, *De ciuitate Dei*, completed only in 426, four years before his death, dedicated to Marcellinus, the imperial commissioner who had presided over the Conference of Carthage in 411, and directed explicitly against the pagans.[3]

In this work he took the opportunity of establishing a theory of the whole relation of Church and State on a broad basis. He started with the thought which had long been in his mind, of the contrast between two societies, the earthly city (*ciuitas terrena*) and the heavenly City of God (*ciuitas Dei*), from which the work takes its title. These he identifies with the kingdom of the Devil and the kingdom of God. It is probable that he derived the distinction from the *Book of the Rules* of the Donatist

---

[1] Hieron. *Ep.* CXXVI; CXXVII: 'haeret uox et singultus intercipiunt uerba dictantis: Capitur urbs quae totum cepit orbem.'

[2] Opt. III, 3: 'non enim respublica est in ecclesia, sed ecclesia in republica, id est in imperio Romano.'

[3] See Robertson, op. cit. pp. 206–9; Figgis, op. cit. pp. 6 sq.; Dill, op. cit. pp. 59–73.

Tyconius.[1] He had already used this doctrine of the two cities in 400, in writing the *De catechizandis rudibus*,[2] and now he was to expand and illustrate it in his greatest work and to refer to it the whole of human history. The two cities were first of all separated in the fall of the rebellious angels, and with them the *ciuitas terrena* first started on its iniquitous course. That course is traced through the descendants of Cain, the tower of Babel, and the empires of Nineveh, Babylon, Persia, Macedonia and Rome. The course of the *ciuitas superna*, the City of God, comes down through Noah, Abraham, Israel and Christ. Now they dwell side by side on earth, waiting for their final separation, when tares will be separated from the wheat and burned in eternal flames. Although now mingled corporally, and to man indistinguishably, they are, and have always been, spiritually disparate.[3] Both the earthly and the supernal cities include angels as well as men.[4]

These two societies rest upon divergent principles. The heavenly rests upon the love of God carried to the point of contempt of self, and the earthly upon the love of self carried to the point of contempt of God.[5] The earthly represents the principle of evil, the heavenly of righteousness; the earthly is the exemplification of pride, the heavenly of humility.[6]

Now every city and society is a concordant assembly of men united for the attainment of some special purpose.[7] In the case of the earthly

[1] See F. C. Burkitt, 'The Book of the Rules of Tyconius', in vol. III, § 1 of J. A. Robinson, *Texts and Studies* (Cambridge, 1894).

[2] Aug. *De cat. rud.* XIX, 31.

[3] Ibid. XIX, 31: 'duae ciuitates una iniquorum, altera sanctorum, ab initio generis humani usque in finem saeculi perducuntur, nunc permixtae corporibus, sed uoluntatibus separatae, in die uero iudicii etiam corpore separandae.'

[4] Aug. *Enchir.* CXI, 29: 'ciuitates duae, una scilicet Christi, altera diaboli, una bonorum, altera malorum, utraque tamen et angelorum et hominum.'

[5] Aug. *De ciu. Dei*, XIV, xxviii: 'fecerunt itaque ciuitates duas amores duo, terrenam scilicet amor sui usque ad contemptum Dei, caelestem uero amor Dei usque ad contemptum sui. denique illa in se ipsa, haec in Domino gloriatur. illa enim quaerit ab hominibus gloriam: huic autem Deus conscientiae testis maxima est gloria. illa in gloria sua exaltat caput suum: haec dicit Deo suo: Gloria mea, et exaltans caput meum. illi in principibus eius uel in eis quas subiugat nationibus dominandi libido dominatur: in hac seruiunt inuicem in caritate et praepositi consulendo et subditi obtemperando. illa in suis potentibus diligit uirtutem suam: haec dicit Deo suo: Diligam te, Domine, uirtus mea.' See also *De Gen. ad litt.* XI, xv, 20. [6] Aug. *De ciu. Dei*, XIV, xiii.

[7] Aug. *Ep.* CXXXVIII, ii, 10: 'quid est ciuitas nisi multitudo hominum in quoddam uinculum reducta concordiae?' *Ep.* CLV, iv, 9: 'cum aliud ciuitas non sit quam concors hominum multitudo.' *De ciu. Dei*, XV, viii: 'ciuitas nihil est aliud quam hominum multitudo aliquo societatis uinculo conligata.'

city that purpose is the attainment of earthly peace (*pax terrena*); but in the case of the heavenly city it is the attainment of the peace of heaven.[1] And that may be identified with the *summum bonum*, the Vision of God. The earthly city seeks such agreement among its citizens as may produce peace within its walls and plenteousness within its palaces: it is, in other words, a mere external peace with a view to temporal convenience. The heavenly city uses the earthly peace that through it it may seek the peace of heaven with which it will not be crowned till hereafter.[2] The earthly city cannot aspire to the heavenly peace, for it lacks the resources necessary to attain it; and its object is in any case necessarily lower than that of the heavenly city. Moreover, since its moral resources are not even commensurate with its own end, it has to fall back on force, and herein lies another distinction between the two cities. The motive and unitive power of the City of God is love, but of the earthly city force. Apart from justice, which can only derive from the *ciuitas Dei*, the *ciuitas terrena* is nothing but 'flat thievery'.[3]

And yet in this world the two cities, which in thought can be thus distinguished, are inseparably intermingled, and dependent upon one another. Without the aid of the earthly city, the heavenly, in so far as it is identified with the Visible Church, cannot perform its functions, for it possesses property and is defended from its enemies only by the civil power.[4] On the other hand, the earthly society can only hold together because of the concord of its citizens, and such concord implies justice at the least, if not a measure of love; and those gifts are the gifts of the supernal city.[5] Yet the earthly must always be subject to the heavenly, and must serve it according to the will of God.[6] It is in accordance with this line of thought that Saint Augustine justified in the Donatist controversy the appeal which the Church was making to the State over a question which was spiritual and ecclesiastical as well as temporal: 'immo seruiant reges terrae Christo, etiam leges ferendo pro Christo.'[7]

---

[1] Aug. *De ciu. Dei*, XIX, xiv: 'omnis igitur usus temporalium refertur ad fructum pacis terrenae in terrena ciuitate; in caelesti autem ciuitate refertur ad fructum pacis aeternae.'   [2] Aug. *De ciu. Dei*, XIX, xvii.
[3] As J. Healey rendered the 'magna latrocinia' of *De ciu. Dei*, IV, iv: 'remota itaque iustitia, quid sunt regna nisi magna latrocinia? quia et ipsa latrocinia quid sunt nisi parua regna?'
[4] Aug. *In Ioan. Evang. tract.* VI, 25: 'iure regum possidentur possessiones.'
[5] Aug. *De ciu. Dei*, V, xxiv.
[6] H. Reuter, op. cit. Studien III und VI.
[7] Aug. *Ep.* XCIII, v, 19. See references on p. 141 of Reuter, op. cit.

It must, however, be borne in mind that the term *ciuitas superna* is not synonymous with the Church Militant. Sometimes Augustine seems to identify them, but usually the *ciuitas superna* is the whole Church when it is *in patria* and not the Church *in uia*. Similarly the *ciuitas terrena* is not always to be identified with the State as such. Sometimes Augustine does speak in this way, as when he cites Assyria and Rome as examples of the *ciuitas terrena*. And in any case he is not, in the *De ciuitate Dei*, discussing a purely Christian State, which did not exist in his day, but attacking the pagan or semi-pagan State.[1]

But if such a State has the virtue of justice, and even a measure of love, it derives them from the heavenly society by borrowing, and in it we see God overruling evil for good ends. For rulers can render service to God in a way that is not open to any other man.[2] Thus civic duty, at its highest, can proceed from the love of God.[3] And yet, on the other hand, no human government is free from sin; and at its best an earthly society is but the pale image of the true *societas perfecta* which is not of this fallen world.

With the claim that the kings of the earth must by their legislation serve Christ Saint Ambrose would have been in full accord.[4] But Saint Augustine could not have subscribed to the opinion of his teacher Saint Ambrose that the spheres of Church and State were distinct, and that it was only in certain strictly limited departments (for example the suppression of paganism and the maintenance of the Christian moral law) that interpenetration was allowable. For Augustine the whole concept of political and civil authority is that it is merely a concession to human frailty, one of the evils necessitated by man's gratuitous rebellion against God, and the original sin which it entailed. Ambrose would doubtless have allowed that the State possessed and exercised justice. To Augustine such a concept was impossible. The State might

[1] Cf. N. H. Baynes, op. cit. pp. 11, 12.

[2] Aug. *C. Litt. Pet.* II, xcii, 210: 'omnes enim homines seruire Deo debent: aliter communi conditione, qua homines sunt: aliter diuersis donis, quod ille aliud agit in rebus humanis, ille aliud. non enim auferenda idola de terra, quod tanto ante futurum praedictum est [Isa. ii. 18; Zech. xiii. 2], posset quisquam iubere priuatus. habent ergo reges, excepta generis humani societate, eo ipso quo reges sunt, unde sic Domino seruiant, quomodo non possunt qui reges non sunt.'

[3] Aug. *De moribus eccles. catholicae*, I, xxx, 62: 'tu [sc. ecclesia] pueriliter pueros, fortiter iuuenes, quiete senes...exerces et doces...tu ciues ciuibus, gentes gentibus, et prorsus homines primorum parentum recordatione, non societate tantum sed quadam etiam fraternitate coniungis. doces reges prospicere populis; mones populos se subdere regibus....'

[4] Cf. Ambros. *In Ps.* XXXVII, *enarr.* 43.

provide a working arrangement for the preservation of earthly peace; but that is not justice in its fullest sense. For Saint Augustine the State is always and necessarily subordinate and ancillary to the City of God, even when it is not hostile to it. It may be necessary, but it is always a necessary evil, the result of human pride and selfishness, which are brought under restraint by civil government, but which can only be eradicated by the infusion of the divine Spirit of mercy, truth and love. The ends of the earthly society are at their best partial and temporal: therefore it must always be in subjection to that holy society whose ends are complete and eternal. In short, the only true *ciuitas* which exists at all is the eternal one, for the earthly is but the faint and imperfect image of the true and ideal laid up in heaven. And the essential basis of it is righteousness.[1] That is Augustine's greatest legacy in this matter to succeeding ages, and its influence has been incalculable.[2]

Man is a pilgrim on earth, and not a resident citizen, for his true home is on high. He 'seeks a better city, that is an heavenly',[3] and God has prepared it for him. It is not a city, as the city of this world, built upon the shifting sands of human wickedness and ineptitude, but 'a city that hath foundations, whose builder and maker is God'[4]: 'fundamenta eius in montibus sanctis.'[5]

---

[1] Cf. A. Robertson, op. cit. pp. 281, 282.

[2] Cf. A. Robertson, op. cit. Lect. VI, pp. 225 sq.; Figgis, op. cit. Lectures V and VI, pp. 81–117.

[3] Heb. xi. 16.   [4] Heb. xi. 10.   [5] Ps. lxxxvii. 1.

CHAPTER VI

SAINT AUGUSTINE'S DOCTRINE OF THE MINISTRATION OF THE SACRAMENTS

Closely connected with the doctrine of the Church thus forged under the pressure of Donatist teaching is the view which Saint Augustine evolved of the ministration of the sacraments. The question posed to Augustine may be summed up in the words of Professor Turner:[1]

Can the sacramental gifts by which under the Christian dispensation the divine life is imparted to men be validly (however irregularly and improperly) ministered apart from the unity of the Body of Christ? This question, like all other questions of theory, was not consciously formulated till the pressure of circumstances compelled churchmen to try to think out the answer.

Augustine found himself obliged to answer the theory which the Donatists held tenaciously and propagated indefatigably, that the validity of sacraments even within the Church depended on the sanctity of the minister, with the corollary that the unworthiness of the minister hindered the effect of the sacrament. Their attachment to this theory had led them from the beginning to pronounce not merely that Caecilianus, consecrated Bishop of Carthage by Felix, whom they wrongly held to have been a *traditor* under the persecution of Diocletian, was no real bishop, but also that all those in communion with him, whether in Africa or beyond the seas, were implicated in the effects of the crime alleged to have been committed by Felix, and that therefore their sacraments were entirely invalid and ineffective. On this theory the whole body of Christian people dispersed throughout the world was in schism from the true Church, which now remained only in the party of Donatus. We have seen that the sin which, owing to the original circumstances of their schism, they placed in the forefront of their argument was that of *traditio*;[2] and at the Conference of Carthage they refused even to be seated in the same room as the sons of *traditores*. But by this time their claim to exclusive holiness had become ridiculous when contrasted with the violent excesses of their bishops and Circumcellions, and with the dishonest obstructions of their representatives at the Conference. It was now little more than an *a posteriori* attempt to seek a theological basis for the continuance of a schism already inveterate.

[1] C. H. Turner, in Swete, op. cit. pp. 143, 144. [2] Supra, pp. 3-5.

DOCTRINE OF THE MINISTRATION OF THE SACRAMENTS

1. *Earlier views*

When the Donatists adopted this view of the Church as the society of the pure, which they did increasingly as the fourth century progressed and the divisions of African Christianity hardened, it had no novelty about it. Puritanism in discipline was a very primitive and tenacious Christian outlook.[1] Even in New Testament days the author to the Hebrews had refused absolution to those guilty of grievous sin.[2] Such stringency had gradually eased, but it remained vigorous in certain schisms, such as those of Novatian and Donatus.[3] It excluded from the Church, and therefore also from the valid ministration of sacraments, those clergy who committed mortal sins. We must trace briefly the course of such beliefs before we approach the new interpretation for which Saint Augustine was to be responsible.

Some 130 years before the origin of the Donatist schism, we find Saint Irenaeus teaching that the true Church must avoid heretics and evil-thinkers, self-pleasing and self-satisfied schismatics, hypocrites actuated by love of money or of reputation. 'All such we must shun, and cleave to those who keep the Apostles' doctrine and combine with holy orders soundness in word and conduct without offence.'[4] Two classes of bishops are here ruled out, those who are heretics or schismatics, and those who are orthodox, but who are unworthy because their lives are inconsistent with their faith. If a bishop has been justly ejected on either of these grounds, Saint Irenaeus would have said that his ministerial acts were simply null and invalid, for in the primitive view it is certain that a bishop was not really conceivable apart from his church and people.[5] The precise question posed by Donatism in the fourth century is of course not answered by Irenaeus; but we may be sure that, holding as he does with all primitive Fathers that the Church is the sole fountain of grace, and that outside it none can be assured of salvation or of sacramental grace, he would have ruled out as entirely worthless the sacraments of schismatics or men of impure life.[6] For if the Holy Spirit does not dwell outside the Visible Church, no one can expect the fruits of his grace to be found outside it.[7]

The standpoint of Tertullian is similar, and expressed with his

[1] Supra, pp. 1–3. [2] Heb. vi. 4–6.
[3] See references on supra, pp. 1–3; and Swete, op. cit. p. 149.
[4] Iren. *Adu. haer.* IV, xxvi, 2–5. See Swete, op. cit. p. 125.
[5] Swete, op. cit. p. 126.
[6] E.g. Iren. *Adu. haer.* III, xvii, 2, xxiv, 1; IV, xxxiii, 7. See Swete, op. cit. pp. 125–7.
[7] See Swete, op. cit. p. 127; Iren. *Adu. haer.* III, xxiv, 1.

customary vehemence in the *De baptismo*, written before 200, and in a now lost Greek work on the subject.[1] In Ephesians iv. 5 we find the phrase 'one baptism' coupled with 'one Lord, one faith'. Therefore, says Tertullian, those who have not the one Lord and the one faith cannot possess the one baptism. Only those in the communion of the Church can possess them; and so heretics, when they come into the Church, are baptized as pagans, for anything they have received before is worthless, and is not in any case Christian baptism, which God bestows only through the Church.[2]

But these difficulties became much more acute under the disciplinary difficulties involved in the incidence of persecution. It was especially the persecutions of Decius and Diocletian which compelled the Church to face them. After the Decian persecution arose the Novatianist schism, holding a strictly puritan view, and refusing reconciliation to apostates even at the point of death; and the Donatists followed a similar line in the next century at the conclusion of Diocletian's persecution.

It is of the greatest importance to consider what Saint Cyprian taught on this question, inasmuch as the Donatists rested their case against Catholicism largely on his authority, which had always been very considerable in Africa.[3] The boast of the Donatists that their church was true because it was holy, in contrast to the mixture of good and evil to be found in the communion of Saint Augustine, was answered by the challenge, 'Let them maintain, if they can, that they have a church better and purer than the united church of Saint Cyprian's day'.[4] Saint Cyprian laid it down as axiomatic that the sacraments cannot be ministered except in the one Church which alone can dispense the living water: for him the validity and efficacy of sacraments

[1] Tert. *De bapt.* xv.
[2] Ibid. xv: 'unus omnino baptismus est nobis, tam ex Domini euangelio quam ex apostolicis litteris, quoniam "unus Deus" et "unum baptisma" et una ecclesia in caelis. sed circa haereticos sane quid custodiendum sit digne quis retractet. ad nos enim editum est: haeretici autem nullum habent consortium nostrae disciplinae, quos extraneos utique testatur ipsa ademptio communicationis. non debeo in illis cognoscere quod mihi est praeceptum, quia non idem Deus est nobis et illis, nec unus Christus, id est idem, ideoque nec baptismus unus, quia non idem; quem cum rite non habeant, sine dubio non habent, nec capit numerari quod non habetur. ita nec possunt accipere, quia non habent.'
[3] See, for example, Aug. *C. Cresc.* II, xxxi, 39; *De bapt.* III, i, 1; and on Cyprian's baptismal controversy, see Benson, op. cit. ch. viii, pp. 331–436.
[4] Aug. *C. Ep. Parm.* III, ii, 8: 'dicant ergo, si possunt, meliorem se atque purgatiorem habere nunc ecclesiam, quam erat ipsa unitas beatissimi Cypriani temporibus.'

are synonymous; and the Cyprianic doctrine of sacraments is entirely bound up with his view of the Church, which has already come to our notice.[1]

Saint Cyprian followed Saint Irenaeus and Tertullian in thus restricting valid sacraments to the fold of the One Church. For that Church is, in the words of the Song of Songs, 'hortus conclusus... fons signatus, puteus aquae uiuae'.[2] If the Church is a closed garden, it cannot be open to the strangers and the profane; if a sealed fountain, those who have no access to it cannot drink of its water; if a well of living water, those who are cut off from that water cannot be quickened and sanctified by it.[3] The custodians of this living water are the bishops lawfully appointed by the Church.[4] Or again, the Church is the Paradise of the Old Testament, watered by four streams,[5] and whatever is outside that Paradise is not watered.[6] Consequently it is Saint Cyprian's teaching that the sacraments of Christ can only be conferred within the Church of Christ; they cannot exist, be enjoyed or be transmitted outside that Church. The controversy that caused the amplification of such a view by Cyprian was that about rebaptism, in the course of which, by conciliar action in Africa, Cyprian sought to establish the African practice adopted by a Council of Carthage held about 213 under Agrippinus, Bishop of Carthage next but one before Cyprian, of baptizing as pagan converts those who had already been baptized by heretics and schismatics outside the bounds of the true Church. The lapsed who had originally received Catholic baptism were reconciled by the imposition of hands.[7] This council of Agrippinus was attended by about seventy bishops drawn from the provinces of Africa and Numidia.[8]

On the other hand the Church of Rome took the more liberal view that baptism administered in the name of the Blessed Trinity, and with the intention of incorporating a man into the Church, was valid even

[1] Chapter IV, supra, pp. 96–105.

[2] Cypr. Ep. LXIX, 2: 'una est columba mea, perfecta mea, una est matri suae, electa genetrici suae...hortus conclusus, soror mea sponsa, fons signatus, puteus aquae uiuae.' See Cant. iv. 12; vi. 8.

[3] Cypr. Ep. LXIX, 2; LXXIII, 10, 11.

[4] Ibid. LXXIII, 11: 'nos diuino permissu rigamus sitientem Dei populum, nos custodimus terminos uitalium fontium.' [5] Gen. ii. 10–14.

[6] Cypr. Ep. LXXIII, 10: 'numquid de ecclesiae fontibus rigare potest qui totus in ecclesia non est? numquid paradisi potus salubres et salutares impertire cuiquam potest qui peruersus et a semetipso damnatus et extra paradisi fontes relegatus aruit et aeternae sitis siccitate deficit?' [7] Ibid. LXXI, 2.

[8] Vincent. Lerinen. Commonitorium, I, 6; Aug. De unico bapt. XIII, 22; Ep. LXXI, 4; De bapt. II, vii, 12; III, ii, 2, xii, 17; IV, iv, 8; V, i, 1.

if administered by heretics and schismatics. Thus the baptismal controversy was, from one point of view, one further instance of the rigorist tendency in African churchmanship which we have already noticed. Rebaptism had been after the council of Agrippinus partly accepted in Africa (as it was practised, to some extent, in Asia), but in the next forty years it fell into desuetude in Africa, so that Saint Cyprian tells us that many heretics had been received into the Church without baptism.[1] Moreover, three councils on baptism in a space of less than two years would scarcely have been necessary if in Cyprian's own day rebaptism had been universal.[2]

The first of these councils (Cyprian's fifth Council of Carthage) met in 255, and consisted of twenty-one bishops.[3] The seventieth Epistle of Cyprian is their conciliar declaration, not unanimously promulgated, that the baptism of heretics is worthless, and that baptism is necessary on reception into the Church from heresy.[4] This letter was addressed to eighteen Numidian bishops who held the doctrine of rebaptism, but had asked for a synodical declaration because of disputes with their colleagues about it.

The second of the baptismal councils met in the following year, 256, and seventy-one bishops, from Africa and Numidia, were present.[5] They used the phrase, which became popular with those who supported rebaptism, of the 'stain of profane water bespotting' those washed in it, and ordered all converts to be baptized. This decision was unanimous, and it was transmitted to Stephen, Bishop of Rome, in a synodical letter. Stephen, through some bishop who sat in the council, and who sympathized with the Roman view, circulated a paper admitting even the baptism of Marcion,[6] a copy of which was submitted to Saint Cyprian by Iubaianus, a Mauretanian bishop. Cyprian answered it in the Epistle to Iubaianus, which he later read to the third council on baptism as the final statement of his own doctrine.[7] The bishops who took the synodical letter of the second council to Rome were not even granted an audience by Stephen.[8] But the letter was answered by post,[9] and in the reply Stephen vituperated Cyprian with some vigour, calling him a false Christian, a false apostle, and

[1] Cypr. *Ep.* LXXIII, iii, 23.
[2] Aug. *De bapt.* III, xii, 17.
[3] For these three synods, see Hefele, op. cit. vol. I, pp. 98–116, and Benson, op. cit. pp. 349 sqq.
[4] Cypr. *Ep.* LXXI, 1.   [5] Ibid. LXXIII, 1.
[6] Ibid. LXXIII, 4; Aug. *De bapt.* VII, xvi, 30.
[7] Cypr. *Ep.* LXXIII.   [8] Ibid. LXXV, 25.
[9] Ibid. LXXIV, 1.

a deceitful worker.[1] At the same time he wrote also to Asia Minor, threatening to excommunicate the whole Church there if it persisted in its support of the practice of rebaptism.[2]

In the same year, on 1 September 256, the third and greatest council on baptism assembled at Carthage. Eighty-seven bishops came from the provinces of Africa, Numidia and Mauretania, and gave their opinions in the audience of a great assembly of clergy and laity. Saint Cyprian, who presided once more, is praised by Saint Augustine for the *perseuerantissima tolerantia* of his introductory speech, in which he urged the bishops to speak each his own mind, and recognized the right of every bishop to hold his own opinion without being forced into excommunication or schism on account of it. We have preserved in the last two books of Augustine's *De baptismo* the very words of all these bishops. They delivered their judgements in order of seniority, and after the council Cyprian wrote to his supporter, Firmilian, Bishop of Caesarea and Metropolitan of Cappadocia, to inform him of the decision.[3]

Cyprian had thus won unanimous African support for his thesis that all who came into the Church from heresy must be baptized. Like Tertullian[4] Cyprian maintained that as Christians have not the same faith as heretics, so they cannot share in one baptism.[5] Moreover, the sole authority to baptize was committed by Christ to the Church,[6] and those who usurp it must expect the judgement of Korah, Dathan and Abiram.[7] The mere use of the name of Christ cannot invest heretical baptism with Christian effectiveness, for it is ministered in falsity by those to whom it has not been committed.[8]

---

[1] Ibid. LXXV, 25: 'et tamen non pudet Stephanum...Cyprianum pseudo-Christum, et pseudo-apostolum et dolosum operarium dicere.'

[2] Ibid. LXXV, 25; Euseb. *H.E.* VII, 5.   [3] Cypr. *Ep.* LXXIII, LXXIV.

[4] Tert. *De bapt.* XV (quoted supra, p. 146).

[5] Cypr. *Ep.* LXXIII, 4.   [6] Ibid. LXXIII, 7.

[7] Ibid. LXXIII, 8: 'quod supplicium manet eos qui alienam aquam baptismo inferunt falso, ut diuina censura ulciscatur et uindicet id haereticos contra ecclesiam gerere quod non nisi soli licet ecclesiae.'

[8] Ibid. LXXIII, 16: 'non est autem quod aliquis ad circumueniendam christianam ueritatem Christi nomen opponat ut dicat, "in nomine Iesu Christi ubicumque et quomodocumque baptizati gratiam baptismi sunt consecuti", quando ipse Christus loquatur et dicat, "non omnis qui mihi dicit, Domine, Domine, introibit in regnum caelorum", et iterum praemoneat atque instruat ne quis a pseudoprophetis et pseudoChristis in nomine suo facile fallatur... unde apparet non ea statim suscipienda et adsumenda quae iactantur in Christi nomine, sed quae geruntur in Christi ueritate.' Ibid. 21: 'baptisma nobis et haereticis commune esse non potest, cum quibus nec pater Deus nec filius Christus nec sanctus Spiritus nec fides nec ecclesia ipsa communis est.'

The same applies to the celebration of the Eucharist. As heretical baptism defiles instead of cleansing, so to communicate with an heretical celebrant is to eat and drink damnation to oneself.[1] For those who serve the altar must be pure, and what greater impurity can there be than to oppose Christ, to scatter the Church which he purchased with his precious blood, and to forget peace and love in the mad pursuit of hatred?[2] There is here no thought of any indelible character of priesthood or of episcopacy; and no distinction, such as Augustine was to emphasize, between invalid and irregular ministrations. What was not within the Church was outside, and outside the Church there can be no grace. Repudiation by the Church renders a man's ministry ineffective, and he can and should be repudiated for any kind of impurity or grave wickedness. Of such impurity the worst form is schism. In it a man takes a stand against Christ[3] and so severs himself from the Church which is the source of grace and the ark of God, 'cui soli baptisma concessum est'.[4] To approve heretical baptism, therefore, is to do dishonour to God, the giver of the only true baptism.[5]

In thus teaching that valid sacraments are to be found only within the fold of the one Church which has been commissioned by Christ to administer them, Cyprian is on ground of unshakable firmness, and his argument logically unanswerable. The problem is that his argument does not face the real difficulty which arises when we are compelled to consider the case of those who are not clearly outside the Church on the grounds of heresy or of schism, but are otherwise of unworthy life. If a minister is formally deposed from his office (as Cyprian says an unworthy bishop should be), the case is clear. But if a minister has not been deposed, to what degree of obliquity must he descend before we can pronounce that at this point he ceases to become the lawful minister of a sacrament? Cyprian's decision which rules out schismatic ministrations, described by Dr Benson as 'Cyprian's unforeseen contribution to Donatism, the invalidation of an ecclesiastical act on account of the

[1] Ibid. LV, 27; *De bapt.* IV, iv, 6; *De lapsis*, VI; see Aug. *C. Cresc.* IV, xxvi, 33.
[2] Cypr. *Ep.* LXXII, 2.
[3] Ibid. LXXII, 2: 'aduersus Christum stetisse'.
[4] Ibid. LXIX, 2; LXXIII, 7, 8; see I Pet. iii. 20, 21.
[5] Cypr. *Ep.* LXXIV, 8: 'si sic honor Deo datur, si sic a cultoribus eius et sacerdotibus timor Dei et disciplina seruatur; abiiciamus arma, manus demus in captiuitatem, tradamus diabolo ordinationem euangelii, dispositionem Christi, maiestatem Dei, diuinae militiae sacramenta soluantur, castrorum caelestium signa dedantur, succumbat et cedat ecclesia haereticis, lux tenebris, fides perfidiae, spes desperationi, ratio errori, immortalitas morti, caritas odio, ueritas mendacio, Christus antichristo.'

subjective imperfection in the minister', does not answer the problem posed by the conferring of sacraments within the Church by a minister of unworthy life. The Donatists, though professing to rely on Saint Cyprian's principles, had really shifted their ground on this point, and in Saint Augustine's time laid their principal stress not so much on the prerogative of the Church (which is Cyprian's main ground) as on the character of the minister of the sacraments. Saint Cyprian's extant writings give no final answer to this further question, for it was not one which he considered. Saint Augustine touched the weak spot in the whole Cyprianic theory when he pointed out that it lays too much emphasis on the human agent, and too little on the virtue of Christ, the giver of divine grace through the sacraments which he instituted.[1]

But with this criticism goes always the praise of Augustine for Cyprian's love of unity and breadth of charity.[2] By the middle of the fourth century the circumstances of the time, the need for reconciling to the Church the Donatist majority of African Christians, and the shift of emphasis in Donatist teaching on the sacraments which we have just noticed, brought the burning question of the middle third century once again to the fore, and demanded a new and larger answer to this ancient problem. It remained for Saint Optatus to take the next step and, in teaching that sacraments derive their validity from Christ the giver and not from the human minister, to prepare the way for the fully developed doctrine taught by Saint Augustine.

The Bishop of Milevis had to deal, as Saint Augustine later, with Donatists who claimed the authority of Saint Cyprian, but had pressed too far his suggestion that orthodox but morally unworthy ministers cannot confer valid sacraments. Saint Optatus holds that the impossibility of forming a final judgement of the character of men in this world implies that we must go on to reject the Donatist thesis that sacraments derive their validity from the

---

[1] See also L. Saltet, *Les réordinations: Étude sur le sacrement de l'ordre* (Paris, 1907), ch. i.

[2] Cf. Nicolaus Cusanus, *De concordantia catholica* (Basel, 1565), I, v (p. 698): 'nam licet fides una sit funiculus colligantiae, tamen aliquando uarietas opinionum absque pertinacia stat cum unitate. Cyprianus enim et totum concilium LXX episcoporum diuersi fuerunt in fide catholica Ecclesiae, tamen non abscissi, quoniam non praetulerunt opinionem unitati fraternae, quia absque pertinacia fuerunt, ut Augustino placet, libro secundo contra Donatistas' (i.e. *De bapt.* II). There may be hidden sinners, but if they remain, they may, if they have authority, minister sacraments. 'haec est catholica ueritas, quam cuncti fideles fatentur, quam Augustinus libro secundo contra epistulam Parmeniani ad longum prosequitur.' See E. F. Jacob, *Essays in the Conciliar Epoch* (Manchester, 1943), p. 17.

holiness of him by whom they are conferred: 'hoc munus baptismatis esse dantis non accipientis.'[1] This maxim, says Optatus, is true if it be applied to Christ, the giver of all sacramental grace, but not if applied to the human agent of such ministry.[2] The part of the recipient is that he should receive in faith,[3] and men must understand that in baptism they are ministers of God's gift and not lords and masters.[4] For baptism is administered not in the name of the minister, but of the Blessed Trinity; and its gift is good, as being God's gift, whether the minister be good or evil.[5] Whoever plants and whoever waters, it is God who gives the increase.[6] Optatus sums up his teaching in the phrase: 'sacramenta per se esse sancta, non per homines.'[7]

But he goes further, and with Saint Cyprian teaches that sacraments conferred by schismatics are not merely useless, but have an actively defiling effect upon the recipient: 'dum lauant, sordidant.'[8] Christian baptism in the name of the Trinity confers grace, but the pretended conferment of baptism on one who has already received it involves loss of the eternal life conferred at first[9] and logically argues belief in another God and another Christ.[10] Rebaptism therefore not only confers no grace, but inflicts spiritual injury upon the recipients.[11]

2. *Saint Augustine's view*

In the doctrine of the sacraments as of the Church, we have to bear constantly in mind the ardent desire of Augustine for the reunion of African Christians. The Donatist challenge on the subject of the

[1] Opt. v, 7.
[2] Opt. v, 7: 'et utinam de Deo diceretis, qui huius rei dator est. sed quod stultum est, uos dicitis esse datores.'
[3] Opt. v, 7, 8.
[4] Opt. v, 7: 'intelligite uos uel sero operarios esse non dominos.'
[5] Opt. v, 7: 'quisquis in nomine Patris et Filii et Spiritus sancti baptizauerit, apostolorum opus impleuit... nam et ipsis sic mandatum est, ut opus esset illorum sanctificatio Trinitatis, nec in nomine suo tingerent, sed in nomine Patris et Filii et Spiritus sancti: ergo nomen est quod sanctificat, non opus.'
[6] Opt. v, 7: 'ut ostenderet quia hoc totum sacramentum baptismatis Dei est, ut illic sibi nihil uindicet operarius, sic ait: Ego quidem plantaui—id est, de pagano catechumenum feci; Apollo rigauit—hoc est, ille catechumenum baptizauit. sed ut cresceret quod plantatum est aut irrigatum est, Deus fecit.' See also Opt. v, 12.
[7] Opt. v, 4.   [8] Opt. v, 3.
[9] Opt. v, 1: 'baptisma christianorum Trinitate confectum confert gratiam.'
[10] Opt. v, 3: 'si datis alterum baptisma, date alteram fidem; si datis alteram fidem, date et alterum Christum; si datis alterum Christum, date alterum Deum.'
[11] Opt. v, 3: 'tales sunt, quos aut rebaptizatione aut poenitentia sauciastis.' Opt. IV, 6.

necessity of the sacraments being ministered by those who were pure might conceivably have been answered by Augustine along some such lines as these. He might have agreed with them in adopting the Cyprianic standard of exclusiveness, and in ruling out all schismatic ministrations as altogether invalid and worthless; while at the same time challenging the Donatists to establish their impossible thesis that they only were pure Christians. For they had failed to prove their charges of *traditio* levelled against Catholics; and any defence of their claim that they only were pure was impossible in the face of their Circumcellion activities. Such a line of argument would probably have been sufficient to establish Augustine's own position: that it would ever have reconciled any Donatists to the Catholic fold it is impossible to assert. And a desire for reconciliation was never absent from his mind. For in him we find the meeting place of the polemical theologian and the pastor of souls, and no scheme of thought which did not do justice to both aspects of his ministry could ever have satisfied him. Therefore he was impelled to find an answer to the challenge of the Donatists who based themselves mainly on the Cyprianic tradition, and yet had emphasized rather the commission of the minister by those who ordained him than his function as a bestower of a grace that is God's alone. Only a few of his opponents were in any sense dogmatic theologians (and they not very good ones, to judge by what has been preserved of their writings): they were for the most part laity ignorant of the theological issues involved, who had inherited the schism by the accident of their birth and upbringing in the Donatist fold, and had neither the knowledge nor the inclination to think the matter out for themselves, more particularly in view of the uncompromising hostility which the Circumcellions and other extremists invariably showed to any Donatists who were inclined to waver in their allegiance. Augustine's teaching, therefore, must be calculated to win such people to the truth. For they were inheritors of schism, and not implicated in the full guilt of being its originators. Augustine desired to receive the Donatist laity without baptizing them, and the Donatist clergy without ordaining them, recognizing the baptism or ordination which they had already received in schism. In accordance with this practical outlook (which undoubtedly weighed very heavily with him),[1] he found an important distinction between the sacrament itself, and the use and benefit of the sacrament. The sacraments, he taught, are indeed received in schism, but not profitably. For the principal gift which they all confer is the charity which comes of God the Holy Ghost. Saint Paul had taught

[1] See C. H. Turner, in Swete, op. cit. preface to 2nd ed., 1921, p. xxxii.

that even the greatest virtues are useless without this charity which is God's supreme gift.[1] And charity is, moreover, the special gift of Christian unity;[2] the man who separates himself from his Christian brethren proves manifestly that he is destitute of this supreme grace.[3] Now, if the baptism he has received in schism has failed to give him this grace of charity, it is proved to be useless.[4] Yet the grace is there, as it were latent, and will revive when by union with Christ's fold, the Holy Church throughout all the world, a man begins to enjoy and to practise this greatest of God's gifts.[5] It is impossible to confine the grace of the sacraments within the Church. Cyprian had taught that the rivers which water Paradise water nothing outside;[6] but Augustine reminds us that in fact the Book of Genesis says that they flowed outside Paradise, watering Mesopotamia and Egypt.[7]

(a)   *Distinction between validity and regularity of sacraments*

Saint Augustine was thus faced with the same case as Saint Optatus, and he builds on the same principle in answering it. He also invites his opponents to look behind the human minister, and see in the sacraments the operation of Christ, who is the giver of all sacramental grace.[8] This is the main theme of his two most relevant works against the Donatists, the *De baptismo contra Donatistas* and the *De unico baptismo*. The Donatist principle, he rightly maintains, breaks down because it is impossible for us to determine who is pure and who impure.[9] But since a sacrament is God's gift, it is no hindrance to its efficacy that it is administered by

[1] I Cor. xiii.   [2] Aug. *De bapt.* III, xvi, 21.
[3] Aug. *De unico bapt.* xv, 25: 'caritas ista non tenetur nisi in unitate ecclesiae.'
[4] Aug. *C. Ep. Parm.* II, iv, 24: 'quapropter securus iudicat orbis terrarum bonos non esse qui se diuidunt ab orbe terrarum in quacumque parte terrarum.'
[5] Aug. *Ep.* LXI, 1: 'sed propterea dolemus errantes, et eos per caritatem Christi lucrari Deo cupimus, ut sanctum sacramentum quod foris ab ecclesia habent ad perniciem, in pace ecclesiae habeant ad salutem.' See also *Ep.* LXXXIX, 8; XCIII, xi, 46; *De bapt.* VI, v, 7.
[6] See supra, p. 147.   [7] Aug. *De bapt.* IV, i, 1.
[8] Aug. *C. Ep. Parm.* II, xiv, 22; *De bapt.* IV, i, 1: 'sic ergo baptismus ecclesiae potest esse extra ecclesiam, munus autem beatae uitae non nisi intra ecclesiam reperitur: quae super petram etiam fundata est, quae ligandi et soluendi claues accepit. haec est una quae tenet et possidet omnem sui sponsi et domini potestatem; per quam coniugalem potestatem etiam de ancillis filios parere potest: qui si non superbiant, in sortem haereditatis uocabuntur; si autem superbiant, extra remanebunt.' Ibid. IV, x, 16: 'quantum arbitror, iam claret et liquet, in ista quaestione de baptismo non esse cogitandum quis det, sed quid det; aut quis accipiat, sed quid accipiat; aut quis habeat, sed quid habeat.' Ibid. IV, xvii, 24; VI, i, 1.
[9] Aug. *C. Cresc.* IV, xii, 14.

an unworthy minister,[1] for since it is impossible for us to test the worthiness of any particular minister, those who receive the sacraments must have a better guarantee of their validity than the worthiness of a minister can give: they must have the assurance of nothing less than the divine institution of the sacrament.[2] Ministers may vary, but the gift of God is constant and trustworthy.[3] In baptism the cleansing proceeds from the word of God, and not from the merits of the minister.[4]

Augustine shows further why it was that Saint Cyprian and others erred on this question. It was because they failed to distinguish between the sacrament itself, and the use or effect of the sacrament, and concluded that because the effects, namely deliverance from sin and rectitude of heart, were not to be found in heretics and schismatics, therefore no sacrament was to be found with them.[5] It is true that the Church is the home of grace, and alone has the divine authority necessary to give full effect to the sacraments conferred therein. Yet the tradition of Christendom, apart from the Cyprianic tradition in Africa and the remnants in Asia Minor and elsewhere in the East of the strict view, is inclusive and not exclusive; and provided that baptism is ministered with intention to conform to the ordinance of Christ, and in the name of the Blessed Trinity (which is itself a guarantee against Christological and Trinitarian heresies), then Augustine is prepared to follow that tradition in allowing that baptism, and not repeating it. The converted schismatic therefore is received by imposition of hands, for the conferring of the Holy Ghost with his gift of charity, and not by administering baptism to him.[6] Baptism and other sacraments are irregular outside the Church, for it alone dispenses God's grace, and in it alone can we be sure of receiving this in full.[7] But Augustine

[1] Aug. *Ep.* LXXXIX, 5; XCIII, xi, 48. [2] Ibid. XCIII, xi, 46, 48.
[3] Ibid. CV, iii, 12: 'quare ergo non uerum dicimus et recte sapimus, quia semper Dei est illa gratia et Dei sacramentum, hominis autem solum ministerium; qui si bonus est, adhaeret Deo, et operatur cum Deo; si autem malus est, operatur per illum Deus uisibilem sacramenti formam, ipse autem donat inuisibilem gratiam. hoc sapiamus omnes, et non sint in nobis schismata.' *Ep.* XXIII; XCIII, xi, 46; CVIII, i, 3; *C. Cresc.* III, v, 5.
[4] *Serm.* XCIX, xiii, 13; CCLXVI, 3; *Ep.* LXXXIX, 5; XCIII, xi, 48; *De unit.* XXI, 58; *C. Litt. Pet.* II, cviii; III, xxxv, xlii, xlix; *C. Ep. Parm.* II, xiv, 32.
[5] Aug. *De bapt.* IV, xvii, 24; VI, i, 1.
[6] Ibid. V, xxiii, 33: 'propter caritatis autem copulationem quod est maximum donum Spiritus sancti, sine quo non ualent ad salutem quaecumque alia sancta in homine fuerint, manus haereticis correctis imponitur.'
[7] Aug. *Serm.* LXXI, xix, 32: 'potest enim esse uisibilis forma palmitis etiam praeter uitem; sed inuisibilis uita radicis haberi non potest, nisi in uite. proinde corporalia sacramenta, quae portant et celebrant etiam segregati ab unitate corporis

will not say that sacraments outside the Church are altogether worthless.[1] The grace is there, latent and useless, valid but not efficacious to salvation or to the well-being of souls, until it be revivified by the fructifying gift of charity within the fold of the Church.[2] Although he thus distinguishes between *habere* and *salubriter* or *utiliter habere*, and proclaims the reviviscence of baptismal and other grace when a man comes into the Catholic unity, and also explicitly condemns the full doctrine of Cyprian and Optatus that baptism administered outside the Church has an actively defiling effect upon the recipient,[3] yet he does not deny that the recipient is implicated in the negation of charity which schism involves, and wounded spiritually by it.[4] By this line of

Christi formam possunt exhibere pietatis; uirtus uero pietatis invisibilis et spiritualis ita in eis non potest esse, quemadmodum sensus non sequitur hominis membrum, quando amputatur a corpore.'

Serm. CCLXVIII, 2: 'iam uero si membrum praecidatur de corpore, numquid sequitur spiritus? et tamen membrum agnoscitur quid est; digitus est, manus est, brachium est, auris est: praeter corpus habet formam, sed non habet uitam. sic et homo ab ecclesia separatus. quaeris ab illo sacramentum, inuenis; quaeris baptismum, inuenis; quaeris symbolum, inuenis. forma est; nisi intus spiritu uegeteris, frustra foris de forma gloriaris.'

[1] Aug. *Ep.* XXIII; LXXXIX, 5; XCIII, xi, 46, 48; CVIII, i, 3.

[2] Aug. *De bapt.* III, x, 13-15: 'sed aliud est non habere aliquid, aliud non iure habere uel inlicite usurpare. non itaque ideo non sunt sacramenta Christi et ecclesiae, quia eis inlicite utuntur non haeretici solum sed etiam omnes iniqui et impii. sed tamen illi corrigendi aut puniendi, illa uero agnoscenda et ueneranda sunt.' Ibid. VII, xxxiii, 65: 'salus enim propria est bonis, sacramenta uero communia bonis et malis.' *C. Ep. Parm.* II, xiii, 30.

[3] Aug. *De bapt.* III, x, 15: 'non est autem aqua profana et adultera, super quam nomen Dei inuocatur, etiamsi a profanis et adulteris inuocetur; quia nec ipsa creatura, nec ipsum nomen adulterum est. baptismus uero Christi uerbis euangelicis consecratus, et per adulteros et in adulteris sanctus est, quamuis illi sunt impudici et immundi: quia ipsa eius sanctitas pollui non potest, et sacramento suo diuina uirtus assistit, siue ad salutem bene utentium, siue ad perniciem male utentium. an uero solis uel etiam lucernae lux, cum per coenosa diffunditur, nihil inde sordium contrahit, et baptismus Christi potest cuiusquam sceleribus inquinari? si enim ad ipsas res uisibiles quibus sacramenta tractantur, animum conferamus; quis nesciat eas esse corruptibiles? si autem ad id quod per illas agitur, quis non uideat non posse corrumpi, quamuis homines per quos agitur, pro suis moribus uel praemia percipiant, uel poenas luant?'

[4] Ibid. I, v, 6: 'illi uero qui per ignorantiam ibi [sc. in parte Donati] baptizantur, arbitrantes ipsam esse ecclesiam Christi, in istorum [sc. schismatis auctorum] quidem comparatione minus peccant, sacrilegio schismatis uulnerantur non ideo non grauiter quod alii grauius.' Ibid. I, viii, 10: 'itaque illi quod baptizant sanant a uulnere idololatriae uel infidelitatis, sed grauius ferunt uulnere schismatis. idololatres enim in populo Dei gladius interemit (Exod. xxxii), schismaticos autem terrae hiatus absorbuit (Num. xvi) et Apostolus, Si habeam, inquit, fidem, ita

thought, Augustine placed the heretic or schismatic outside the Church in the same position as the man of vicious life or erroneous faith within the Church.[1] Whether this view adequately answers the cogent argument of Saint Cyprian that it is only in the one Church that sacraments can really be conferred or received must be left for consideration after we have examined more closely Saint Augustine's teaching on the sacraments.

(b)   *The baptismal question*

The circumstances of the Donatist controversy, in the framework of which we see Augustine's doctrine of sacraments developed, concentrated attention upon the sacrament of Christian initiation, for rebaptism was the characteristic error of the Donatists.[2] To the Donatists who claimed that true Christian baptism was only administered within their sect, and who rebaptized all Catholics whom they received, Augustine says: 'We charge you with two errors, first that you are wrong on the question of baptism, and secondly that you set yourselves apart from those who do hold the true opinion.'[3] The Donatists claimed the support of Saint Cyprian, and so Augustine's greatest work against them on the baptismal question, the seven books *De baptismo*, is devoted to a careful examination of this question; and in the last two books of this work he records and comments on the opinions of the eighty-seven bishops of Cyprian's third council on baptism held at Carthage on

ut montes transferam, caritatem uero non habeam, nihil sum.' *Ep.* LXI, 1: 'sed propterea dolemus errantes, et eos per caritatem Christi lucrari Deo cupimus, ut sanctum sacramentum quod foris ab ecclesia habent ad perniciem, in pace ecclesiae habeant ad salutem.'

[1] Aug. *De bapt.* III, xiv, 19: 'neque enim parua res est in ipsa intus catholica tenere integram fidem, ita ut omnino non de aliqua creatura sed de ipso Deo nihil aliter credat quam ueritas habet. numquidnam ergo, si in ipsa catholica baptizatus postea legendo audiendo et pacifice disserendo, ipso Domino reuelante, cognouerit aliter se antea credidisse quam debuit, denuo baptizandus est?' Ibid. IV, xx, 27: 'propositis itaque duobus, uno catholico cum his omnibus uitiis, alio haeretico sine his (quae possunt non esse in haeretico), quamuis contra fidem non uterque disputet, et tamen contra fidem uterque uiuat et spe uana uterque fallatur et a caritate spiritali uterque dissentiat et ob hoc uterque ab illius unicae columbae corpore alienus sit, cur in uno eorum sacramentum Christi cognoscimus, in alio nolumus, quasi aut huius aut huius sit, cum in utroque idem sit et non nisi Dei sit et quamuis in pessimis bonum sit?'

[2] Aug. *Ep.* XXIII; XXXIV, 2, 3; XXXV, 3; XLIV, V, 12; CVI; CVIII, 1; *C. Litt. Pet.* I, i, 2 sq.; II, ii, 4 sq., xxxii, 72 sq., xlvii, 109 sq.; *De unico bapt.* XI, 18 sq.; Opt. II, 19–26; III, 11; V, 4–7; VI, 4.

[3] Aug. *C. Cresc.* III, iii, 3: 'duo mala uestra uobis obiicimus; unum, quod erratis in baptismi quaestione; alterum, quod uos ab eis qui de hac re uerum sentiant separatis.'

1 September 256.¹ He applies the general theory of sacraments which has been outlined in the last section, and he refers the reader to the gift which proceeds only from God rather than to the merits of the minister at whose hands we receive that gift in the sacraments.² There is an important distinction between baptizing *per ministerium*, which is the function of the human minister, and baptizing *per potestatem*, which pertains only to Christ.³ Moreover, Christ was careful to preserve this power of conferring baptism in his own hands: if it had been given to his servants, there might have been as many baptisms as there were servants.⁴ But he has committed it to men for them to minister, and that to bad men as well as to good. What they administer is Christ's gift, not theirs, and derives all its virtue from him, and nothing from them.⁵ Only in this way can we have any security concerning the sacraments: if we had to wonder whether he who ministered a sacrament to us was pure, or whether he had some hidden fault that would vitiate the sacrament, we should never be able to know whether we had received the sacrament or not.⁶ What is deficient in schismatic baptism,

¹ Aug. *De bapt.* VI and VII.
² Opt. V, 1 sq.; Aug. *De bapt.* I, i, 2 sq.; *C. Litt. Pet.* I, i, 2 sq.; III, xiv, 16 sq.; *De unit.* XXI, 57 sq.; *C. Cresc.* II, v, 7 sq.; *De unico bapt.* II, 3 sq.; XVII, 32.
³ Aug. *In Ioan. Evang. tract.* V, i, 6: 'aliud est enim baptizare per ministerium, aliud baptizare per potestatem. baptisma enim tale est, qualis est ille in cuius potestate datur; non qualis est ille per cuius ministerium datur...tale..baptisma Domini, qualis Dominus; ergo baptisma Domini diuinum, quia Dominus Deus.'
⁴ Ibid. V, i, 7: 'potuit autem Dominus Iesus Christus, si uellet, dare potestatem alicui seruo suo, ut daret baptismum suum tamquam uice sua, et transferre a se baptizandi potestatem, et constituere in aliquo seruo suo, et tantam uim dare baptismo translato in seruum, quantam uim haberet baptismus datus a Domino. hoc noluit ideo, ut in illo spes esset baptizatorum, a quo se baptizatos agnoscerent. noluit ergo seruum ponere spem in seruo...et potuit hanc potestatem seruis dare et noluit. si enim daret hanc potestatem seruis, id est, ut ipsorum esset quod Domini erat, tot essent baptismi quot essent serui.' Ibid. VI, 6: 'si enim, ut iam dixi, fratres mei, transferretur potestas a Domino in ministrum, tot baptismata essent quot ministri essent, et iam non staret unitas baptismi'; VI, 8: 'illud quod datum est, unum est, nec impar propter impares ministros; sed par est et aequale, propter, Hic est qui baptizat.'
⁵ Ibid. V, i, 11: '...potestatem dominici baptismi in nullum hominem a Domino transituram, sed ministerium plane transiturum; potestatem a Domino in neminem, ministerium et in bonos et in malos. non exhorreat columba ministerium malorum, respiciat Domini potestatem. quid tibi faciat malus minister, ubi bonus est Dominus? quid te impedit malitiosus praeco, si est beneuolus iudex?'
⁶ Aug. *Enarr. in Ps.* CXLV, 9: 'non eris tu plane auctor salutis meae; ille erit de quo securus sum; de te incertus sum.' *C. Ep. Parm.* II, x, 21 sq., xiv, 32 sq.; *De bapt.* I, i, 2; *C. Litt. Pet.* I, i, 2 sq.; II, v, 11, vi, 13, xxxiii, 78; *C. Cresc.* III, iv sq.; *De unico bapt.* II, 3 sq.; *Breu. Coll.* III, viii, 12.

as in any other schismatically conferred sacrament, is the gift of charity. It is not baptism which is the nuptial garment required of those who would sit at God's feast, nor is it the altar, nor fasting, nor churchgoing, nor the working of miracles. It is charity, and not every kind of charity, but charity with a pure conscience and an unfeigned heart.[1] For in baptism we are born from the womb of our mother the Church,[2] in which alone true charity can be possessed. If our first birth is of woman, our second is of God and the Church,[3] a birth from the Spirit, and not from the flesh. Schismatic baptism constitutes a man a member of Christ's Church, but since it cannot confer the charity without which any gift is useless, he cannot be endued with the Spirit or endowed with his gifts, until by submission to the Church he enters the home of grace, and becomes capable of receiving God's gifts in the company of God's faithful people.[4] Yet, in spite of the inutility of baptism in a schismatic or an heretic, its indelible character remains, and sets him apart from men as a member of the Church.[5] His position is to be compared to that of an army deserter, who on his return is not enrolled afresh, but begins to exercise his duties as a soldier which have till then been pretermitted.[6] But, although the grace of baptism is thus susceptible of reviviscence, it is of no use to, and will not save, a man who remains obdurately in schism. Its effect may in such a case be said to be mortal to the soul, for it wounds the recipient with the sacrilege of schism.[7]

So there is a clear distinction between *baptismum* and *ius dandi baptismum*. The right of conferring baptism reposes only in the Church, as the Body

[1] Aug. *Serm.* XC, 5.   [2] Ibid. CXIX, iv, 4: 'uulua matris, aqua baptismatis'.
[3] Ibid. CXXI, 4: 'prima natiuitas ex masculo et femina, secunda natiuitas ex Deo et ecclesia.'
[4] Ibid. CCLXIX, 2: 'nec inmerito recte intelligitur, quamuis ipsos baptismum Christi habere fateamur, haereticos accipere uel schismaticos Spiritum sanctum, nisi dum compagini adhaeserint unitatis per consortium caritatis. tunc enim gentium linguae etiam ipsorum erunt; quia ubi sunt illae, ibi et ipsi erunt, in eodem scilicet Christi corpore ubique crescente, seruantes unitatem spiritus in uinculo pacis.'
[5] Aug. *C. Ep. Parm.* II, xiii, 28.
[6] Aug. *De symbolo*, VIII, 16: 'sed haereticis baptismum non mutamus. quare? quia sic habent baptismum, quomodo desertor habet characterem; ita et isti habent baptismum; habent, sed unde damnentur, non unde coronentur. et tamen si desertor ipse correctus incipiat militare, numquid audet quisquam et characterem mutare?'
[7] Aug. *De bapt.* I, v, 6; *C. Faustum*, XII, xx: 'quod post dies quadraginta emissus coruus non est reuersus...significat homines inmunditia cupiditatis teterrimos, et ob hoc ad ea quae foris sunt in hoc mundo nimis intentos, aut rebaptizari, aut ab his quos praeter arcam, id est praeter ecclesiam, baptismus occidit, seduci et teneri.'

of Christ; and only when so conferred and received can it have its full value. Yet where it exists among schismatics, it is not to be rejected, but completed by the imposition of hands for reconciliation, to make a man able in the fold of the Church to enjoy all the blessings of the Holy Spirit.[1]

This case answered the Donatist argument that the impure cannot make others pure, and that a man without grace cannot confer grace. They had appropriated from Saint Cyprian the catchword, 'qui non habet, quomodo dat?',[2] but it was easy for Optatus and Augustine to answer it with 'Deum esse datorem'; and nothing is stronger in Augustine's sacramental doctrine than this reference of the validity of baptism to its divine source, where it is independent of the merits of the minister which no one is able to assess in this world.

(c) *Other sacraments*

On the sacrament of baptism the Roman theology thus anticipated very nearly the developed formulas of Saint Augustine. But whereas Saint Augustine extended the same principle to cover all the sacraments, and so was able to arrive at a consistent and coherent conception of the relation of the sacraments to the Church, the Roman opponents of Saint Cyprian carefully limited the application of their principle to the one sacrament only. They were statesmen not theologians, and were reluctant to deal with more than the problem that had actually arisen: moreover, so far as it was the instinct of Christian charity that had dictated their policy, that instinct was satisfied when it was conceded that Christians outside the communion of the Church possessed, truly and validly, the sacrament primarily necessary to salvation. However much Stephen and Cyprian differed about baptism, it was common ground to them, and it would seem not only to all their contemporaries but to their successors of the next generations for another hundred years, that no other sacrament could be validly administered in heresy or schism. The gift of the Holy Spirit, whether in confirmation or in ordination, was recognised on both sides as reserved to the Holy Church.[3]

From this summary, it will be seen what a great step Augustine took in extending the application of his principle to other sacraments than baptism. Of these the most important is ordination, for the Donatists not merely rebaptized all who came into their fold from Catholicism, but also reordained any Catholic clergy whom they were able to convert. And in smoothing the path for returning Donatists, Augustine

[1] Aug. *De bapt.* I, xi, 18; IV, x, 16; V, viii, 9; VI, v, 7; *C. Ep. Parm.* II, 28; *C. Litt. Pet.* I, 8.
[2] Cypr. *Ep.* LXIX, 11.
[3] C. H. Turner, in Swete, op. cit. pp. 160, 161.

DOCTRINE OF THE MINISTRATION OF THE SACRAMENTS

and his supporters promised Donatist clergy who submitted that they should retain their orders. This was contrary to the general practice of the Western Church, which received all such converted heretical and schismatic clergy into lay communion,[1] and required synodical sanction in Africa, which was obtained by Augustine, who pleaded that it was necessary for the reconciliation of schismatics.[2] Cyprian had followed the ancient tradition in holding that an erring bishop loses the power of conferring holy orders, which, like other sacraments, must be derived from the Church alone.[3] But Augustine, having introduced a new distinction between the validity and regularity of sacraments, is able to apply to ordination the principle which he taught in relation to baptism, and to say that ordination confers indelible character. That character is unprofitable in schism, where none of God's grace can be effective to salvation, but it lies there latent, and will revive when unification with the Church bestows on a man the revivifying power of the Holy Spirit. Then for the first time a schismatic can exercise the authority committed to him by ordination. This distinction between the indelible marking of every recipient of orders, which takes place whoever administers the sacrament, and the administration of the grace of the sacrament of orders, which only takes place within the fold of the Church, solved for Augustine the problem of receiving Donatist bishops and clergy. When they are received they already possess the first, and are now able to receive the second, and proceed in their ministrations without further ordination.[4] In one of his treatises on marriage, he introduced an

---

[1] C. H. Turner, in Swete, op. cit. p. 151: 'In the case of baptism, the claim for its recognition was extended step by step to one class of separatists after another. But the process was very much slower in the case of holy orders. There is no sign that before Saint Augustine any theologian had worked out the theory, or any church had adopted the practice, of the general recognition of orders conferred outside the Catholic Church.'

[2] Fifth Council of Carthage, 401. See Hefele, op. cit. vol. II, p. 422; and Chapter III, supra, pp. 49, 50.

[3] Aug. *Ep.* LXV, 2.

[4] Aug. *C. Ep. Parm.* II, xiii, 28: 'nulla ostenditur causa cur ille qui ipsum baptismum amittere non potest, ius dandi possit amittere. utrumque enim sacramentum est, et quadam consecratione utrumque homini datur, illud cum baptizatur illud cum ordinatur, ideoque in catholica utrumque non licet iterari. nam si quando ex ipsa parte uenientes etiam praepositi bono pacis, correcto schismatis errore, suscepti sunt, etiam si uisum est opus esse ut eadem officia gererent quae gerebant, non sunt rursus ordinati, sed sicut baptismus in eis ita ordinatio mansit integra; quia in praecisione fuerat uitium, quod unitatis pace correctum est, non in sacramentis, quae ubicumque sunt ipsa sunt...sicut autem habent in baptismo quod per eos dari possit, sic in ordinatione ius dandi; utrumque quidem ad perniciem suam, quamdiu caritatem non habent unitatis. sed tamen

interesting comparison between this problem of ordination and the blessing of children to married people. Although the first end of marriage is the procreation of children, yet there are cases in which, by continence or sterility, this blessing is denied to married people. In that case there still remain for them the other two blessings of marriage, faith between consorts, and the sacramental grace which marriage confers, and which shows forth the unity of Christ and the Church; and theirs is still an indissoluble union, for the holiness of the sacrament is more important than fecundity.¹ It is even so with ordination. By it an indelible gift of grace is conferred; and when it is conferred in the Church a man is given authority to minister in a particular see or congregation. But if no congregation assembles to which he can minister, his orders are not thereby rendered void, and he retains his status and the right of administering such sacraments as pertain to his order, although in fact he is not doing so. The same applies if he has been removed from office, and the principle holds good in the case of the Donatists ordained in schism.²

In the case of confirmation, difficulty and confusion had arisen through the use of imposition of hands both in confirmation and in the reconciliation of heretics.³ We have seen that the Roman practice, in contrast to the African, was to receive schismatics by imposition of hands, and not by baptism. Cyprian violently opposed Stephen on this point. But on both sides confusion reigned as to the purpose of this imposition of hands. A comparison of Stephen⁴ and Cyprian⁵

aliud est non habere, aliud perniciose habere, aliud salubriter habere.' Ibid. II, xiii, 30: 'si enim utrumque sacramentum est, quod nemo dubitat, cur illud non amittitur et illud amittitur? neutri sacramento iniuria facienda est.'

¹ Aug. *De bono coniug.* III, XVIII, XXIV; cf. *De nupt. et conc.* I, x–xii.

² Aug. *De bono coniug.* XXIV: 'quemadmodum si fiat ordinatio cleri ad plebem congregandam, etiamsi plebis congregatio non subsequatur, manet tamen in illis ordinatis sacramentum ordinationis; et si aliqua culpa quisquam ab officio remoueatur, sacramento Domini semel imposito non carebit, quamuis ad iudicium permanente.' See G. G. Willis, *An Analysis, with Commentary, of S. Augustine of Hippo's Treatises on Marriage* (M.A. dissertation, University of Manchester Library, 1939), p. 107.

³ See Saltet, op. cit. ch. i; and Benson, op. cit. pp. 420–1.

⁴ Cypr. *Ep.* LXXIV, 1: 'etiam illud adiunxit [Stephanus] ut diceret: si quis ergo a quacumque haeresi uenerit ad uos, nihil innouetur nisi quod traditum est, ut manus illi imponatur in poenitentiam, cum ipsi haeretici proprie alterutrum ad se uenientes non baptizent, sed communicent tantum.'

⁵ Ibid. LXXII, 1: 'de eo uel maxime tibi scribendum et cum tua grauitate ac sapientia conferendum fuit, quod magis pertineat et ad sacerdotalem auctoritatem, et ad ecclesiae catholicae unitatem pariter ac dignitatem de diuinae dispositionis ordinatione uenientem, eis qui sunt foris extra ecclesiam tincti, et apud haereticos

shows us that the laying-on of hands for penitence and that for receiving the Holy Ghost are parallel. This confusion is corrected in the anonymous treatise *De rebaptismate*, where the author says that the bestowal of the Holy Ghost by imposition of hands is preceded by penitence.[1] That this was not approved by Cyprian is clear from his attack on it, in which he says that if heretics have indeed received true baptism in heresy, they have been able to receive the gift of the Holy Spirit; and that if they have not received true baptism, they have received nothing at all, and must start again from the beginning as if they were pagans.[2] Crescens of Cirta, one of the eighty-seven bishops of Cyprian's final council on baptism, spoke of it as a reconciliation in penitence.[3] In the next century, in 385, Siricius, Bishop of Rome, had confirmed this settled Roman view of heretical reception by confirmation.[4]

It was Augustine who attacked this view at its basis. He held that in this case the imposition of hands is not confirmation at all, but an act

et schismaticos profanae aquae labe maculati, quando ad nos atque ad ecclesiam, quae una est, uenerint, baptizari oportere; eo quod parum sit eis manum imponere ad accipiendum Spiritum sanctum, nisi accipiant et ecclesiae baptismum. tunc enim demum plene sanctificari et esse filii Dei possunt, si sacramento utroque nascantur.'

[1] *Auctor de Rebaptismate*, x: 'idcircoque poenitentiam agentibus correctisque per doctrinam ueritatis et per fidem ipsorum, quae postea emendata est purificato corde eorum, tantummodo baptismate spiritali, id est manus impositione episcopi et Spiritus sancti subministratione, subueniri debeat.'

[2] Cypr. *Ep.* LXXIII, 6: 'quod si secundum prauam fidem baptizari aliquis foris et remissam peccatorum consequi potuit, secundum eandem fidem consequi et Spiritum sanctum potuit, et non est necesse ei uenienti manum imponi ut Spiritum sanctum consequatur et signetur. aut utrumque enim fide sua foris consequi potuit, aut neutrum eorum qui foris fuerat accepit.'

[3] *Sent. episc.* 8; in Aug. *De bapt.* VI, xv, 24: 'censeo ego omnes haereticos siue schismaticos, qui ad catholicam ecclesiam uenire uoluerint, non ante ingredi nisi exorcizati et baptizati fuerint; exceptis his sane qui in ecclesia catholica fuerint ante baptizati, ita tamen ut per manus impositionem in poenitentiam ecclesiae reconcilientur.'

[4] Siric. *Ep.* I, i, 2 (*P.L.* XIII, 1133): 'prima itaque paginae tuae fronte signasti, baptizatos ab impiis Arianis plurimos ad fidem catholicam festinare, et quosdam de fratribus nostris eosdem denuo baptizare uelle: quod non licet, cum hoc fieri et Apostolus uetet (Eph. iv. 5), et canones contradicant, et post cassatum Ariminense concilium missa ad prouincias a uenerandae memoriae praedecessore meo Liberio generalia decreta prohibeant, quos nos cum Nouatianis aliisque haereticis, sicut est in synodo constitutum, per inuocationem solam septiformis Spiritus episcopalis manus impositione Catholicorum conuentui sociamus; quod etiam totus Oriens Occidensque custodit: a quo tramite uos quoque posthac minime conuenit deuiare, si non uultis a nostro collegio synodali sententia separari.'

of reconciliation.[1] Communicants are received without further confirmation, but by this imposition of hands they receive the greatest gift of the Holy Ghost, which until now has been ineffective in them, and that is the gift of charity, which is only possessed in Catholic unity.[2] For Augustine, confirmation, like baptism, confers indelible character, and cannot be repeated. But here again a useful distinction is introduced: in confirmation there are two gifts, the imposition of hands, and the *consignatio* of the soldier of Christ.[3] Grace thus received in schism will remain latent till fructified by union with the Church.

The same principle applies to the Eucharist. Schismatics may receive the outward sign, but they cannot receive the inward grace of refection by the Body and Blood of Christ, for they do not belong to the bond of peace which is signified and set forth in the sacrament of unity. Moreover, they eat and drink damnation to themselves, for they cannot discern the Lord's Body, which is given only to the faithful.[4] The

[1] Cf. *Constit. Apostol.* VIII, 9 (tit.): Χειροθεσία καὶ εὐχὴ ὑπὲρ τῶν ἐν μετανοίᾳ.

[2] Aug. *De bapt.* v, xxiii, 33: 'manus autem impositio, si non adhiberetur ab haeresi uenienti, tamquam extra omnem culpam esse iudicaretur; propter caritatis autem copulationem, quod est maximum donum Spiritus sancti, sine quo non ualent ad salutem quaecumque alia sancta in homine fuerint, manus haereticis correctis imponitur.' Ibid. III, xvi, 21: 'manus autem impositio non sicut baptismus repeti non potest. quid est enim aliud nisi oratio super hominem?'

[3] Aug. *C. Litt. Pet.* II, civ, 239: 'et in hoc unguento sacramentum chrismatis uultis interpretari: quod quidem in genere uisibilium signaculorum sacrosanctum est, sicut ipse baptismus; sed potest esse in hominibus pessimis, in operibus carnis uitam consumentibus, et regnum caelorum non possessuris... discerne ergo uisibile sanctum sacramentum, quod esse et in bonis et in malis potest, illis ad praemium, illis ad iudicium, ab inuisibili unctione caritatis, quae propria bonorum est.'

[4] Aug. *De ciu. Dei*, XXI, xxv: 'quamobrem quod ait Dominus Iesus, "hic est panis qui de caelo descendit, ut si quis ex ipso manducauerit, non moriatur. ego sum panis uiuus qui de caelo descendi; si quis manducauerit ex hoc pane, uiuet in aeternum", quomodo sit accipiendum merito quaeritur. et ab istis quidem quibus nunc respondemus, hunc intellectum auferunt illi quibus deinde respondendum est: hi sunt autem qui hanc liberationem, nec omnibus habentibus sacramentum baptismatis et corporis Christi, sed solis catholicis, quamuis male uiuentibus, pollicentur; quia non solo, inquiunt, sacramento, sed re ipsa manducauerunt corpus Christi, in ipso scilicet eius corpore constituti, de quo corpore ait Apostolus, "unus panis, unum corpus multi sumus". qui ergo est in eius corporis unitate, id est in christianorum compage membrorum, cuius corporis sacramentum fideles communicantes de altare sumere consueuerunt, ipse uero dicendus est manducare corpus Christi et bibere sanguinem Christi. ac per hoc haeretici et schismatici ab huius unitate corporis separati possunt idem percipere sacramentum, sed non sibi utile, immo uero etiam noxium, quo iudicentur grauius, quam uel tardius liberentur. non sunt quippe in eo uinculo pacis, quod illo exprimitur sacramento.'

DOCTRINE OF THE MINISTRATION OF THE SACRAMENTS

principle of reviviscence is no use here, for the Eucharist is a sacrament that may be repeated. It is certain that in Augustine's eyes it conveys no gift to those who are separated from the unity of Christ which is signified by the sacrament. But to those who receive it in faith within the Church's fold it confers the gift of unity.[1] Again, in speaking to the children on the blessed sacrament, he emphasizes this showing forth of Christian unity in the sacrament, and uses Cyprian's illustration of the unity prefigured by the compacting of many grains in bread, and of many grapes in wine.[2] For the Eucharist, with its significance of unity, is the special gift of God through the Church to his children.

Donatists were therefore (says Richard Hooker) in process of time, though with much ado, wearied and at the length worn out by the constancy of that truth which teacheth, that evil ministers of good things are as torches, a light to

---

[1] Aug. *Serm.* LVII, 7: 'ergo eucharistia panis noster quotidianus est; sed sic accipiamus illum, ut non solum uentre sed et mente reficiamur. uirtus enim ipsa quae ibi intelligitur, unitas est, ut redacti in corpus eius, effecti membra eius, simus quod accipimus. tunc erit uere panis noster quotidianus.'

[2] Ibid. CCLXXII: 'si ergo uos estis corpus Christi, et membra, mysterium uestrum in mensa dominica positum est; mysterium uestrum accipitis... quare ergo in pane? nihil hic de nostro afferamus, ipsum Apostolum identidem audiamus, qui cum de isto sacramento loqueretur, ait, "unus panis, unum corpus multi sumus". intelligite et gaudete: unitas, ueritas, pietas, caritas. "unus panis": quis est iste unus panis? "unum corpus multi". recolite quia panis non fit de uno grano, sed de multis. quando exorcizabamini, quasi molebamini. quando baptizati estis, quasi conspersi estis. quando Spiritus sancti ignem accepistis, quasi cocti estis. estote quod uidetis, et accipite quod estis. hoc apostolus de pane dixit. iam de calice quid intelligeremus, etiam non dictum, satis ostendit. sicut enim ut sit species uisibilis panis multa grana in unum consperguntur, tamquam illud fiat, quod de fidelibus ait scriptura sancta,"erat illis anima una et cor unum in Deum"; sic et de uino. fratres, recolite unde fit uinum. grana multa pendent ad botrum, sed liquor granorum in unitate confunditur. ita et Dominus Christus nos significauit, nos ad se pertinere uoluit, mysterium pacis et unitatis nostrae in sua mensa consecrauit. qui accipit mysterium unitatis, et non tenet uinculum pacis, non mysterium accipit pro se, sed testimonium contra se.' Cf. Cypr. *Ep.* LXIII, 13: 'quo et ipso sacramento populus noster ostenditur adunatus; ut, quemadmodum grana multa in unum collecta et commolita et commista panem unum faciunt, sic in Christo, qui est panis caelestis, unum sciamus esse corpus, cui coniunctus sit noster numerus et adunatus.' Ibid. LXXVI, 6: 'denique unanimitatem christianam firma sibi atque inseparabili caritate connexam etiam ipsa dominica sacramenta declarant. nam quando Dominus corpus suum panem uocat de multorum granorum adunatione congestum, populum nostrum quem portabat indicat adunatum; et quando sanguinem suum uinum appellat de botris atque acinis plurimis expressum atque in unum coactum, gregem item nostrum significat commistione adunatae multitudinis copulatum.'

others, a waste to none but themselves only, and that the foulness of their hands can neither any whit impair the virtue nor stain the glory of the mysteries of Christ.[1]

In part Saint Augustine is the inheritor of the classical doctrine of Christian antiquity that as the authority to administer the sacraments of Christ was committed by him to the Apostles, and through them and their successors the bishops to the ministers of the Catholic Church, therefore it is only within that Church that sacraments have the value which Christ intended for them. Like other gifts of God, they are useless without the all-embracing gift of charity. And since by its very uncharitableness of separation schism demonstrates that its supporter has not the grace of charity, which includes not only love of God but also love of the brethren, it is clear that he is not competent to receive the gifts which God bestows through his Church. We have seen that the general view before Saint Augustine's time, taught by Irenaeus, Cyprian and others, had been that this principle excludes as invalid any sacrament administered otherwise than in the fold of the Church. Now this is a very strong position. It is the only purely logical position adopted on the matter in the first five centuries. It is able to settle at a glance any problem of the ministration of sacraments. For it is easy to say who is in the unity of the Catholic Church, and therefore by authority of his ordination able to minister the sacraments, and who does not possess this authority. It involves neither the difficulty, introduced by the puritan schisms, of attempting in this world to adjudicate on the quality of the lives of ministers, nor the problems which Saint Augustine's more liberal doctrine postulates. It simply inquires whether a minister has the authorization of the Church for his ministerial acts, and it enables the recipients of sacraments to rest not upon the merits of ministers but on the promises of God made to them in the sacraments. From this principle men can derive security and confidence in the use of sacraments.

Of all this Augustine is aware. And yet he felt compelled in the circumstances of his time to seek a wider basis for his doctrine of the ministration of sacraments. Was there any possible position between the completely authoritarian attitude of the earlier Fathers and an utter antinomianism? It was clear that if such a position was to be discovered, distinctions must be sought. Augustine found one which satisfied him in teaching that in a sacrament there are two things to be considered, the sacrament itself and the use or benefit of the

[1] Richard Hooker, *Ecclesiastical Polity*, v, lxii, 10.

sacrament.¹ When the outward sign of a sacrament is performed according to the institution of Christ, when, for instance, the person is baptized with water with the Trinitarian formula, and with the intention of doing what the Church does in that sacrament, namely incorporating a person into the fold of Christ, then the sacrament is there according to Christ's promise. But then we must go further and consider the use and benefit of the sacrament. The sacrament itself is not limited to members of the visible Catholic Church, but its use is. Those on whom it is conferred in schism possess it, whether it be baptism, or confirmation, or holy orders, but it is no use to them outside the Church. No grace is available, though the empty shell of the sacrament is possessed. If they remain outside the Church all their lives, they receive nothing. But when they enter the fold of the Church, and are reconciled by the imposition of hands, the latent grace revives, and what was possessed before uselessly, and more probably to the damnation of the recipient, is now crowned with the gift of charity, and begins to fructify the life of the recipient. On this principle, Augustine admitted to lay communion those baptized in schism, and to the exercise of their orders in the Catholic Church those who had been ordained in schism. Thus the work of God in the sacraments is recognized, and not repudiated as it was on the old theory, and the position of the Church as the sole home of grace is at the same time triumphantly vindicated. The Donatist principle, 'qui non habet, quomodo dat?', had found its answer in the words of Augustine, 'quod fieri non debuit, factum ualet'.

And yet in some ways the sacramental theory of Augustine is not so satisfying as the old theory of Cyprian.² Professor Turner says:

> The historian of Christian doctrine may venture the judgement that in order to achieve this short-cut to reunion Saint Augustine sacrificed something of even higher value when he threw over the inherited tradition of the Church on the subject of the sacraments. The divorce of the theology of the sacraments from the theology of the Church was a heavy price to pay even for the union with the Donatists.³

If on the one hand it may be regarded as somewhat surprising that a theologian of such caution as was Professor Turner should thus commit himself to the extreme view that Augustine 'threw over the inherited tradition of the Church on the subject of the sacraments', when

¹ Aug. *In Ioan. Evang. tract.* XXVI, 11: 'aliud est sacramentum, aliud uirtus sacramenti.'
² See Swete, op. cit. preface, pp. xxxii–xxxiv; and C. H. Turner, 'Apostolic Succession', Sect. B, 'The Problem of Non-Catholic Orders', ibid. pp. 143 sq.
³ Swete, op. cit. preface, p. xxxiii.

in fact he did all he could to save this principle within the framework of a wider principle, yet there is no one who will not subscribe to his judgement that 'in the temper of his approach to the problem of a divided African Christianity, Augustine set a good example',[1] and few will be unconscious of the danger involved in the Augustinian divorce of the theology of the sacraments from the theology of the Church. It is true that we cannot find in Augustine the imposing unity of Church and sacraments which we find in the rigid Cyprianic theory; and there seems little doubt that all the earlier writers whom we have considered would have been most uncomfortable about Augustine's position. If logic is the only guide, it is probably impossible to undermine the case of which Saint Cyprian is the most powerful exponent. If his doctrine is thought to be too rigid, it can always be answered that it, and it only, does full justice to the profound truth that only in the fold of the one Church can we be sure of the outpouring of God's gifts. Augustine's case is weaker than Cyprian's in so far as it does not fulfil this condition. And yet, on the other hand, Saint Augustine makes a valiant and not entirely unsuccessful attempt to effect a reconciliation between the ancient view that only in the Church is God's grace given through the sacraments, and the practical view which he himself adopted, that the broader charity demands a less exclusive criterion, and urges us to believe that, though faithful Christians must labour to preserve unity, yet God's gifts are still more widely given. Augustine so far agrees with Cyprian as to assert that no sacramental gift is of any use to a man still separated from Catholic unity; but he does not deny the existence of any such gift, and claims that it lies there dormant until awakened by the gift of charity which invests a man on his entry into unity with Christ's people. Comprehensiveness can be a great strength to the Church but, if it is pushed too far, may result in disaster and in further schism. With Saint Augustine it was not pushed too far, but in the hands of men with a weaker view of Christian unity and charity it might be a great potential danger. Therefore, Saint Augustine left to the Church in this matter, as in the problem of State intervention in religious disputes, a viewpoint which in his case was adequately safeguarded, but which in the hands of lesser men was destined to be productive of great evils.

[1] Ibid. p. xxxiii.

CHAPTER VII

CONCLUSION

1. *The controversy with the Donatists*

This campaign against Donatism occupied Saint Augustine for a longer period than any other of the many controversies in which during the course of his ministry of forty years he was engaged. Not even Pelagianism claimed his attention for so long a period. But, like all his controversies, it was intensely pastoral in nature, and his work on it is almost entirely casuistical. There is nothing in Saint Augustine of the academic theologian who, like Saint Thomas Aquinas and others, could sit down in his study and write a *Summa Theologica* which should be an exhaustive treatment of either the whole field of theology or of selected parts of it. His genius was utterly different. As he was by early training a rhetorician, so in his religious controversies as a bishop he is not concerned so much with elucidating a complete problem which he sets before himself as with answering questions as they are forced on his attention by the circumstances of his pastorate. Throughout his life he retained the rhetorician's approach to controversy. He was concerned to demolish his opponent's case and to establish his own. His thoroughness in this policy is seen in the care with which he quotes the exact words of his opponents, and answers them point by point. It is a characteristic which is apt to weary the reader with its prolixity. So often we read the same answer to the same statement in practically the same words. But we are compelled to admire the thoroughness of his method. Nothing is left to chance, or to the perverse stupidity of opponents. The simplest mind would feel itself compelled by the exhaustiveness and repetition of the argument to consent to Saint Augustine. And then it may also be said of him that in this as in all his struggles he is never led into vast irrelevancies, into the examination of questions much wider than those proposed to him. Every treatise on Donatism which he wrote, every letter and every sermon, is intensely casuistical. He writes and speaks only under the stimulus of a challenge, and is content if he can answer it without wide divagations. But because the challenges he faces are so varied, the doctrine he teaches is wide, and in fact touches almost the whole theory of Church, Ministry and sacraments.

It may not be irrelevant to illustrate this characteristic of the theology of Augustine by reference to two other of his disputes. That against the Pelagians, which filled the last twenty years of his life, was precisely similar to the dispute with the Donatists in that the great questions involved—those of grace and free will, of election and predestination—were not handled in detail by Augustine until he was compelled to do so by the insistence of what he thought to be the dangerous teaching of the Pelagians. And, as with Donatism, the protracted course of the struggle led him to face all these questions in turn, and to consider them, stage by stage, on the widest scale.[1] Again, in a smaller field, in the three treatises he wrote on marriage, *De bono coniugali*, *De adulterinis coniugiis* and *De nuptiis et concupiscentia*, the whole theology of marriage is embraced, not because Saint Augustine composed an exhaustive treatise on the subject, but because the three controversies which evoked these works happened to be different, and to cover amongst them nearly every aspect of the sacrament of marriage. Thus the first work showed that the prevalent orthodox exaltation of celibacy above marriage did not amount to a condemnation of marriage as evil, and went on to show what the blessings of Christian marriage are; the second answered questions specifically submitted by Pollentius about the Christian rule of indissolubility of marriage, and therefore dealt with adultery and divorce; and the third really formed part of the Pelagian controversy, since it set out to show that the evil of concupiscence, though in fact transmitted on Augustine's theory by means of the matrimonial act, does not imply that marriage is an evil, since such transmission is accidental to marriage, and not constitutionally inherent in it.[2]

So it was with Donatism. The unhappy divisions of African Christianity presented the Bishop of Hippo with an insistent pastoral anxiety in his own diocese, and in the whole Church of Africa, which was impeding the Church's work, distressing the faithful, and exposing the clergy to constant peril. It must be faced, and the schism must be opposed in the councils of the Church, in the advice offered by the Church to the civil government, and in the instruction of the flock committed to Augustine's charge. So his doctrine of unity and schism, of Church, Ministry and sacraments, is inevitably moulded by the schism, and forged under its pressure.

His works against the Donatists may be divided into three classes, the pastoral works designed primarily for the edification of the laity, the

[1] See N. P. Williams, *The Ideas of the Fall and of Original Sin*, Bampton Lectures, 1924 (London, 1927), pp. 315 sq.
[2] See G. G. Willis, op. cit. pp. 49–63.

CONCLUSION

polemical works in which he answers the writings of Donatists, and the more purely theological, in which particular doctrines are worked out more fully.[1] It would be possible to include some works in more categories than one, but the general division of them will stand.

To the first class the first anti-Donatist work, the *Psalmus contra partem Donati* undoubtedly belongs.[2] It was for popular use in instructing the laity in the principles involved in the dispute. The lost work *Contra partem Donati* seems to have been a pastoral letter against the schismatics.[3] Another pastoral to his own flock was the first book *Contra Litteras Petiliani*,[4] as was the *De unitate ecclesiae*, of which the original title is *Ad Catholicos epistula contra Donatistas*,[5] and which was addressed to the people of the diocese of Hippo. The summary of the official minutes of the Conference of Carthage, *Breuiculus Collationis*, was composed expressly for the use of the laity and others who had neither the time nor the patience to read the full report.[6] After the Conference a further pastoral was addressed to the Donatists, entitled *Ad Donatistas post collationem*[7] and designed to prevent their being further seduced by their leaders. Among the more popular works must of course be numbered the many sermons preached on the subject of the schism during the long course of the campaign.

The second class, the polemical works, is by far the most numerous. Above everything else, it displays the care and thoroughness of Saint Augustine's dialectical method. To this class may be assigned most of the anti-Donatist epistles, some of which[8] approach in bulk the full-sized treatises. The works of this class include, in chronological order, the *Contra Epistulam Donati*, *Contra Epistulam Parmeniani*, *Contra quod attulit Centurius a Donatistis*, *Contra Litteras Petiliani* (Books II and III), *Contra Cresconium*, *Probationum et testimoniorum contra Donatistas liber*, *Contra Donatistam nescio quem*, *Admonitio Donatistarum de Maximianistis*, *De unico baptismo*, *De Maximianistis contra Donatistas*, *Ad Emeritum episcopum Donatistarum post collationem*, *Sermo ad Caesariensis ecclesiae plebem*, *Gesta cum Emerito*, and finally *Contra Gaudentium*.

The longest of the works against Donatists stands rather in a class by itself, though it might be included in the list of polemical works. The *De baptismo contra Donatistas* is the most purely theological of the works, and deals in considerable detail with the principal theological question

[1] For an analysis of these anti-Donatist works, see supra, Chapter III, pp. 36–92.
[2] See supra, pp. 36 sq.   [3] See supra, p. 42.
[4] See supra, p. 44.   [5] See supra, pp. 53, 54.
[6] See supra, p. 76.   [7] See supra, p. 79.
[8] E.g. *Ep.* XCIII, CV, CLXXXV.

of the dispute, namely the authority of Saint Cyprian in the baptismal controversy.[1] It concludes, in Saint Augustine's best controversial style, with a detailed examination in order of the judgements of the eighty-seven bishops assembled in Cyprian's final council on baptism in 256.[2]

This intensive literary campaign must not obscure in our minds the very important activity directed by Saint Augustine against the Donatists in other fields. Councils of the African provinces, of Africa proper, Numidia and Mauretania, were meeting frequently, and Augustine was present at most or all of them. Little remains of them except their canons and synodical letters, but we shall not be far wrong in supposing that Saint Augustine was a leading figure in them, when theological questions were under discussion. He stood out among the seven Catholic *actores* who conducted the case at the Conference of Carthage before Marcellinus; but it is to be noted that, according to the verbatim report of that Conference, he said almost nothing on the first two days, leaving to others the conduct of the business in the face of Donatist obstructions. Only when, in the third session, the purely historical and theological controversies arose, did he begin to take a leading part in the business. Perhaps it was the same in the councils of the period. We may well be right in picturing him leading the debates on such matters, and in most cases swaying the assemblies, composed of bishops who have left little or no mark on history, and winning them to his own well-thought-out views. The exception to this statement is of course the problem of appeal to the State, in which he explicitly informs us that his view was changed by the constant pressure of his fellow-bishops.[3] It was the councils, and not Augustine as an individual bishop, who appealed for the assistance of the State in combating Donatism. The policy was justified by its results, for not only did it succeed in reducing Donatism to an insignificant and impotent sect, from being nearly the national church of Africa, but it ensured freedom of conscience to the large number of Donatist laity who were anxious to be united to the Church, but who dared not come over for fear of the persecutions threatened by their fellow-Donatists.

2. *The doctrinal principles involved*

There is no doubt that throughout this wearisome controversy one principle above all others was kept in view by Saint Augustine, and that is summed up in the Catholic watchword of Africa at the time,

[1] See supra, pp. 43, 44.   [2] Aug. *De bapt.* VI and VII.
[3] See, for example, Aug. *Ep.* CLXXXV, vii, 25–31.

CONCLUSION

Pax. The word is woven into the fabric of all Augustine's writing on the subject, and to it we are constantly brought back. Those who came from Donatism were said to seek it; and so we read of the deacon Nabor, himself a converted Donatist who suffered death at the hands of the schismatics,

> conuersus pacem pro qua moreretur amauit.[1]

The end of all Saint Augustine's activity against the schism was one dear to the heart of the wearied and exhausted Church of Africa, the establishment of the unity of the spirit in the bond of peace. The note of this passionate longing for unity and peace is struck at the beginning of the struggle. In his first work on the subject, the *Psalmus contra partem Donati*, the re-echoing refrain

> omnes qui gaudetis de pace, modo uerum iudicate

sets forth the claim of Catholicism to give to all men the peace which passes understanding. Again, the heading of the pastoral letter *De unitate ecclesiae* wishes its readers salvation and the peace which comes from unity and charity.[2] Similarly the final appeal of the pastoral of 403 to the Donatists is an appeal for salvation, peace and unity.[3] But above all these examples is the constant insistence on the desire for peace which marks the sermons preached in Carthage by Saint Augustine as an immediate preparation for the Conference in the fortnight preceding its convocation. In them the faithful were urged to pray for peace, which is the fruit of love, and the sole object of the Catholic bishops at the impending Conference.[4] For unity is the fruit of charity and its manifestation; while schism is the product of uncharitableness and hatred of the brethren.

Peace, then, is the principle of Saint Augustine's conduct of the

---

[1] Epitaph by S. Augustine on the deacon Nabor, quoted supra, p. 41, n. 3.

[2] Aug. *De unit. eccl.*, ad init.: 'Augustinus episcopus dilectissimis fratribus ad nostrae dispensationis curam pertinentibus, Salus quae in Christo est, et pax unitatis et caritatis eius sit uobiscum.'

[3] Aug. *Ep.* LXXVI, 2: 'euigilate ad salutem, amate pacem, redite ad unitatem.'

[4] Aug. *Serm.* CCCLVII and CCCLVIII. Especially *Serm.* CCCLVIII, 1: 'curam nostram pro uobis et pro inimicis nostris et uestris, et pro salute omnium, pro quiete, pro pace communi, pro unitate quam Dominus iussit, Dominus diligit, adiuuent preces Sanctitatis uestrae, ut de illa identidem et ad uos loquamur et uobiscum gaudeamus.' Ibid. 6: '...per nomen ipsius Domini, per auctorem pacis, plantatorem pacis, dilectorem pacis, oramus uos, ut eum pacifice oretis, pacifice deprecemini, et memineritis esse filii eius, a quo dictum est, Beati pacifici, quoniam filii Dei uocabuntur.'

whole controversy. In the course of it three great doctrines were evolved and expounded by him, his doctrine of the Church, his teaching on the relations between Church and State, and his view of the ministration of the sacraments. As these have already been discussed in the course of this inquiry, it will now only be necessary to recapitulate the conclusions to which these studies have led us.

In the doctrine of the Church it was Augustine's task to find the answer to the claim of the Donatists that they were the inheritors of the classical African ecclesiology established by the authority of Cyprian.[1] Augustine does not deny this claim, but he does deny that the Cyprianic doctrine is in any sense Catholic. It had never taken root in Christendom at large; and had been officially abandoned in the West by the Council of Arles, which repudiated the teaching that those baptized outside the Church should be treated as pagans, and baptized when they entered its fold. If Cyprian had been cursed with the uncharitableness of the present-day Donatists, he would have founded a schism because he disagreed with the see of Rome and other foreign churches. But with Cyprian the charity which manifests itself in unity was such a predominant passion that he steadfastly refused to break off communion with those who held the Roman view, thereby teaching the lesson which the Donatists above all others would do well to learn, that charity is greater than truth. The difficulty which Cyprian felt in believing that grace may flow outside the Visible Church is solved by distinguishing between the Visible and the Invisible Church. Augustine's Platonism here assists him in enforcing such a distinction. The Visible Church is but the phenomenal Church, the mere pattern of the real Church Invisible in the heavens, which is the true fullness of him that filleth all in all. The fullness of the Church as Christ's Body, embracing all the truly faithful, is not of this world but of the world beyond the veil: it is the communion of those who are holy and spiritual, who have been tested in the fire, and not found wanting. The most glorious City of God has her perfection in the stability of her eternal abode, and not in this mutable world. She is the home of the predestined elect, of the only true and perfect communion and fellowship of the saints. But here, with the introduction of the thought of predestination, the valuable distinction between a Visible and an Invisible Church becomes blurred. Ultimately an extreme doctrine of predestination cannot be reconciled with a view of the Church on earth as containing both good and evil in unresolved tension. And this problem was never completely worked out by Saint Augustine.

[1] On this see supra, pp. 120 sq.

CONCLUSION

Secondly, the Donatist controversy forced upon Augustine the consideration of the relations of Church and State.[1] The course of the struggle witnesses a transmutation of his mind from a complete belief in the efficacy of persuasion as the only lawful Christian method in controversy to a qualified acceptance of the rightfulness and necessity of compulsion in spiritual matters. This was accomplished partly by the insistent pressure of his fellow-bishops, who had less reluctance than he had in resorting to methods of compulsion; and partly by an increasing realization that true freedom of conscience could only be attained by the Donatists of the rank and file when the constraint of the cruel discipline of the sect was removed from them. It was no use to exhort them to unity and to preach the need of charitableness when they were intimidated by the outrageous bitterness invariably directed against any who presumed to leave the sect for the Church. If they were to be free to choose, and were to become susceptible to logical and charitable argument, they must first be delivered from this tyranny. The only way of achieving this end was to have the whole matter publicly discussed and, when the verdict was given in favour of the Catholic Church, to put down the insolent pride of the Donatist leaders. Milder measures of restraint, those directed against violence and brutality, had failed, and no prospect of the triumph of free judgement lay open but through the outlawing of the sect. Augustine was finally convinced, after many years, that this would be the only effective policy; and in the Conference of Carthage he achieved his ambition. Nothing then remained but to carry the judgement of Marcellinus into effect, and to this he directed his attention until victory could be said to have been won.

The pursuit of this inquiry into the rightfulness of religious coercion combined with the acute problem raised by pagan attacks on the Church subsequent upon the fall of the Eternal City to compel Augustine to think out the wider questions of the relation of Church and State. His general conclusion, as we have seen,[2] is that the earthly city and the heavenly are essentially in conflict, since they rest upon divergent principles, the former upon the love of self, and the latter upon the love of God; and seek divergent ends, the former the peace of earth, and the latter the peace of heaven. They seek them by divergent means, the former by force and the latter by love. Therefore if righteousness and stability of government are to be assured, the earthly city, which borrows from the heavenly city even the justice which alone holds it together, must also borrow the grace of love, and must be prepared to

[1] See supra, Chapter V, pp. 127 sq.   [2] Supra, pp. 139 sq.

serv · Christ by being subject to his Church, and by seeking its good and serving its higher ends by its own legislation. 'Immo uero seruiant reges terrae Christo, etiam leges ferendo pro Christo.'[1]

Finally, not the least important of Saint Augustine's contributions to Western theology is the teaching on the ministration of sacraments. Here again his thought is guided by the circumstances of the Donatist controversy. For the Donatists had taken the theory of Saint Cyprian that it is only within the Catholic Church and by the authority of Christ committed solely to that Church that valid sacraments can be administered, and had warped it by teaching that even within that Church the sacraments can only validly be administered by men of spotless life. When they were asked how it was possible for man to determine who was pure and who impure, they ignored all kinds of unholy conduct except *traditio* during the persecution of Diocletian. They claimed for themselves the title of saints, and for their bishops that of leaders of the saints. It was irrelevant, as far as they were concerned, what violence or cruelty was inflicted on fellow-Christians in the interests of their schism: they thought nothing of theft or incendiarism, or even of suicide. The one thing that mattered was that a minister should be free from the actual or inherited taint of *traditio* in the late persecution. Their claim was that they were pure, and in no wise implicated in having handed over sacred books. This was untrue. Their charge against the Catholics was that they were the descendants of *traditores* and the inheritors therefore of the *traditio* of those like Felix and Caecilianus through whom their orders had been derived. This also was untrue, as the trial of the matter by the Emperor Constantine had shown. Like all puritans, they so insisted on one aspect of holiness as to lose the whole balance of Christian morality and faith. It is untrue to describe the classic Donatist doctrine of the late fourth and early fifth centuries as being Cyprianic, for it had shifted its emphasis from the divine commission of the Church (which was Cyprian's test) to the personal holiness of the minister. Thus it was easy for Saint Augustine to demolish their pretensions, and to indicate the absurdity of pretending that the true Church was now restricted to Africa, and that Christians overseas who had never heard the name of Caecilianus could have been contaminated and excluded from the ministration and reception of Catholic sacraments by the supposed crimes of an unknown foreigner.

Such is the first stage of Augustine's answer to them on this point. The second lies in the distinction which he introduced between valid

[1] Aug. *Ep.* XCIII, v, 19.

CONCLUSION

and regular sacraments. While holding with Cyprian that Christ's sacraments are only perfectly ministered in all things necessary to the same within the one Church, he rejects Cyprian's corollary that all other sacraments are worthless. He directs the reader's thought away from the human minister towards the divine giver of all grace and all sacraments. He recognizes the force of the Cyprianic teaching when he says that the sacraments are only fully efficacious to salvation for those who share in the gift of divine charity which is conferred by union with the Catholic Church. He diverges from it when he distinguishes between the sacrament and the use of the sacrament, and holds that the former is invariably conferred, whether within or without the Church, so long as the sacrament is ministered according to Christ's ordinance, and with the intention of doing what Christ does in that sacrament; but that the latter, the conferment of divine grace efficacious to salvation, is only present to those who receive a sacrament within Christ's unity or, by their subsequent reunion to the Church from schism, find the gift of the sacrament, hitherto useless, reviving under the showers of divine grace which is only to be had within the Church. This line of thought was applied by Saint Augustine first of all to the sacrament of baptism, which circumstances had placed in the forefront of the dispute; but also to confirmation, ordination and the Eucharist, which were involved as well. It represents a middle course between a complete insecurity about sacramental grace and the rigidity of the pure Cyprianic doctrine, and it is safeguarded from the dangers of each of these views.

Saint Augustine's contribution to the development of Christian doctrine made in the course of his struggle against the Donatists may therefore be said to comprise interpretations of the doctrines of the Church as the Body of Christ, of the relation of Church to State, of the theory of compulsion for religious ends, and finally of the ministration of sacraments within and without the Church.

3. *The importance of these principles for the future*

We have traced the development of these lines of thought down to the work of Saint Augustine. It may not be without value to glance at their subsequent importance, and see how they rooted themselves in later theology, and particularly in the post-Reformation theology of the Church of England, which adopted them so widely. Any detailed consideration of them would be far beyond the compass of this study, and yet an indication of their later use may serve to show what it is valuable to remember, namely how Saint Augustine's thought dominates ages after him. Of the pre-Reformation period it may be allowable to select the dominant figure of the scholastic period, Saint Thomas Aquinas in the thirteenth century; and in the fifteenth Cardinal Nicolas of Cues (Cusanus), papal legate in Germany and Bishop of Brixen, who had studied Augustine's anti-Donatist works in detail, and applied many of their principles to the circumstances of his own time. Of the Church of England after the Reformation Richard Hooker will stand as a typical representative, and to him we may add Bishops Pearson and Hall and others of the seventeenth century. All these men knew and valued the work of Saint Augustine, and it is interesting to observe how they use it and apply it to their own purposes.

It may be said without contradiction that the spirit of ἐπιείκεια in which Saint Augustine approached the Donatist problem has rooted itself in Anglican theology of the post-Reformation period, and especially in its classic age of the sixteenth and seventeenth centuries. In all questions of ecclesiastical division charity and truth must be combined, and the solution of practical problems must not evade the maintenance of sound principle. Saint Augustine's view of schism as being the negation of charity became a commonplace of theologians. Accordingly we find that Saint Thomas Aquinas teaches that unity and charity are rent by schism.[1] Like Saint Augustine he insists that the unity of the Church is an unity of the members with one another, and with Christ as the head; but goes beyond him in insisting on unity with the visible head of the Church on earth, the Bishop of Rome.[2] The proper penalty for the breach of this unity is excommunication, to be followed by compulsion at the hands of the temporal power.[3]

In his letters to the Bohemians on the disputed subject of utraquism, Cusanus attacks the Bohemians not primarily for their divergence from Catholic custom in the use of the blessed sacrament, but for the spirit of dissension which prompts their attitude. He urges that unity is the

---

[1] S. Thos. Aq. *Summa Theologica*, II, ii, qu. xxxix, art. i (conclusio): 'schismatis peccatum speciale est uitium caritati oppositum.' Ibid. (corpus): 'peccatum schismatis proprie est speciale peccatum, ex eo quod intendit se ab unitate separare, quam caritas facit; quae non solum alteram personam alteri unit spirituali dilectionis uinculo, sed etiam totam ecclesiam in unitate Spiritus. et ideo proprie schismatici dicuntur, qui propria sponte et intentione se ab unitate ecclesiae separant, quae est unitas principalis.'

[2] Ibid.

[3] Ibid. II, ii, qu. xxxix, art. iv (conclusio): 'cum schismatici uoluntarie se ab ecclesiae unitate separent, et nolint per spiritualem potestatem coerceri, conueniens est eos non modo excommunicationis sententia puniri, sed etiam per temporalem potestatem coerceri.'

CONCLUSION

principal desire of Christians, and that it is shown forth particularly in this sacrament.[1]

[1] Nicolaus Cusanus, *Ep.* II, 'de usu communionis ad Bohemos' (*Opera*, Basel, 1565, p. 830): 'uos uero Bohemi, qui quadam singularitate sub religionis specie, quo ad usum diuinissimae Eucharistiae, a reliquo corpore Ecclesiae cum pacis et unitatis ruptura abscissi estis, contrarium huius agitis, quod praedicatis. nam cum hoc summum conuiuium non solum sit sacramentum unitatis corporis Christi in altaris sacramento, sed et etiam in pacis uinculo, ut uult Augustinus in "de ostensione Ecclesiae ad Donatistas" (est enim mysterium unionis cum capite et membris Christi, ut idem ait de sacramentis fidelium, feria secunda Paschae) non recte ueneramini unitatis sacramentum quod ipso in schismaticam diuisionem utimini. non rectam fidem sacramenti tenetis, si separati a corpore Christi uiuere uos putatis. Christus quidem caput Ecclesiae, uita est quae non uiuificat nisi unita membra. quare cum extra pacem et unitatem ecclesiae sitis, non uitam sed mortis iudicium expectatis....'

Ibid. p. 832: '...multa tamen quae agitis reprehensibilia sunt; inter quae hoc maxime, quod non cum pace ecclesiae, sed temere et uestra sponte (auctoritate prohibente etiam ecclesiastica) ritum communionis iam non sine causa quoad sanguinis speciem, quo ad laicos inconsuetum renouastis, potius eligentes abscindi ab ecclesia, quam a renouatione desistere. ubi haec egistis putantes plus utilitatis uos ex bibitione calicis in separatione quam esu Agni paschalis tantum in unitate et pace consequuturos, non recte iudicastis. non enim utiliter calix Domini unionis et pacis pro causa diuisionis sumitur, nec uitam conferre potest extra ecclesiam, quae corpus Christi est, abscisso membro. nec uobis satis est, nisi diceretis reliquum corpus ecclesiae a uobis abscissum, uosque ueram ecclesiam in paruam Bohemiae partiunculam coarctatam, perniciosius astereretis. in eadem quidem ecclesia remanente unitate, uarium posse ritum esse sine periculo, nemo dubitat; ubi uero praesumptuosa temeritas quemcumque ritum unitati et paci profert, etiamsi in se bonus, sanctus, laudabilisque foret, damnabilis est.'

Ep. VII, 'de amplectenda unitate ecclesiae ad Bohemos' (ibid. pp. 851, 852): 'ex superioribus litteris nostris satis ostensum putamus, Iacobellianos ex compactis pro se allegatis, conuictos sua confessione, extra catholicam ecclesiam esse, quae est sponsa Christi, et nobis solum sufficit sic ostendisse, pro nostra contra eos uictoria, etiamsi in omnibus sacramentis nobiscum concurrerent, ut elegantissime arguit magnus Augustinus contra Rogatistas et Donatistas in multis locis, et late de catholica ecclesia praemissu in epistola quam ipse et Siluanus senex, Valentinus, Aurelius, Innocentius, Optatus, et ceteri episcopi de concilio Zertensi scripserunt ad Donatistas, cuius initium est—"cum in auribus nostris fama crebresceret" (Aug. *Ep.* CXLI). et quod illa sit catholica quae unitur successori Petri apostoli et quod anathema sit aliam esse, ostendit Augustinus in epistola quam ipse et Fortunatus ad Generosum scripserunt (Aug. *Ep.* LIII). ...audiant Iacobelliani quid ait idem Augustinus in epistola ad Bonifacium comitem, quae incipit, "laudo et gratulor et admiror", circa finem; sic enim dicit—"isti autem cum quibus agimus, non sunt desperandi: adhuc enim sunt in corpore; sed non quaerant Spiritum sanctum, nisi in Christi corpore, cuius habent foris sacramentum, sed rem ipsam non tenent intus cuius est illud sacramentum; et ideo sibi iudicium manducant et bibunt. unus enim panis sacramentum est unitatis, quoniam sicut apostolus dicit, unus panis, unum corpus multi sumus. proinde ecclesia catholica

Like Saint Optatus and Saint Augustine, Richard Hooker distinguishes between heresy, schism and apostasy,[1] and stigmatizes schism as the breaking of the bond of unity.

Secondly, in the doctrine of the Church, we find the distinction of Saint Augustine between the Visible and Invisible Church accepted. The Church is imperfect in holiness on earth, and must wait for its perfection hereafter, when all those of the visible society who are unworthy of it shall have been separated, and the invisible society of holy men, now known only to God, shall have been made manifest to all.[2] For Cusanus, writing the *De concordantia catholica* for the Council of Basel (1431), the catholicity of the Church is manifested in its uniformity of faith throughout the world.[3] Hooker uses the illustration of Cyprian of the Church as the Ark, outside which there is, and can be, no salvation; and says that even inside the Ark are some who are separated from the kingdom of God, while yet belonging to the visible body.[4] Of the Church Visible perfect holiness of life is not a sure and

sola corpus est Christi, cuius ille caput est saluator corporis sui. extra hoc corpus neminem uiuificat Spiritus sanctus" (Aug. *Ep.* CLXXXV, xi, 50). haec et plura de hoc ibidem.'

[1] Hooker, *Serm.* v, 11: 'When they separate themselves, they are αὐτοκατάκριτοι, not judged by us but by their own doings. Men do separate themselves either by heresy, schism or apostasy. If they loose the bond of faith, which then they are justly supposed to do, when they frowardly oppugn any principal point of Christian doctrine, this is to separate themselves by heresy. If they break the bond of unity, whereby the body of the Church is coupled and knit in one, as they do which wilfully forsake all external communion with saints in holy exercises purely and orderly established in the Church, this is to separate themselves by schism. If they willingly cast off and utterly forsake both profession of Christ, and communion with Christians, taking their leave/of all religion, this is to separate themselves by plain apostasy.'

[2] S. Thos. Aq. *S.T.* III, qu. viii, art. iv (corpus).

[3] Cusanus, *De conc. cath.* XIII (*Opera*, Basel, p. 706): 'de hoc et Augustinus et Cyprianus et sancti patres scripta nobis maxime reliquerunt, unde ex hoc elicitur, quia fides nostra hodierna est concordans cum ea fide quae fuit illis temporibus per orbem diffusa necessario uera est, quia una est fides inuariabilis, licet de ducentis et quinque episcopis, qui in Africanis partibus commorarunt, et se in conciliis subscripserunt, nullus Christianus sit, neque in orientalibus partibus, tamen inter tot scismata et uarias haereses in fide christiana nostra haec unica fides diffusior est quam aliqua secta scismaticorum aut haereticorum. unde ex hoc argumento omnis haeretica prauitas uicta iacet.'

[4] Hooker, *Eccl. Pol.* III, i, 2: 'That Church of Christ, which we properly term his Body mystical, can be but one; neither can that one be sensibly discerned by any man, inasmuch as the parts thereof are some in heaven already with Christ, and the rest that are on earth (albeit their natural persons be visible) we do not discern under this property, whereby they are truly and infallibly of that body....

CONCLUSION

distinctive mark,[1] but there is always in that Church, as Augustine teaches, a mixture of good and evil.[2] The Scriptural illustrations are those used by Saint Augustine—the net cast into the water, and gathering good fish and bad; the great supper, to which good and evil men are invited; and the tares growing together with the wheat until the harvest.[3] Similarly John Pearson, the seventeenth-century Bishop of Chester, dealing with this subject, cites the actual Donatist controversy.[4]

They who are of this society [sc. the invisible Church] have such marks and notes of distinction from all others, as are not object to our sense; only unto God, who seeth their hearts and understandeth all their secret cogitations, unto him they are clear and manifest.'

[1] Ibid. III, i, 7: 'If by external profession they be Christians, then are they of the visible Church of Christ; and Christians by external profession they are all, whose mark of recognisance hath in it those things which we have mentioned, yea, although they be impious idolaters, wicked heretics, persons excommunicable, yea and cast out for notorious improbity. Such withal we deny not to be the imps and limbs of Satan, even as long as they continue such.'

[2] Ibid. III, i, 8: 'Howbeit of the visible Body and Church of Jesus Christ, those may be, and oftentimes are, in respect of the main parts of their outward profession, who, in regard of their inward disposition of mind, yea, of external conversation, yea, even of some parts of their very profession, are most worthily both hateful in the sight of God himself, and in the eyes of the sounder part of the visible Church most execrable. Our Saviour therefore compareth the kingdom of heaven to a net, whereunto all which cometh neither is nor seemeth fish: his Church he compareth to a field, where tares manifestly known and seen by all men do grow intermingled with good corn, and even so shall continue till the final consummation of the world.'

[3] Hooker, *Serm.* v, 8: 'Noah at the commandment of God built an ark, and there were in it beasts of all sorts, clean and unclean. A husbandman planteth a vineyard, and looketh for grapes, but when they come to the gathering, behold, together with grapes there are found also wild grapes. A rich man prepareth a great supper, and biddeth many; but when he sitteth him down, he findeth among his friends here and there a man whom he knoweth not. This hath been the state of the Church sithence the beginning. God always hath mingled his saints with faithless and godless persons; as it were the clean with the unclean, grapes with sour grapes, his friends and children with aliens and strangers.'

[4] J. Pearson, *An Exposition of the Creed*, ed. E. Burton (Oxford, 1864), 'Article IX', quoted in P. E. More and F. L. Cross, *Anglicanism, The Thought and Practice of the Church of England, illustrated from the Religious Literature of the Seventeenth Century* (London, 1935), p. 33: 'I conclude, therefore, as the ancient Catholics did against the Donatists, that within the Church, in the public profession and external communion thereof, are contained persons truly good and sanctified, and hereafter saved, and together with them other persons void of all saving grace, and hereafter to be damned; and that Church containing these of both kinds may well be called "holy", as Saint Matthew calleth Jerusalem the "holy city", even at that time when our Saviour did but begin to preach, when we know there was in that city a general corruption in manners and worship.'

Although holiness is now mingled with evil, it will be pure in the glorious Church of the next world, and without taint of infection or corruption.[1] The usual illustrations from Scripture applied by Saint Augustine to the distinction between the Visible and the Invisible Church appear again at this time in the work of Joseph Hall, Bishop of Norwich.[2]

[1] Ibid. pp. 33, 34: 'Of these promiscuously contained in the Church, such as are void of all saving grace while they live, and communicate with the rest of the Church, and when they pass out of this life, die in their sins, and remain under the eternal wrath of God; as they were not in their persons holy while they lived, so are they no way of the Church after their death, neither as members of it, nor contained in it. Through their own demerit they fall short of the glory unto which they were called, and being by death separated from the external communion of the Church, and having no true internal communion with the members and the head thereof, are totally and finally cut off from the Church of Christ. On the contrary, such as are efficaciously called justified and sanctified, while they live are truly holy, and when they die are perfectly holy; nor are they by their death separated from the Church, but remain united still by virtue of that internal union by which they were before conjoined both to the members and the head. As therefore the Church is truly holy, not only by an holiness of institution, but also by a personal sanctity in reference to these saints while they live, so is it also perfectly holy, in relation to the same saints glorified in heaven. And at the end of the world, when all the wicked shall be turned into hell, and consequently cut off from the communion of the Church, when the members of the Church remaining being perfectly sanctified shall be eternally glorified, then shall the whole Church be truly and perfectly holy. Then shall that be completely fulfilled, that Christ shall "present unto himself a glorious Church", which shall be "holy and without blemish". Not that there are two churches of Christ, one in which the good and bad are mingled together, another in which there are good alone; one in which the saints are imperfectly holy, another in which they are perfectly such; but one and the same Church, in relation to different times, admitteth or not admitteth the permixtion of the wicked, or the imperfection of the godly. To conclude, the Church of God is universally holy in respect of all, by institutions and administrations of sanctity; the same Church is really holy in this world, in relation to all godly persons contained in it, by a real infused sanctity; the same is farther yet at the same time perfectly holy in reference to the saints departed, and admitted to the presence of God; and the same Church shall hereafter be most completely holy in the world to come, when all members actually belonging to it shall be at once perfected in holiness and completed in happiness.'

[2] J. Hall, *Works* (ed. Peter Hall, 1837), vol. IV, p. 151 (quoted in *Anglicanism*, p. 44): 'As the Church, or spiritual kingdom of God here upon earth, is thus largely diffused through efficacy of his Gospel, so it may not be conceived to be pure and free from all sinful mixtures while it is here below. Rather is it like unto a drag-net, which is cast into the sea, and fetches up much variety, not of great and little fishes only, but of stones and seaweed and shells and mud altogether; which when it is drawn to the shore, is disburdened of all the unprofitable loan thereof, and yieldeth the good provision of fish unto the vessels of the owner. So doth the Church of God. Here for the outward and visible composition of it,

CONCLUSION

And such is also the official doctrine of the Church of England, as expressed in Article XIX.[1]

In the classical Anglican theology of the sixteenth and seventeenth centuries we find that the balance of thought on the matter of compulsion for religious purposes has been redressed after the excesses of the Inquisition; and that the doctrine of Augustine on the rightfulness of the Church's appeal to the State, not for the death penalty, but for compulsion short of that, is an accepted principle. It is clearly set forth by Hooker in these words:

Again, the custom which many Christian churches have to fly to the civil magistrate for coercion of those that will not otherwise be reformed—these things are proof sufficient that even in Christian religion, the power wherewith ecclesiastical persons were endued at the first is unable to do of itself so much as when secular power doth strengthen it; and that, not by way of ministry or service, but of predominancy, such as the kings of Israel in their time exercised over the Church of God.[2]

To this Robert Sanderson, Restoration Bishop of Lincoln, and William Beveridge, Bishop of St Asaph, assent. The former asserts that the power of the sword is committed to princes by God;[3] the latter, that the Church is within the Empire, as Optatus, but not Augustine, had taught; but that on the other hand it is the duty of the State to enforce with its own power the laws and canons of the Church.[4] Article

it containeth not only sound and holy and faithful men, but even the secretly vicious, sly hypocrites, hollow and faithless professors. But at the end of the world, when this great net is drawn up to the shore, the angels shall come forth and make a due separation of the wicked from among the just.'

[1] Art. XIX: 'ecclesia Christi uisibilis est coetus fidelium, in quo uerbum Dei purum praedicatur, et sacramenta, quoad ea quae sunt necessario exigantur, iuxta Christi institutum recte administrantur.'

[2] Hooker, *Eccl. Pol.* VIII, iii, 4.

[3] R. Sanderson, *Works* (ed. W. Jacobson, 1854), vol. v, p. 210 (quoted in More and Cross, *Anglicanism*, p. 692): '*Ius gladii*, the right and power of the sword (which is really the sovereign power) belongeth, we know, to kings. But it is by the ordinance of God, not the donation of the people, for he beareth the sword, Saint Paul telleth us, as God's minister from whom he received it, and not as the people's minister, who had no right to give it because they never had it themselves.'

[4] Wm Beveridge, Συνόδικον, *siue pandectae canonum sanctorum Apostolorum et Conciliorum ab ecclesia graeca receptorum* (Oxford, 1672), Prolegomena, 1: 'etiamsi ecclesia in imperio sit, unumque cum eo in singulis regnis caput commune habeat, reapse nihilominus ab eo distinguitur, non secus atque anima a corpore; hoc enim medici, illa theologi curae committitur: proinde homo ex duabus istis conflatus partibus, commune est utriusque regiminis subiectum, sub diuerso tamen respectu,

XXXVII is much more cautious, and says nothing directly concerning the coercion of spiritual delinquents by the civil power, though it vindicates the Church's authority in matters of doctrine and sacraments.[1] We find that Saint Thomas teaches the same doctrine of sacramental administration as Saint Augustine, namely that sacraments are useless in schism, but that they exist there, since in the administration of them man always acts as the instrument of God.[2] This is also the exact position

imperio quidem quatenus ζῷον πολιτικόν est, ecclesiae autem quatenus ζῷον ἀθάνατον, sempiternae scilicet felicitatis uel miseriae capax. enimuero homo conuenientis sibi societatis ex natura appetens, istiusmodi necesse est subiiciatur legibus, quibus talis societas conseruetur; ad eum autem integre conseruandam nihil amplius requiritur, quam ut caueatur, ne unus alteri noceat, sed singuli sibi inuicem prospiciant, et suum cuique tribuatur.' Ibid. II: 'quidquid autem a synodis ecclesiasticis decretum est, a ciuili etiam potestate confirmari solenne fuit. unde et omnes propemodum canones qui hoc libro continentur, ab imperatore Iustiniano Rhinotmeto iis subscribente corroborati sunt. nimirum principes christiani, ut ad ecclesiae praesidium, aeque ac ad imperii regimen, ciuilem sibi commissam habentes potestatem, ea ecclesiasticam per imperii sui prouincias stabilire auctoritatem, canonicas tueri leges, et cauere ut ecclesia pace sub suo fruatur patricinio, et auctoritatem ipsi concreditam libere exerceat, ex officio suo tenentur; ut ueteres etiam ecclesiae patres docuerunt. et idcirco, etiamsi ipsi imperatores inconsulta ecclesia ecclesiasticas numquam ferant leges, ut latae tamen in imperio cuiusque conseruentur, ipsis etiam per ciuilem suam auctoritatem prouidere incumbit.'

[1] Art. XXXVII: '... cum regiae maiestati summam gubernationem tribuimus... non damus regibus nostris aut Verbi Dei aut Sacramentorum administrationem... sed eam tantum praerogatiuam, quam in sacris Scripturis a Deo ipso, omnibus piis principibus, uidemus semper fuisse attributam: hoc est, ut omnes status atque ordines fidei suae a Deo commissos, siue illi ecclesiastici sint, siue ciuiles, in officio contineant, et contumaces ac delinquentes gladio ciuili coerceant.'

[2] S. Thos. Aq. S.T. II, ii, qu. xxix, art. iii (corpus): 'quamquam schismatici habere ordinis potestatem possint, iurisdictionis tamen auctoritate priuantur. respondeo dicendum, quod duplex est spiritualis potestas: una quidem sacramentalis, alia iurisdictionalis. sacramentalis quidem potestas est quae per aliquam consecrationem confertur. omnes autem consecrationes ecclesiae sunt immobiles, manente re quae consecratur, sicut etiam patet in rebus inanimatis; nam altare semel consecratum, non consecratur iterum, nisi fuerit dissipatum. et ideo talis potestas secundum suam essentiam remanet in homine, qui per consecrationem eam est adeptus, quamdiu uiuit, siue in schisma, siue in haeresim labatur; quod patet ex hoc quod rediens ad ecclesiam non iterum consecratur... si tamen usi fuerint, eorum potestas effectum habet in sacramentalibus; quia in his homo non operatur, nisi sicut instrumentum Dei. unde effectus sacramentales non excluduntur propter culpam quamcumque conferentis sacramentum. potestas autem iurisdictionalis est quae ex simplici iniunctione hominis confertur. et talis potestas non immobiliter adhaeret: unde in schismaticis et haereticis non manet.' Cf. S.T. III, qu. lxiv, art. i (corpus), art. iv (corpus), art. v (corpus): 'ministri ecclesiae, cum instrumentaliter operentur in sacramentis, sacramenta conferre possunt, siue boni

CONCLUSION

of Cusanus on the subject. Both in the *De concordantia catholica* and in the Epistles to the Bohemians he states his view that an evil minister cannot abrogate the divine promise, which is always secure in the sacrament.[1]

uel mali sint. respondeo dicendum, quod sicut dictum est (art. i et iii) ministri ecclesiae instrumentaliter operantur in sacramentis, eo quod quodammodo eadem est ratio ministri et instrumenti. sicut autem supra dictum est (qu. lxxii, art. i et iv) instrumentum non agit secundum propriam formam aut uirtutem, sed secundum uirtutem eius a quo mouetur. et ideo accidit instrumento, in quantum est instrumentum, qualemcumque formam uel uirtutem habeat, praeter id quod exigitur ad rationem instrumenti: sicut quod corpus medici, quod est instrumentum animae habentis artem, sit sanum uel infirmum, et sicut quod fistula per quam transit aqua, sit argentea uel plumbea. unde ministri ecclesiae possunt sacramenta conferre, etiamsi sint mali.' Art. ix (corpus): 'quemadmodum mali ministri extra caritatem existentes ministrare sacramenta possunt, ita et infidelis, dummodo ea non omittantur quae de necessitate sunt sacramenti' (in this passage he cites Aug. *C. Litt. Pet.* II, xxi, 47, and pseudo-Aug. *De fide ad Petrum*, 36; Aug. *De unico baptismo*, VIII, 13). *S.T.* III, qu. lxxxii, art. v (corpus), art. vii (corpus) (quoting Aug. *C. Ep. Parm.* II, xiii), art. viii, ix.

[1] Cusanus, *De conc. cath.* v (*Opera*, p. 698): 'adhuc pensandum est, quoniam ecclesia ab unitate et concordantiali congregatione dicitur, quod ipsa ex fraternitate constituitur, cui nihil proprie tantum contrariatur, quantum discissio siue schisma. nam licet fides una funiculus colligantiae, tamen aliquando uarietas opinionum absque pertinacia stat cum unitate. Cyprianus enim et totum concilium 70 episcoporum diuersi fuerunt in fide catholica ecclesiae, tamen non abscissi, quoniam non praetulerunt opinionem unitati fraternae, quia absque pertinacia fuerunt, ut Augustino placet, libro secundo contra Donatistas (*De bapt.* II, v, 6). ideo ministerium illius occulti haeretici, quod in unitate ecclesiae in salutem dispensari credit recte, licet dispensatori obsit, non sibi recte disposito in unitate ecclesiae capienti: haec est catholica ueritas, quam cuncti fideles fatentur, quam Augustinus libro secundo contra epistulam Parmeniani ad longum prosequitur (*C. Ep. Parm.* II, i, 3–v, 10). perfectissimus itaque Deus et homo, qui est mediator Dei et hominum, perfectissime et infallibili ordinatione ita ordinauit, quod, sicut Augustinus ad Paulinum epistula 42 scribit (Aug. *Ep.* XLII) ac altissimo ingenio Ambrosio in epistula Ad Iustum 56, tunc Christus est totum illud, quod quaeritur, et medium concordantiae ad Deum, per quem solum omnia. igitur non obest malus minister, quoniam sanctus Spiritus per praelatum propositum et ministrum etiam fictum operatur. qui ficte in ecclesia est, ita operatur euangelizando, consecrando, regenerando, quod salus ex hoc ministerio non minus praestabitur digne recipienti. quoniam non homo sed Christus hominis ministerio per sanctum Spiritum hoc agit. haec infallibilis ueritas quam Augustinus contra Parmenianum prosequitur....'

Ep. II *ad Bohemos*, ibid. p. 835: '...haec ligandi et soluendi potestas non minor est in ecclesia quam in Christo. unde Augustinus quarto libro de baptismo: munus beatae uitae non nisi intra ecclesiam reperitur, quae supra petram etiam fundata est, quae ligandi et soluendi claues accepit. haec est una, quae tenet et possidet omnem sponsi sui Domini potestatem.'

Ep. VII *ad Bohemos*, ibid. p. 860: 'nemo potest per se accipere et manducare

Hooker likewise emphasizes the divine gift of the sacrament and the fact that man is but the minister of it, by the authority of God. Such is the dignity of the ministry, and the security of the recipient of the sacrament.[1] Again, Article XXVI expresses the pure doctrine of Augustine on the subject.[2] Francis White expounds this same view with a most curious illustration.[3]

Eucharistiam, nisi qui consecrauit. simul hic traditur potestas consecrandi, et accipiendi per se et tradendi aliis. unde dicit Augustinus eos potestatem circa modum sacramenti habuisse, sed facultas tradendi aliis potestatem, aut distribuendi, non est praeceptum.'

[1] Hooker, *Eccl. Pol.* v, lxxvii, 1: 'The ministry of things divine is a function which as God himself did institute, so neither may men undertake the same but by authority and power given them in lawful manner...They are therefore ministers of God, not only by way of subordination as princes and civil magistrates whose execution of judgement and justice the supreme hand of divine providence doth uphold, but ministers of God as from whom their authority is derived, and not from men. For in that they are Christ's ministers and his labourers, who should give them their commission but he whose most inward affairs they manage? Is not God alone the Father of spirits? Are not souls the purchase of Jesus Christ? What angel in heaven could have said to man as our Lord did to Peter: Feed my sheep; preach; baptize; do this in remembrance of me; whose sins ye retain they are retained; and their offences in heaven pardoned whose faults you shall on earth forgive? What think we? Are these terrestrial sounds, or else are they voices uttered out of the clouds above? The power of the ministry of God translateth out of darkness into glory, it raiseth men from the earth, and bringeth God himself down from heaven, by blessing visible elements it maketh them invisible grace, it giveth daily the Holy Ghost, it hath to dispose of that flesh which was given for the life of the world and that blood which was poured out to redeem souls, when it poureth malediction upon the heads of the wicked they perish, when it revoketh the same they revive. O wretched blindness if we admire not so great power, more wretched if we consider it aright and notwithstanding imagine that any but God can bestow it!'

[2] Art. XXVI: 'quamuis in ecclesia uisibili, bonis mali semper sint admixti, atque interdum ministerio uerbi et sacramentorum administrationi praesint; tamen cum non suo sed Christi nomine agant, eiusque mandato et auctoritate ministrent, illorum ministerio uti licet, cum in uerbo Dei audiendo tum in sacramentis percipiendis. neque per illorum malitiam effectus institutorum Christi tollitur, aut gratia donorum Dei minuitur, quoad eos qui fide et rite sibi oblata percipiunt, quae propter institutionem Christi et promissionem efficacia sunt, licet per malos administrentur. ad ecclesiae tamen disciplinam pertinet ut in malos ministros inquiratur, accusenturque ab his qui eorum flagitia nouerint, atque tandem iusto conuicti iudicio deponantur.'

[3] Francis White, *A reply to Jesuit Fisher's answer to certain questions propounded by His Most Gracious Majesty, King James* (London, 1624), p. 52 (quoted in *Anglicanism*, p. 415): 'The promises of Christ made to the Church concerning his presence and assistance to his word and sacraments, preached and administered according to his commandment, are fulfilled when wicked persons execute the office, and

4. Conclusion

We have thus summarized the course of Saint Augustine's controversy with the Donatists, and the theological principles which that struggle elicited from him. We have glanced at some passages of later authors which will perhaps suffice to indicate how firmly Augustine's teaching on the unity of the Church, and on her Ministry and sacraments, as well as on her relations with the civil power, rooted itself in the thought of later ages. In this, as in many other departments of thought, the dominance of his principles in subsequent ages leads us to realize afresh, even if we cannot fully assent to it, the point of Dr Harnack's contention that Augustine is the first modern man. For in him we see the transition from primitive to later notions on all these subjects. Truly he was a theological pioneer, and the history of Christian doctrine could never have been quite the same had he not been raised up to bear his witness to the faith at such a critical period as the turn of the fourth century. Augustine's is the genius of following lines of thought dimly adumbrated by earlier thinkers, and investing them with a freshness and relevance to life which makes them part of the permanent heritage of Christ's Church. If the test of a man's thought be its ability thus to root itself in the minds of his successors throughout many generations, here is confirmation of the high place accorded to Saint Augustine in the line of Christian scholars and bishops, of scholars because of his intellectual triumphs, of bishops because his pastoral care and enthusiasm numbers him, as far as this controversy is concerned, and to say nothing of the others in which he engaged, in the ranks of those who can be described as 'sufferentes inuicem in dilectione, studentes seruare unitatem Spiritus in uinculo pacis'.[1]

perform the work of outward ministry. For although wicked persons, like the carpenters of Noah's Ark, reap no benefit to themselves, yet God Almighty concurreth with their ministry (being his own ordinance) for the salvation of all devout and worthy communicants.'

[1] Ephes. iv. 2, 3.

BIBLIOGRAPHY

DICTIONARIES, GENERAL WORKS OF REFERENCE, AND COLLECTIONS OF SOURCES

BAUDRILLART, H. M. A. (ed.). *Dictionnaire d'histoire et de géographie ecclésiastiques* (Paris, 1909), in progress.
CABROL, F. (ed.). *Dictionnaire d'archéologie chrétienne et de liturgie* (Paris, 1901), in progress.
HERGENRÖTHER & KAULEN. *Kirchenlexicon* (Freiburg, 1882-1903).
HERZOG-HAUCK. *Realenkyklopädie für protestantische Theologie und Kirche* (Leipzig, 1896-1913).
MIGNE, J. P. *Dictionnaire des Conciles* (Paris, 1847).
DE ROSSI, G. B. *Inscriptiones christianae urbis Romae VII saeculo antiquiores* (Rome, 1857-88).
TURNER, C. H. *Ecclesiae Occidentalis Monumenta Iuris Antiquissima* (Oxford, 1899-1939).
VACANT, MANGENOT & AMANN. *Dictionnaire de théologie catholique* (Paris, 1923), in progress.
VOELLI & IUSTELLI. *Fulgentii Ferrandi, Carthaginensis ecclesiae diaconi, Breuiatio Canonum*, in *Bibliotheca Iuris Canonici*, vol. I (Paris, 1661).

PERIODICALS

Analecta Gregoriana (Rome).
Antiquity (London).
Bulletin archéologique du Comité des travaux historiques (Paris).
Journal of Theological Studies (Oxford).
Mélanges de l'École française de Rome (Rome).
Revue Bénédictine (Maredsous).
Revue de l'histoire des religions (Paris).
Revue des questions historiques (Paris).
Revue internationale de théologie (Paris).
Texte und Untersuchungen (Leipzig).
Zeitschrift für Kirchengeschichte (Berlin).

PRIMARY SOURCES

AMBROSIUS:
  De officiis. P.L. XVI.
  Epistulae. P.L. XVI.
Auctor de Rebaptismate. P.L. III, 1231 sq.
AURELIUS AUGUSTINUS:
  Ad Donatistas post collationem. P.L. XLIII; C.S.E.L. LIII.
  Breuiculus Collationis. P.L. XLIII; C.S.E.L. LIII.
  Confessiones. P.L. XXXII; C.S.E.L. XXXIII.
  Contra Cresconium. P.L. XLIII; C.S.E.L. LII.

BIBLIOGRAPHY

Contra Epistulam Fundamenti. P.L. XLII; C.S.E.L. XXV.
Contra Epistulam Parmeniani. P.L. XLIII; C.S.E.L. LI.
Contra Faustum Manichaeum. P.L. XLII; C.S.E.L. XXV.
Contra Gaudentium. P.L. XLIII; C.S.E.L. LIII.
Contra Iulianum. P.L. XLIV.
Contra Litteras Petiliani. P.L. XLIII; C.S.E.L. LII.
De adulterinis coniugiis. P.L. XL; C.S.E.L. XLI.
De agone christiano. P.L. XL; C.S.E.L. XLI.
De anima et eius origine. P.L. XLIV.
De baptismo contra Donatistas. P.L. XLIII; C.S.E.L. LI.
De bono coniugali. P.L. XL; C.S.E.L. XLI.
De catechizandis rudibus. P.L. XL.
De ciuitate Dei contra paganos. P.L. XLI; C.S.E.L. XL.
De correptione et gratia. P.L. XLIV.
De doctrina christiana. P.L. XXXIV; Florilegium Patristicum, Fasc. XXIV.
De fide et operibus. P.L. XL; C.S.E.L. XLI.
De fide et symbolo. P.L. XL; C.S.E.L. XLI.
De Genesi ad litteram. P.L. XXXIV; C.S.E.L. XXVIII.
De haeresibus. P.L. XLII.
De nuptiis et concupiscentia. P.L. XLIV; C.S.E.L. XLII.
De patientia. P.L. XL; C.S.E.L. XLI.
De peccatorum meritis et remissione. P.L. XLIV; C.S.E.L. LX.
De symbolo. P.L. XL.
De uita beata. P.L. XXXII; C.S.E.L. LXIII.
De unico baptismo. P.L. XLIII; C.S.E.L. LIII.
De unitate ecclesiae. P.L. XLIII; C.S.E.L. LII.
De utilitate credendi. P.L. XLII; C.S.E.L. XXV.
Enarrationes in Psalmos. P.L. XXXVI, XXXVII.
Enchiridion. P.L. XL.
Epistulae. P.L. XXXIII; C.S.E.L. XXXIV, XLIV, LVII, LVIII.
Gesta cum Emerito. P.L. XLIII; C.S.E.L. LIII.
In Epistulam Ioannis ad Parthos tractatus. P.L. XXXV.
In Ioannis Euangelium tractatus. P.L. XXXV.
Opus imperfectum contra Iulianum. P.L. XLV.
Psalmus contra partem Donati. P.L. XLIII; C.S.E.L. LI.
Quaestiones in Heptateuchum. P.L. XXXIV; C.S.E.L. XXVIII.
Retractationes. P.L. XXXII; C.S.E.L. XXXVI.
Sermo ad Caesariensis ecclesiae plebem. P.L. XLIII; C.S.E.L. LIII.
Sermones. P.L. XXXVIII, XXXIX.

PSEUDO-AUGUSTINUS:
Contra Fulgentium. P.L. XLIII; ed. C. Lambot, Revue Bénédictine, 1948.
De fide ad Petrum. P.L. XL.

CLAUDIANUS. *Bellum Gildonianum.* P.L. XI.

CYPRIANUS (THASCIUS CAECILIUS):
Epistulae. P.L. III, IV; C.S.E.L. III.
De lapsis. P.L. IV; C.S.E.L. III.
De oratione dominica. P.L. IV; C.S.E.L. III.
De unitate. P.L. IV; C.S.E.L. III.
De zelo et liuore. P.L. IV; C.S.E.L. III.

BIBLIOGRAPHY

EUSEBIUS PAMPHILI. *Historia Ecclesiastica*. P.G. XX.
GENNADIUS. *De uiris illustribus*. P.L. LVIII.
Gesta apud Zenophilum. P.L. XLIII.
Gesta Collationis Carthaginensis. P.L. XI, 1223 sq.
GREGORIUS NAZIANZENUS. *Orationes*. P.G. XXXV, XXXVI.
HERMAS. *Pastor*. P.G. II.
HIERONYMUS (EUSEBIUS):
    Aduersus Pelagianos. P.L. XXIII.
    De uiris illustribus. P.L. XXIII.
HIPPOLYTUS. *In Proverbia*. P.G. X.
IRENAEUS. *Aduersus haereses*. P.G. VII.
OPTATUS (EP. MILEUITANUS). *Libri VII*. P.L. VII; C.S.E.L. XXVI.
OROSIUS (PAULUS). *Historiarum libri*. P.L. XXXI; C.S.E.L. V.
PHILASTER BRIXENSIS. *Liber de haeresibus*. P.L. XII; C.S.E.L. XXXVIII.
POSSIDIUS:
    Index Operum Augustini. P.L. XXXII.
    Vita Augustini. P.L. XXXII.
PRIMASIUS. *Commentarium super Apocalypsim Beati Ioannis*. P.L. LXVIII.
RUFINUS. *Historia Ecclesiastica*. P.L. XXI; C.S.E.L. XLVI.
Sententia Concilii Bagaiensis. C.S.E.L. LIII, pt iii, pp. 276–7.
SIRICIUS. *Epistulae*. P.L. XIII.
SOCRATES. *Historia Ecclesiastica*. P.G. LXVII.
SOZOMENUS. *Historia Ecclesiastica*. P.G. LXVII.
TERTULLIANUS:
    De baptismo. P.L. I; C.S.E.L. XX.
    De oratione. P.L. I; C.S.E.L. XX.
    De praescriptione haereticorum. P.L. II; C.S.E.L. XX.
    De pudicitia. P.L. II; C.S.E.L. XX.
THEODORETUS (EP. CYRENSIS). *Haereticarum fabularum compendium*. P.G. LXXXIII.
TYCONIUS. *Liber Regularum*. Ed. F. C. Burkitt, in vol. III, § 1 of J. A. Robinson, *Texts and Studies* (Cambridge, 1894).
VINCENTIUS LERINENSIS. *Commonitorium*. Ed. R. S. Moxon (Cambridge, 1915).
ZOSIMUS. *Epistulae*. P.L. XX.

SECONDARY SOURCES

AUDOLLENT, A. 'Mission épigraphique en Algérie', in *Mélanges de l'École française de Rome* (1890).
BAXTER, J. H. 'The Martyrs of Madaura', in *J.T.S.*, vol. XXVI (October 1924), pp. 21 sq.
BAYNES, N. H. 'Optatus', in *J.T.S.*, vol. XXVI (1924–5).
—— *The Political Ideas of Saint Augustine's 'De ciuitate Dei'* (London, 1936).
BENSON, E. W. *Cyprian, his Life, his Times, his Work* (London, 1897).
BERNARD, J. H. 'The Cyprianic Doctrine of the Ministry', in Swete, *Early History of the Church and the Ministry*.
BERTHIER, A. *Les vestiges du christianisme antique dans la Numidie centrale* (Alger, 1943).

BIBLIOGRAPHY

BETHUNE-BAKER, J. F. *Introduction to the Early History of Christian Doctrine* (London, 1929).
BÉVENOT, M. 'Saint Cyprian's *De Unitate*, Chapter IV, in the light of the manuscripts', in *Analecta Gregoriana*, vol. XI, Series Facultatis Theologicae, Sectio B, N. 5 (Rome, 1938).
BEVERIDGE, W. Συνόδικον, *siue pandectae canonum sanctorum Apostolorum et Conciliorum ab ecclesia graeca receptorum* (Oxford, 1672).
BRIGHT, W. *The Age of the Fathers* (London, 1903).
BURNABY, J. *Amor Dei: A Study in the Religion of Saint Augustine*, Hulsean Lectures, 1938 (London, 1938).
BURY, J. B. *History of the Later Roman Empire* (London, 1923).
CHAPMAN, J. 'Les interpolations dans le traité de Saint Cyprien sur l'Unité de l'Église', in *Revue Bénédictine* (Maredsous, 1902–3) and in *J.T.S.* (London, 1902–3).
COCHRANE, C. N. *Christianity and Classical Culture, A study of thought and action from Augustus to Augustine* (Oxford, 1940).
CUSANUS (NICOLAS OF CUES). *De concordantia catholica. Epistulae ad Bohemos.* (In D. Nicolai Cusani, *Opera*, Basel, 1565.)
D'ARCY, M. C., and others. *A Monument to Saint Augustine* (London, 1934).
DILL, S. *Roman Society in the last Century of the Western Empire* (London, 1910).
DUCHESNE, L. *Histoire ancienne de l'Église* (Paris, 1910–11); E. T., *Early History of the Church* (London, 1922).
—— 'Le dossier du Donatisme', in *Mélanges de l'École française de Rome* (1890).
DUDDEN, F. HOMES. *The Life and Times of Saint Ambrose* (Oxford, 1935).
DUPIN, ELLIES (ed.). *Optatus* (Paris, 1845).
FIGGIS, J. N. *Political Aspects of Saint Augustine's 'City of God'* (London, 1921).
FREND, W. H. C. 'The Revival of Berber Art', in *Antiquity* (December 1942).
—— 'Note on the Berber Background in the Life of Augustine', in *J.T.S.*, vol. XLIII, Nos. 171, 172 (July–October 1942).
HALL, J. *Works*, ed. Peter Hall (London, 1837).
HARNACK, A. *Dogmengeschichte*; E.T., *History of Dogma* (London, 1896).
—— *Geschichte des altchristliche Litteratur* (Leipzig, 1893).
HEFELE, C. J. *Conciliengeschichte*; E.T., *History of the Christian Councils*, trans. W. R. Clark (Edinburgh, 1872).
HOOKER, R. *The Ecclesiastical Polity. Sermons.* (In *Works*, Oxford, 1865.)
HORT, F. J. A. *The Christian Ecclesia* (London, 1897).
JACOB, E. F. *Essays in the Conciliar Epoch* (Manchester, 1943).
JALLAND, T. G. *The Church and the Papacy*, Bampton Lectures, 1942 (London, 1944).
KIRK, K. E. *The Vision of God*, Bampton Lectures, 1928 (London, 1931).
KOCH, H. 'Cyprian und der Römische Primat', in *Texte und Untersuchungen*, vol. XXXV (Leipzig, 1910).
DE LABRIOLLE, P. *Histoire de la littérature latine chrétienne*; E.T., *Latin Christianity* (London, 1924).
LACEY, T. A. *Unity and Schism*, Bishop Paddock Lectures, 1917 (London, 1917).
LIGHTFOOT, J. B. *The Christian Ministry* (London, 1901).
MARROU, H. I. *Saint Augustin et la fin de la culture antique* (Paris, 1938).
MICHAUD, E. 'La théologie d'Optat de Milève, d'après son *De schismate Donatistarum*', in *Revue Internationale de Théologie*, vol. XVI (1908).

BIBLIOGRAPHY

MONCEAUX, P. *Histoire littéraire de l'Afrique chrétienne* (Paris, 1901–23).
MORE, P. E. and CROSS, F. L. *Anglicanism, The Thought and Practice of the Church of England, illustrated from the Religious Literature of the Seventeenth Century* (London, 1935).
PEARSON, J. *An Exposition of the Creed*, ed. Burton (Oxford, 1864).
PHILLIPS, VASSALL. *The Work of Saint Optatus against the Donatists* (London, no date).
RABY, F. J. E. *A History of Christian Latin Poetry* (Oxford, 1927).
REUTER, H. *Augustinische Studien* (Gotha, 1887).
ROBERTSON, A. *Regnum Dei: Eight Lectures on the Kingdom of God in the History of Christian Thought*, Bampton Lectures, 1901 (London, 1901).
ROSE, H. J. 'Saint Augustine as a forerunner of mediaeval hymnology', in *J.T.S.*, vol. XXVIII (July 1927).
SALTET, L. *Les réordinations: Étude sur le sacrement de l'ordre* (Paris, 1907).
SANDERSON, R. *Works*, ed. W. Jacobson (London, 1854).
SEECK, O. 'Quellen und Urkunden über die Anfänge des Donatismus', in *Zeitschrift für Kirchengeschichte*, vol. X (1889).
SPARROW SIMPSON, W. J. *Saint Augustine and African Church Divisions* (London, 1910).
SOUTER, A. 'Tyconius' Text of the Apocalypse: a partial restoration', in *J.T.S.*, vol. XIV (1913).
SPECHT, T. *Die Lehre von der Kirche nach dem h. Augustin* (Paderborn, 1892).
SWETE, H. B. *The Holy Catholic Church* (London, 1916).
—— (ed.). *Essays on the Early History of the Church and the Ministry* (London, 1921).
THOMAS AQUINAS (ST). *Summa Theologica*.
LE NAIN DE TILLEMONT. *Histoire des Empereurs* (Paris, 1700–38).
—— *Mémoires pour servir à l'histoire ecclésiastique des six premiers siècles* (Paris, 1701–12).
TIXERONT, J. *Histoire des Dogmes dans l'antiquité chrétienne* (Paris, 1912–19).
TURNER, C. H. 'Aduersaria Critica, Notes on the anti-Donatist dossier and on Optatus', in *J.T.S.*, vol. XXVII.
—— 'Apostolic Succession', in Swete, *Early History of the Church and the Ministry*.
WATKINS, O. D. *History of Penance* (London, 1920).
WHITE, F. *A reply to Jesuit Fisher's answer to certain questions propounded by His Most Gracious Majesty, King James* (London, 1624).
WILLIAMS, N. P. *The Ideas of the Fall and of Original Sin*, Bampton Lectures, 1924 (London, 1927).
WILLIS, G. G. *An Analysis, with Commentary, of Saint Augustine of Hippo's Treatises on Marriage* (1939). Unpublished thesis in University of Manchester Library.
ZIWSA, C. 'Praefatio in Optatum', in *C.S.E.L.*, vol. XXVI (Vienna, 1893).

INDEX OF PROPER NAMES

Abiram, 103, 115, 149
Abitina, 34
Abraham, 90, 93
Adeodatus, Donatist bishop of Milevis, 71
Adeodatus, son of Augustine, 26
Agonistici (Circumcellions), 11
Agrippinus, Bishop of Carthage, 19, 147
Alaric, 139
Alexandria, 104
Alypius, Bishop of Tagaste, 26, 39, 46, 50, 56, 57, 71, 81
Ambrosius, Bishop of Milan, 127, 137, 138, 142
Ammianus Marcellinus, 21
Anastasius, Bishop of Rome, 49, 120
Antigonus, Bishop of Madaura, 14, 15
Antonius, Bishop of Fussala, 85, 86
Antonius, of Egypt, 127
Anulinus, proconsul of Africa, 4, 6, 7
Apringius, 77, 84, 85
Arcadius, Emperor, 50, 131, 132
Arians, 89
Arius, 47, 69
Asia, Churches of, 108, 155
Athanasius, Bishop of Alexandria, 136
Auctor ad Hebraeos, 145
Auctor de Rebaptismate, 105, 163
Augustine, Bishop of Hippo, works:
  Ad Donatistas post collationem, 79, 170
  Ad Emeritum episcopum Donatistarum post collationem, 80, 171
  Admonitio Donatistarum de Maximianistis, 64, 171
  Breuiculus Collationis, 76, 80, 171
  Confessiones, 54, 124
  Contra Cresconium, 54, 55, 171
  Contra Donatistam nescio quem, 63, 64, 171
  Contra Epistulam Donati haeretici, 38, 171
  Contra Epistulam Parmeniani, 42, 49, 51, 128, 171
  Contra Faustum Manichaeum, 107
  Contra Gaudentium, 82, 83, 171
  Contra Iulianum, 83
  Contra Litteras Petiliani, 44, 52, 54, 55, 171
  Contra partem Donati, 42, 43, 128, 171
  Contra quod attulit Centurius a Donatistis, 44, 171

De adulterinis coniugiis, 170
De agone christiano, 42
De anima et eius origine, 83
De baptismo contra Donatistas, 43, 44, 49, 122, 124, 149, 154, 157, 158
De bono coniugali, 170
De catechizandis rudibus, 140
De ciuitate Dei, 21, 39, 124, 138-43
De fide et operibus, 79
De fide et symbolo, 30
De haeresibus, 83
De Maximianistis contra Donatistas, 64, 171
De nuptiis et concupiscentia, 170
De patientia, 80
De unico baptismo, 64, 154, 171
De unitate ecclesiae, 53, 54, 173
Enarrationes in Psalmos, 39, 47, 48, 57, 58, 87, 88
Enchiridion, 83
Epistulae, 38, 39, 44-6, 55-7, 64-8, 80, 83-6
Gesta cum Emerito, 171
Opus imperfectum contra Iulianum, 83
Probationum et testimoniorum contra Donatistas liber, 52, 63, 171
Psalmus contra partem Donati, 36-8, 40, 171, 173
Retractationes, 38, 42-4, 53, 63, 64, 75, 80, 85, 128
Sermo ad Caesariensis ecclesiae plebem, 81, 171
Sermones, 40, 58-60, 69-70, 86-92

Babel, 140
Babylon, 140
Bagai, 10, 13, 33, 41, 61
Basilica Fausti, 78
Basilica Nouorum, 4
Basilica Regionis Secundae, 50, 62
Basilica Restituta, 41, 49, 87, 91
Benson, Edward White, Archbishop of Canterbury, 100, 104, 105, 110, 111, 150
Bernard, John Henry, Archbishop of Dublin, 111, 112
Bévenot, Maurice, 111, 112
Beveridge, William, Bishop of S. Asaph, 183

INDEX

Bonifacius, Count of Africa, 80, 85
Bonifacius, Donatist bishop at Rome, 9
Botrus, 5
Byzacium, 32, 33

Cabarsussa, 32, 58
Caecilianus, Bishop of Carthage, 5–8, 10, 43, 47, 64, 65, 73, 74, 79, 81, 83, 86, 89, 117, 119, 144, 176
Caecilianus, governor of Numidia, 57, 85
Caelestinus, Bishop of Rome, 85, 86
Caelestius, 5
Caesarea, in Mauretania, 22, 81, 82
Caesariana, in Numidia, 61
Calama, 7
Callistus, Bishop of Rome, 2
Cartenna, 21, 116, 119
Cassianus, 16
Castellum Lemellense, 17
Castorius, 50, 56
Celer, 29, 46
Centurius, 44
Chapman, Dom John, 111, 112
Circumcellions, 11–13, 15, 16, 21, 22, 29, 31, 34, 38–41, 45, 47, 59, 61, 63, 65, 67, 68, 75, 77, 83, 117, 130, 144, 153
Cirta (or Constantina), 4, 10, 23, 34, 44, 52, 76, 80, 81, 84
Claudianists, 21, 31
Claudianus, Donatist bishop at Rome, 9, 31
Claudianus, the poet, 22
Constans, Emperor, 10, 16, 25
Constantina. *See* Cirta
Constantinople, 104
Constantinus, Emperor, 9, 16, 74, 132, 136, 176
Constantinus, friend of Augustine, 64
Constantius, Emperor, 136
Crescens, Bishop of Cirta, 163
Cresconius, 54, 55
Crispinus, Donatist bishop of Calama, 30, 46, 56, 65
Crispinus, priest of Calama, 56, 130
Cusanus (Nicolas of Cues), Bishop of Brixen, 178–80, 185
Cyprianus, Thascius Caecilius, Bishop of Carthage, 2, 19, 25, 43, 44, 55, 64, 66, 68, 79, 82, 90, 93, 96–126, 146–63, 167, 168, 172, 174, 176, 177

Damasus, Bishop of Rome, 23, 31
Daniel, 134
Dathan, 103, 115, 149
Datiuus, Donatist bishop of Noua Petra, 14
Decius, Emperor, 146

Demetrius, 32, 33
Deuterius, Bishop of Caesarea, 20, 81, 82
Diocletian, Emperor, 3, 11, 23, 52, 144, 146, 176
Diotimus, 51
Donatus a Casis Nigris, 7–9, 38
Donatus, Bishop of Calama, 4
Donatus, Bishop of Mascula, 4
Donatus, Donatist bishop of Bagai, 10, 11, 13, 14
Donatus, Donatist priest of Mutugenna, 84
Donatus, martyr of Mauretania, 17
Donatus, proconsul of Africa, 62, 65
Donatus, the Great, 7–10, 14, 17, 38, 47, 69, 90, 91, 119, 145
Dulcitius, tribune, 82, 85

Egypt, 154
Elias, the prophet, 134
Emeritus, Donatist bishop of Caesarea in Mauretania, 64, 65, 71, 80–2
Esau, 90
Eucolpius, 9
Eunomians, 89
Eunomius, 7
Euodias, 26, 50
Euphrates, 84
Eusebius, 45

Fasir, 11
Fausta, 7
Faustinus, Donatist bishop of Hippo Regius, 28
Felicia, Donatist nun, 86
Felicianus, Donatist bishop of Musti, 34, 46
Felix, Bishop of Aptunga, 5–8, 117, 144, 176
Felix, deacon, 5
Felix, Donatist bishop of Idicra, 17
Festus, 61, 65
Firmilianus, Bishop of Caesarea and Metropolitan of Cappadocia, 149
Firmus, 21–3
Fortunatianus, Bishop of Sicca, 71
Fortunatus, Bishop of Cirta, 71
Fortunatus, Manichee, 29
Fortunatus, priest of Carthage, 32, 33
Fortunius, Donatist bishop of Thubursicum Numidarum, 41, 45, 46, 128
Fussala, 27, 29, 77, 85

Gaudentius, Donatist bishop of Thamugadi, 71, 82, 83
Generosus, Bishop of Constantina, 46
Genethlius, Bishop of Carthage, 10, 31

194

INDEX

Gennadius, 19
Gildo, Count of Africa, 22, 34, 41, 62
Glorius, 45
Gratianus, Emperor, 22
Gratus, Bishop of Carthage, 10, 14
Gregorius Nazianzenus, 105
Gregorius, *praefectus praetorio*, 25

Hagar, 89
Hall, Joseph, 178, 182
Harnack, Adolf von, 125, 187
Hartel, Gulielmus, 111
Hasna, 30
Henchır-el-Guesseria, 28
Heraclianus, Count of Africa, 63, 77
Hermas, 2
Hezekiah, King, 134
Hierius, Vicar of Africa, 30
Hieronymus, Eusebius, 96, 139
Hippolytus, 2
Hippo Regius, 26–30, 36, 38, 40, 51, 53, 57, 61, 66, 67, 76, 81, 85
Honoratus, Donatist bishop, 46, 128
Honorius, Emperor, 22, 30, 50, 51, 62, 75, 77, 78, 130, 131
Hooker, Richard, 165, 178, 180, 181, 183, 186
Hosius, Bishop of Cordova, 19

Iacob, 90
Iacopone da Todi, 37
Ianuarius, Donatist bishop of Casae Nigrae and primate of Numidia, 61, 65
Icosium, 22
Igmazen, 22
Ignatius, 94, 95
Innocentius, agent of the praetor, 26
Innocentius, priest of Hippo Regius, 83
Irenaeus, Bishop of Lugdunum, 95, 145, 147
Isaflenses, 22
Ishmael, 89
Iubaianus, 105, 148
Iudas, Iscariotes, 15
Iulianus, Bishop of Eclanum, 83
Iulianus, Emperor, 11, 16, 17, 58
Iulianus, proconsul of Africa, 77
Iustina, Empress, 137

Koch, Hugo, 111, 112
Korah, 103, 115, 149

Lacey, T. A., Canon of Worcester, 103, 111
Leontius, Bishop of Hippo, 29, 39

Lucianus, 9
Luciferians, 88
Lucilla, 5, 6

Macarius, 10, 14, 24
Macedonia, 140
Macedonius, Vicar of Africa, 85
Macrobius, Donatist bishop of Hippo Regius, 61, 63, 67
Macrobius, Donatist bishop of Rome, 9
Maiorinus, Donatist bishop of Carthage, 6, 9, 38
Manichaeans, 83, 89, 127
Mappalia, 56
Marcellinus, 60, 63, 68, 70–6, 77, 79, 81, 83–5, 139, 172, 175
Marcion, 148
Marculus, 10, 14
Marinus, Bishop of Aquae Tibilitanae, 4
Marinus, Bishop of Arelatum, 7
Marinus, Count of Africa, 77, 85
Mascezel, 22, 23
Maternus, Bishop of Cologne, 7
Mauretania, 21, 22, 104
  M. Caesariensis, 17, 21
  M. Sitifensis, 17
Maxentius, consul, 5
Maximianists, 33–5, 39, 40, 46, 47, 54, 55, 57, 58, 64, 65, 67, 68, 71, 80, 82, 86
Maximianus, Bishop of Bagai, 130, 131
Maximianus, Bishop of Vaga, 50, 56
Maximianus, Donatist bishop of Carthage, 32, 33, 47
Maximinus, Donatist bishop of Sinitum, 38, 39, 61, 128
Maximus, grammarian of Madaura, 13, 26
Maximus, usurping Emperor, 22
Megalius, Primate of Numidia, 40, 74
Menalius, 4
Mensurius, Bishop of Carthage, 4, 5
Mesopotamia, 47, 154
Migne, J. P., 111
Milan, 23, 127
Milevis, 4, 23, 34, 61, 62
Miltiades, Bishop of Rome, 7, 83
Moesia, 22
Montanus, Donatist bishop of Zama, 71
Montenses (Donatists at Rome), 9

Nabor, deacon, 41
Naucelio, 57
Nineveh, 140
Noah, 140

INDEX

Noua Petra, 14
Novatian, Roman schismatic, 101, 102, 145, 146
Numidia, 10, 15, 17, 21, 26, 34, 40, 41, 55, 57, 65, 77 etc.
Nundinarius, 9

Olympius, Bishop, 7
Olympius, minister of state, 62, 65, 132
Optantius, Donatist bishop of Madaura, 14, 15
Optatus, Bishop of Milevis, 9, 14, 16–18, 23–5, 43, 105–10, 133, 139, 151, 152, 154, 156, 160, 180, 183
Optatus, Donatist bishop of Thamugadi, 11, 22, 23, 34, 41
Ostia, 5

Palladius, Bishop of Tigabis, 81
Pammachius, senator, 55
Pannonia, 22
Parmenianus, Donatist bishop of Carthage, 17–20, 24, 31, 42
Patricius, father of Augustine, 26
Paul, Apostle, 65, 84, 93, 99, 101, 102, 127, 131, 134
Paulina, wife of Pammachius, 55
Paulus, Bishop of Cirta, 4
Paulus, commissioner of Constans, 10, 14
Pearson, John, Bishop of Chester, 178, 181, 182
Pelagians, 89, 169
Pelagius II, 111
Persia, 140
Peter, Apostle, 99, 120
Petilianus, Donatist bishop of Cirta, 44, 52–5, 64, 71
Photinians, 89
Photinus, 47
Pollentius, 170
Pontius, Donatist, 16, 58
Porphyrius, proconsul of Africa, 62
Possidius, Bishop of Calama, 53, 56, 57, 74, 81, 83, 130, 132
Praetextatus, Donatist bishop of Assuras, 34, 46
Primianists, 41, 62, 71
Primianus, Donatist bishop of Carthage, 31–4, 41, 67, 71
Primosus, Bishop of Castellum Lemellense, 17
Primus, Catholic of Castellum Lemellense, 17
Primus, subdeacon of Hippo Regius, 45

Proculeianus, Donatist bishop of Hippo Regius, 44, 45, 61, 69, 128
Protasius, Donatist bishop of Thubunae, 71
Purpurius, Bishop of Limata, 4, 6

Quoduultdeus, 72

Ravenna, 77
Razias, 14
Restitutus, Bishop of Carthage, 10
Restitutus, priest of Hippo Regius, 83
Reticius, Bishop of Autun, 7
Rogatianus, 16, 58
Rogatists, 20, 21, 31, 66, 83, 116, 119
Rogatus, Donatist bishop of Assuras, 34
Rogatus, Donatist bishop of Cartenna, 21, 66
Rome, Church of, 104, 108, 110–12, 147, 148
Rome, Donatist church at, 9
Romanianus, 26
Romanus, Count of Africa, 21
Rotaria, 61
Rusticus, Bishop of Cartenna, 81

Sabellians, 89
Saluius, Donatist bishop of Membressa, 34
Sanderson, Robert, Bishop of Lincoln, 183
Saturninus, 84
Secundus, Bishop of Tigisis, 4, 5, 9
Seuerinus, 46
Seuerus, 26
Sidonius, 132
Siluanus, Bishop of Cirta, 4
Siluanus, Primate of Numidia, 85, 86
Siluester, Bishop of Rome, 8
Siluester, Count of Africa, 10
Sinitum, 29, 61, 67
Siricius, Bishop of Rome, 163
Sitifi, 80
Stephanus, Bishop of Rome, 64, 99, 122, 148, 149, 162
Stilicho, 22, 23, 62

Tagaste, 26, 76, 81
Tarsus, Twenty Martyrs of, 68
Tertullian, 2, 95, 96, 145, 146, 147, 149
Thamugadi, 41
Thasius, 50
Theodorus, 55
Theodosius, Emperor, 29, 30, 51, 56
Theodosius, father of Emperor, 22
Theoprepia, Donatist basilica, 71, 77
Thermae Gargilianae, 70
Thibilis, 61

INDEX

Thomas Aquinas, 169, 178, 184
Thubursicum Numidarum, 41
Tigisis, 4
Tipasa, 17, 22
Tucca, 62
Turner, C. H., 144, 167
Tyconius, 17–21, 42, 43, 139, 140

Valentinianus I, Emperor, 17, 21, 22
Valentinianus III, Emperor, 78
Valerius, Bishop of Hippo, 26, 40, 44
Vegesela, 10
Venerius, Bishop of Milan, 49
Victor a Garba, 9
Victor, Bishop of Russicade, 4

Victorianus, 67
Victorinus a Munaciana, 32
Vincentius, Bishop of Culusi, 71
Vincentius, Rogatist bishop of Cartenna, 66, 83, 116
Vincentius Victor, 31, 83
Vrbanistae, 21
Vrbanus, Donatist bishop of Formae, 17
Vrbanus, of Cirta, 4
Vrsus, *Rationalis Africae*, 6

White, Francis, 187

Zenophilus, 9, 58

INDEX OF SUBJECTS

Absolution, 1, 2
Actores, at Conference of Carthage, 44, 65, 71–3, 80, 81
Apostasy, 2, 3, 101, 106, 116, 125, 180
Apostolic succession, 95, 96, 108, 120
Assessors, at Conference of Carthage, 71–3

Baking of bread, 28
Baptism, 19, 24, 31, 38, 39, 43, 49, 52, 55, 57–61, 64, 79, 87, 89, 97, 101, 104–6, 109, 119, 122, 123, 146–60, 162–4, 167, 172
Basilicas, 10, 16, 17, 21, 29, 33, 34, 39, 41, 49, 50, 52, 56, 61–3, 70, 71, 77, 78, 81, 82, 87, 91
Blasphemy against the Holy Ghost, 4, 90, 91, 116
Bribery, 6
Burial customs, 11, 12, 28

Charity, 24, 60, 64, 69, 70, 80–2, 86, 88, 89, 91, 93, 95, 100–2, 105, 107, 113–17, 122, 125, 126, 135, 140, 141, 151, 153–6, 159, 164, 166, 168, 173–5, 177, 178, 187
Church, 93–126
  and State, 127–43, 170, 172, 174–7, 183–4
  Body of Christ, 1, 94, 106, 107, 113, 115, 174, 177
  City of God, 21, 124, 126, 139–43, 175, 176
  Corpus permixtum, 40, 43, 48, 59, 69, 90, 94, 101, 102, 117, 118, 121, 123, 180–3
  New Israel, 93–4
  Visible and Invisible, 90, 94, 105, 123–5, 141–3, 167, 174, 180–2
Ciuitas superna and *ciuitas terrena*, 127, 138–43, 175–6
Communion of saints, 124–5
Conference of Carthage, 5, 9, 14, 23, 44, 50, 60, 65, 70–6, 81, 86, 131, 144, 172, 173, 175
Conferences, 39, 41, 44–6, 50, 56, 68, 70–6, 81, 82, 128, 132, 171–3
Confirmation, 58, 162–4
Conversion of Augustine, 127
Conversions of Donatists, 14, 50, 55–7, 61–2, 66–8, 84–5

Councils:
  Arles, 314   7, 8
  Byzacium, 24 Feb. 418   78
  Carthage, early councils, 44, 98–100, 103–4, 147–9, 157–8, 172
  28 Aug. 397   41
  16 June 401   49
  13 Sept. 401   49, 50
  25 Aug. 403   50
  16 June 404   50, 130
  23 Aug. 405   51
  13 June 407   62, 132
  16 June 408   62, 132
  13 Oct. 408   62, 65, 66, 132
  14 June 410   63
  1 May 418   63
  25 May 419   79
  Cirta, 14 June 412   80, 84
  Hippo, 8 Oct. 393   30
  Milevis, 27 Aug. 402   50
  Numidia, 14 June 412   77

Dancing, 29
Dating of documents, 4 n. 2, 5
Deo gratias, 58
Deo laudes, 12, 27, 47, 58
Discipline, 1–4, 42, 86, 118
Division of dioceses, 14, 15, 27, 61, 62, 77, 78, 85, 86
Drag-net, parable of the, 40, 59, 181, 182 n. 2
Drunkenness, 29

Edicts of unity, 25, 51, 60, 75, 77
Elections of bishops, 4, 5, 50
Emperor, appeals to, 6–8, 16, 34, 35, 49–51, 58, 62–3, 65–9, 75, 77, 83, 85
Episcopacy, 94–100, 103–5, 150, 166
Estates, 29, 55, 56, 61, 65, 67, 75
Exhibition of notices, 51, 52, 63, 74, 76

Fall of Rome, 139
Feasts in churches, 29, 31, 39

Grace, 21, 150–2, 154–6, 159, 162, 167

Heresy, 2, 47, 55, 69, 90, 106, 110, 114, 122, 124, 129, 130, 149
Heretics, 30, 31, 42, 43, 58, 68, 88, 89, 95, 99, 106, 129, 131, 137, 145

198

INDEX

Idolatry, 2, 48
Imposition of hands, 162–4
Israeles, 11, 58

Legal functions of bishops, 132–3
Libellatici, 3
Liberalism, 1–3

Marriage, 28, 161–2
Martyrdom, 102–3
'Martyrs', Donatist, 11, 14–16, 23, 27, 68, 134
    Feasts of (*Laetitiae*), 15, 27, 39
Mass, 28, 58, 101, 150, 164, 165
Ministers of sacraments, 88, 144–68, 184–6
Murder, 4, 85

Notes of the Church:
    Apostolicity, 94, 120
    Catholicity, 19, 20, 42, 66, 73, 87, 94, 115, 119, 120
    Holiness, 19, 28, 42, 53, 54, 65, 89, 90, 94, 101, 102, 108, 117–19
    Unity, 94, 97, 113–17

Orders, holy, 161–2

Peace, 173–4
Penance, 2, 6, 163
Persecution, 3, 4, 7, 67, 74
Platonism, 123
Predestination, 124–5, 170, 174
Primacy of Rome, 99–100
Psalms, metrical, 18, 36–8
Punic language, 26, 27, 49, 85

Rebaptism, 22, 26, 31, 38, 39, 44, 51, 56, 61, 68, 115, 122, 130, 147–9, 157, 160
Reviviscence, 43, 126, 154, 159, 161, 167
Rigorism, 1–4, 145, 148, 156, 176

Sacraments, 103, 107–9, 144–68, 176–7
    Defiling effect of schismatic sacraments, 109, 110, 148, 156
    Invalidity and irregularity, 103, 107, 109, 146, 153–7, 176–7
Sacrificati, 3
Sacrilege, 16, 17
Sacrilege of schism, 85, 107, 110, 115, 116, 125, 135
Schism, 2, 9, 52, 66, 69, 76, 80, 85, 87, 90–4, 100–1, 106–9, 114–15, 118, 122, 124, 130, 150
Schisms within Donatism, 21, 31–5, 46, 57, 58, 64, 82, 83, 89
State, appeal to, 16, 23, 24, 35, 42, 49–53, 66, 83, 110, 127–34, 172, 175–6, 183–4
Suicide, 14, 15, 48, 80, 82

Toleration of evil, 48, 86, 90, 102, 109
Traditio, 3, 4, 7, 9, 55, 118, 144, 153, 176
Traditores, 3, 4, 6, 8, 18, 19, 108, 117, 144, 176

Unworthiness of ministers, 166
Utraquism, 178

Violence of Donatists, 10, 11, 16, 17, 22, 24, 29–34, 38–41, 45, 47, 56, 61, 65, 77, 83, 110, 117, 127–43, 153

www.ingramcontent.com/pod-product-compliance
Lightning Source LLC
Chambersburg PA
CBHW070323230426
43663CB00011B/2204